Date Due

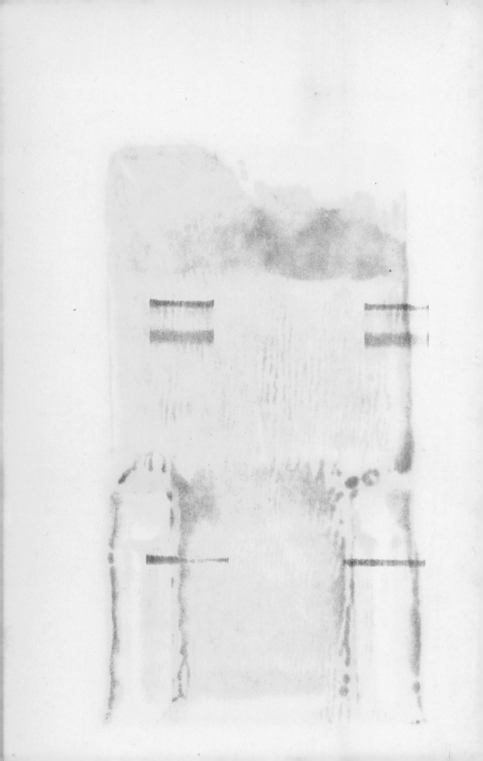

THE SPECTER

THE SPECTER

Original Essays on the Cold War and

the Origins of McCarthyism

EDITED BY
ROBERT GRIFFITH
AND
ATHAN THEOHARIS

NEW VIEWPOINTS
A Division of Franklin Watts, Inc.
New York
1974

Library of Congress Cataloging in Publication Data

Griffith, Robert, 1940–
  The specter; original essays on the cold war and
the origins of McCarthyism.
  Includes bibliographical references.
  1. Subversive activities—United States—Addresses,
essays, lectures. 2. McCarthy, Joseph Raymond, 1908–
1957—Addresses, essays, lectures. 3. Internal
security—United States—Addresses, essays, lectures.
4. United States—Politics and government—1945–1953—
Addresses, essays, lectures. I. Theoharis, Athan C.,
ed. II. Title.
E743.5.G74   1974   322.4'2'0973   73-17191
ISBN 0-531-06364-X
ISBN 0-531-06493-X (pbk.)

For
Matthew,
Jonathan,
Terri,
Jeanne,
and
George Thomas

CONTENTS

INTRODUCTION

The time: February 9, 1950, three days before Lincoln's birthday. The place: Wheeling, West Virginia, a meeting of the Republican Women's Club. The speaker: The junior senator from Wisconsin, the Honorable Joseph R. McCarthy. The speech: a harsh attack on the treachery of the Truman Administration and on the State Department, where "the bright young men who are born with silver spoons in their mouths are the ones who have been the most traitorous." The high point of the talk came when the senator held aloft a sheaf of papers and declared that "I have here in my hand a list of 205 . . . a list of names that were made known to the Secretary of State as being members of the Communist Party and who nevertheless are still working and shaping policy in the State Department."

McCarthy's accusations were carried out over the wire services and in the weeks that followed the senator became the center of national controversy. Responding to the press's reception of McCarthy's charges, the Democratic leadership of the Senate launched an investigation of the State Department. The special subcommittee created to effect this purpose, chaired by the powerful conservative senator from Maryland, Millard Tydings, and dominated by the Democrats, concluded, following four months of bitterly partisan hearings, that McCarthy's charges were "a fraud and a hoax." The Republicans refused to endorse such a conclusion. While differing widely in the extent of their support or tolerance of the Wisconsin senator, Republican leaders gave McCarthy what amounted to a vote of confidence.

In the months that followed, the senator's attacks on Truman, the State Department, and other high government officials mounted in intensity. At one point he called Truman a "son of a bitch" and charged that the President's decision to dismiss General Douglas MacArthur in April 1951 had been made "with the aid of bourbon and benedictine." He called Secretary of State Dean Acheson the "Red Dean of Fashion" and repeatedly referred to the State Department's "crimson clique," which he charged had sold out China to the Communists. In 1951 he even accused Secretary of Defense and former General of the Army George C. Marshall of having participated in a conspiracy to betray his country. McCarthy's charges were incorporated into Republican campaign strategy for 1952. That effort was summed up in the formula of the conservative senator from South Dakota, Karl Mundt, by the letters C_2K ("Communism, Corruption, and Korea"). McCarthy was given a national platform to reiterate these charges at the Republican National Convention and during the closing days of the 1952 presidential campaign the Republicans aired a nationwide attack by the senator on the Democratic presidential candidate, Adlai Stevenson.

For nearly five years McCarthy monopolized national attention with such charges and sought, often with alarming success, to intimidate the federal bureaucracy, two Presidents (Truman and Eisenhower), the press, and a host of fellow senators, Democrats and Republicans alike. On one occasion he even denounced a critical Republican colleague as "a living miracle in that he is without question the only man in the world who has lived so long with neither brains nor guts." More than that, McCarthy pointedly charged that critics of his methods were aiding the Communists and thereby undermining national security. Such charges, broadcast by McCarthy and other partisans, soon came to be called "McCarthyism," and the senator himself became the symbol for one of the most contentious eras in American history.

At the time, many observers saw McCarthy as a charismatic leader with a unique talent for probing the dark reaches of the American mind. He was, wrote Richard Rovere, "the most gifted demagogue" in American history. Many compared him to

Hitler, and it was even suggested that he was an avid reader of *Mein Kampf*. Still others stressed the dangerous volatility and irrationality of the senator's popular following. McCarthyism, they argued, was a mass movement rooted in the status resentments of the lower-middle- and working-class Americans, a populistic alliance of "hick Protestants" and "South Boston Celts." They feared that such movements, led by demagogues like McCarthy, posed a dangerous threat to the very foundations (liberal and conservative) of American society.

In recent years historians and other social scientists have begun to challenge these conventional explanations of McCarthyism and to construct new and alternative interpretations of the strident politics of the mid-twentieth century. The essays in this collection are a part of that effort.

McCarthy himself, in this new view, was not very important. He was the product of America's cold-war politics, not its progenitor; and his success can be fully appreciated only by reference to the issues he symbolized. What was called "McCarthyism," moreover, is better understood in political, not sociopsychological terms. Indeed, the vague and imprecise use of status theory has tended to confuse attempts to explain the nature of McCarthyism. This is not to deny the social base of American politics, or to falsely dichotomize a complex experience, but rather to emphasize the role of political institutions—interest groups, parties, the presidency, the Congress—in generating McCarthyism. The anti-Communist politics that created McCarthyism and sustained the career of Joe McCarthy was not, finally, a mass politics springing simply and spontaneously from popular fears and discontents. Rather, as Michael Paul Rogin has suggested and the present collection demonstrates, it was a conventional politics rooted in the actions and inactions of conservative and liberal elites.

This reassessment of the McCarthy phenomenon is no mere

academic exercise, for the earlier interpretations of the mass character of McCarthyism have continued to shape political debate in this country. The catch-all term "McCarthyism" has been used by conservative politicians (most recently, former Vice President Spiro Agnew and Senator Barry Goldwater) to dismiss criticism of executive authority and to smear appeals for popular support. In the current debate over United States policy in Indochina, even astute critics of the Administration (Senator J. William Fulbright, *New York Times* columnist James Reston, and Daniel Ellsberg as late as 1970) have been hesitant to support a public debate, fearful that the abrupt termination of United States involvement might contribute to a "new McCarthyism," which would exploit popular beliefs in American omnipotence. And, while these critics have condemned recent Administrations for their obsession with Communism, they have attributed this to popular pressures. Thus, in 1965 Senator Fulbright was reluctant to have the Senate Committee on Foreign Relations institute public hearings on Administration policy in Vietnam. Seven years later, in an otherwise thoughtful article ("Reflections: In Thrall to Fear," the *New Yorker,* January 8, 1972,) on the legacies of the Truman Doctrine, Fulbright concluded that "Every American President since that time [the McCarthy era] has been under intense pressure to demonstrate his anti-Communist orthodoxy."

The idea that exposure and publicized surveillance of Administration policy is harmful to the national interest, another legacy of this earlier interpretation of McCarthyism, has been a powerful rationale for executive secrecy and classification. McCarthy did not pioneer, though he did dramatize, the Republicans' postwar assault on executive privilege and secrecy. Yet, when the Republicans secured control of the presidency in 1953, they abandoned their earlier condemnations of executive secrecy to support executive privilege on national security grounds. Significantly, the first occasion for this restatement of executive privilege occurred in the context of Senator McCarthy's confrontation with the Eisenhower Administration during the now-famous Army-McCarthy hearings of early 1954. This fear of the public and of public exposure of executive decisions and secrets has contributed to a profound shift in American politics in the post-McCarthy years. Not only has a more conservative politics ensued, but a more elitist politics as well. As the Pentagon Papers have disclosed, however, the resulting insulation of executive decisions from public accountability has not insured a more rational, enlightened foreign policy but rather has only reinforced anti-democratic political procedures. It is time, then, for an assessment of this aspect of the McCarthy legacy.

These essays seek to provide that assessment. The editors, in inviting young scholars to contribute, have not attempted to impose a uniform interpretive framework. The standard for selection was simply how our understanding of the politics of the postwar years might be expanded. Thus, some of the authors have examined groups traditionally identified with McCarthyism (Catholics, businessmen, conservatives). Others have studied liberal groups (the American Civil Liberties Union, the Congress of Industrial Organizations, and Americans for Democratic Action), which, heretofore, have not been examined as part of the repressive politics of the period. Lastly, an attempt has been made to assess McCarthy's impact by examining the process leading to the enactment of internal security legislation, the factors shaping the 1950 congressional election results, and Senator McCarthy's pre-1950 use of the anti-Communist issue.

The essays themselves reflect a diversity of viewpoints. A majority of the contributors might loosely be described as revisionist historians, though several clearly are not. At least two of the contributors write out of an implicitly Marxist framework, though the others do not. The arguments set forth in any single

Introduction

essay do not therefore necessarily reflect the views of the other contributors or even, for that matter, those of the editors. The contributors do share, however, a common commitment to scholarship and to the attempt, untrammeled by the conventions of the past, to understand the politics of the McCarthy era.

Robert Griffith
Amherst, Massachusetts
Athan Theoharis
Milwaukee, Wisconsin
February 1973

THE SPECTER

AMERICAN POLITICS AND THE ORIGINS OF "McCARTHYISM"

BY
ROBERT
GRIFFITH

For nearly two decades American scholars and journalists have described "McCarthyism" in terms of a popular uprising, a mass movement of the "radical right" that threatened the very fabric of American society. Inchoate, irrational, it swept across the political landscape like an elemental force of nature carrying all before it. Its sources, these scholars maintained, lay not so much in the emergent cold war, but in the "social strains" and status tensions produced by a century of modernization. McCarthyism, like populism, was seen as an attack by paranoid provincials upon the educated and the wealthy. Politicians, in this view, were but the passive instruments of the popular will, reflecting the hysteria that welled up from the grass roots. McCarthy himself, of course, was something of an exception. Indeed, he was credited with a demonic talent for probing "the dark places of the American mind." He was "the most gifted" demagogue in American history, succeeding where others had failed in arousing the American masses and inciting them to action "outside of and against the established channels of constitutional government." [1]

I

But was McCarthyism really a popular movement? Probably not. To be sure, anti-Communism was an element in the American political culture, and popular attitudes toward Communism, conditioned as they were by several decades of misinformation and strident propaganda, were mostly negative. It is also true that public opinion polls showed a rather high level of support for McCarthy (around 35 percent for most of 1953–54), combined with frequently intolerant attitudes toward nonconformists and dissenters. But popular intolerance and anti-Communism, however important, have tended to be constants. Even in the supposedly radical thirties, for example, most Americans seemed to favor denying freedom of speech, press, and assembly to native Communists.[2] What needs to be explained, therefore, is not the mere existence of such attitudes, but how, during the late 1940's and early 1950's, they were mobilized and became politically operational.

Second, as even Seymour Martin Lipset and other proponents of the "radical right" thesis admit, intense negative feelings about McCarthy were usually more common than strongly favorable ones. McCarthy aroused more opposition than support.[3] Third, as Nelson Polsby has suggested in a critique of the radical right thesis, the most common characteristic of McCarthy supporters was not class, religion, or ethnicity, but political affiliation. Support for McCarthy was strongest among Republicans. Socioeconomic factors were not unimportant—when party affiliation was held constant, those with lower status, less education, and of the Catholic faith tended to support McCarthy disproportionately. But these last factors seem clearly less significant than party.[4] There was, moreover, no continuity between populism and McCarthyism, as some historians have argued. Indeed, as Michael Paul Rogin has shown, nearly the reverse was true—agrarian radicalism, where cohesive, contributed not to the Republican right, but to the constituency of Democratic liberalism.[5]

Fourth, while the polls did show substantial support for McCarthy and extremely negative feelings about Communism, as well as a low level of support for the civil liberties of Communists and other political dissidents, the intensity of these feelings was apparently not very strong. When people were asked, for example, whether they favored allowing Communists to teach in their schools, the response (both in the thirties and in the fifties) was largely and unsurprisingly negative. But in 1953, at the height of the McCarthy era, when people were asked a simple, nondirective question ("What kinds of things do you worry about most?"), less than 1 percent listed the threat of Communism as a major concern and only 8 percent mentioned the tangentially related area of world problems. Even when the

American politics and the origins of "McCarthyism"

interviewer sought to lead the respondent ("Are there other problems you worry about or are concerned about, especially political or world problems?"), the level of concern was not great. The number expressing anxiety about Communism increased only from 1 percent to 6 percent. The number concerned over international affairs rose more substantially, from 8 percent to 30 percent. Significantly, more than half of those so questioned added nothing to their initial response. Thus, as Samuel Stouffer concluded in his 1954 study, *Communism, Conformity and Civil Liberties,* Americans were not very deeply concerned over domestic Communism. The "picture of the average American as a person with the jitters, trembling lest he find a Red under the bed, is clearly nonsense." [6]

Finally, what is all too often overlooked is the congruence between popular attitudes toward Communism and the attitudes of influential public figures. Many prominent Republicans, for example, were constantly accusing the Roosevelt and Truman Administrations of selling out to Communism at home and abroad. Nor were such charges limited to conservatives. Some liberal Republicans, such as Senator Ralph Flanders of Vermont who would later lead the movement to censure McCarthy, believed that "our late departed saint Franklin Delano Roosevelt was soft as taffy on the subject of Communism and Uncle Joe." Even Democrats such as Massachusetts Congressman John F. Kennedy attacked the Truman Administration's foreign policies, charging that "what our young men saved [in World War II], our diplomats and our President have frittered away." The Truman Administration itself used the Red issue against Henry Wallace and the Progressives and occasionally even against the Republicans. McCarthy, the President charged at one point, was the Kremlin's "greatest asset." [7] In denouncing Communism, then, Joe McCarthy, despite his occasional attacks on "the bright young men who are born with silver spoons in their mouths," was adopting a political issue already sanctioned by much of the nation's political leadership.

The commonly accepted portrait of McCarthyism as a mass movement and McCarthy as a charismatic leader is, thus, badly overdrawn. People were less concerned about the threat of Communism and less favorably inclined toward McCarthy than is generally thought. Support for McCarthy, moreover, was closely identified with partisan Republicanism. Finally, popular attitudes about Communism generally mirrored the views of many prominent political leaders, and McCarthy's use of the issue was unexceptional.

II

But if McCarthyism is not to be understood primarily in terms of popular passion, then how do we explain the contentious and tumultuous politics of the mid-twentieth century? A partial answer to this problem involves a political definition of McCarthyism and, as Michael Paul Rogin has suggested, the actions and inactions of political elites.[8] McCarthyism may not have been only a political phenomenon; it may indeed have reflected the "social strains" of modern American society, as Talcott Parsons and others have maintained. But it was primarily a product of the political system and its leaders. The latter did not simply respond to popular protest, but rather helped to generate the very sense of concern and urgency that came to dominate the decade.

This is not to argue that the politics of McCarthyism was born solely of the postwar period. There was a long history of anti-radicalism in America, a history produced both by conservative resistance to social change and by nativist fears of strangers in the land. It was not a history created by protean mass movements, however, but by the complicated interplay of political manipulation and popular myth and stereotype. The Red Scare

American politics and the origins of "McCarthyism"

of 1919–20 is instructive in this regard both as analogy and as legacy.

The Red Scare was made possible by hostile popular attitudes toward Communists and other radicals—what has been called the "anti-Communist persuasion." [9] The intolerant atmosphere of World War I politics, the triumph of the Bolsheviks in Russia, the organization of the American Communist Party, and widespread labor unrest all served as proximate causes. The Red Scare itself was created, however, by the vigorous activities of conservative businessmen, organized veterans, patriotic societies, and by ambitious politicians in Congress and especially in the federal government. Business organizations such as the National Association of Manufacturers, the National Metal Trades Association, the National Founders Association all worked hard to stir up public opinion against labor unions as part of their crusade for the "American plan," as they called the open shop. Conservative patriotic groups, such as the National Security League, the American Defense Society, the American Protective League, and the National Civic Federation, sought to promote 100 percent Americanism, as did the newly organized American Legion. Even the American Federation of Labor (AFL) joined the crusade, partially to stifle leftist activities within the labor movement and partially to deflect conservative attacks from the AFL. Sensational reporting by conservative newspapers, a category that included most of the American press, further aroused popular anxieties. Finally, the impulses created by these and other groups were mobilized by such politicians as Attorney General A. Mitchell Palmer and translated into political action —the Palmer raids, deportation of alien radicals, and a flood of sedition bills including one designed to attack what Palmer called "the real menace of evil-thinking." Following the federal lead, more than thirty states hurriedly passed criminal syndicalism, criminal anarchy, and red flag laws.[10]

The Red Scare finally subsided, of course. Most Americans

were probably not deeply troubled by the imminence of a red revolution and were aroused only fitfully by politicians and the press. The Red Scare left as its legacy, however, both a substantial body of law and precedent and a reinforced set of popular myths and stereotypes susceptible to future manipulation by interest groups and politicians.

During the depression thirties the rise of domestic radicalism and the reform programs of the New Deal prompted nervous conservatives to again raise the specter of Communism. Anti-Communism, of course, was a traditional tactic of conservative opponents of social reform—used in response to the general railroad strike of the 1870's, the Populists in the 1890's, and the IWW in the early 1900's. During the thirties it simply became sound conservative doctrine to attack the New Deal as the forerunner of an American bolshevism. "If Roosevelt is not a Communist today," charged Robert A. Taft of Ohio, "he is bound to become one." Roosevelt, echoed the Republican National Committee in 1936, was "the Kerensky of the American Revolutionary Movement." [11]

In 1930 and again in 1934, Congress launched investigations into "un-American activities," and in 1938 Congressman Martin Dies, with the support of Democratic House leaders Sam Rayburn and William B. Bankhead and the endorsement of Vice President John Nance Garner, proposed the creation of a Special Committee on Un-American Activities. Approved by a vote of 191 to 41, the committee, under Dies's flamboyant leadership, set out on a celebrated search for Communists in the Roosevelt Administration. In the process it pioneered almost all of the techniques that would later be associated with Senator McCarthy. The committee's activities were generously reported by the press, and popular reaction appeared to be generally favorable. Liberal opposition to the committee, never very potent, virtually disintegrated; and by the end of the decade one-time critic John M. Coffee (Democrat-Washington) was campaigning on

American politics and the origins of "McCarthyism"

the slogan "The Dies Committee endorses John Coffee's reelection." [12]

At the same time, growing concern over domestic radicalism, combined with increasing international tensions, led to a mass of anti-radical and anti-alien bills, three of which were finally enacted into law. The first of these was the McCormack Act of 1938, which required all agents of foreign governments to register with the Department of Justice and which later served as partial precedent for the Communist registration section of the McCarran Internal Security Act of 1950. The following year Congress passed the Hatch Act, which was primarily intended to restrict the political activities of federal employees, but which also excluded from federal employment members of any organization that advocated the forcible overthrow of the government. Finally, the Smith Act of 1940, designed mainly to compel the registration of aliens, also made it illegal to advocate the overthrow of the government by force or violence.[13]

Most of these measures were sponsored and supported by anti-New Deal conservatives. The Roosevelt Administration itself, however, was an indifferent champion of civil liberties. Thus Secretary of Labor Francis Perkins confined her testimony on the Smith bill to relatively minor points, while the Justice Department, under whose jurisdiction the sedition provisions fell, did not testify at all. The Navy Department, which was responsible for placing in the bill a section aimed at pacifists that made it illegal to interfere with or influence adversely the loyalty, morale, or discipline of the armed forces, warmly supported the measure. Roosevelt himself defended the bill's sedition provisions, replying to a critic that "they can hardly be considered to constitute an improper encroachment on civil liberties in the light of the present world conditions." [14]

The activities of the federal government inspired imitation at the state and local level. These activities peaked, as did their national models, during the "little Red Scare" of the mid-thirties

and again toward the end of the decade. Spurred on by the
American Legion and other zealously anti-Communist groups,
a half dozen states initiated investigations of "un-American activities," and several passed bills requiring loyalty oaths for
teachers. A few states sought to exclude Communists from the
ballot, while others attempted, following the example of the
Hatch Act, to bar from public office anyone thought to advocate
the violent overthrow of the government.[15]

Although the success of such activities often depended on the
acquiescence or even passive support of liberals, the anti-
Communist impulse of the thirties remained primarily anti-
reformist, the product of conservative Republican and Democratic attacks on the New Deal. Its appeal was, therefore, always
limited by the widespread popularity of the Roosevelt program.
All this changed, however, with the advent of the cold war and
the subsequent shift from domestic to international concerns.

III

The cold war transformed the climate of American politics,
overlaying traditional political issues with a new and emotionally
charged set of concerns. The growing power of the Soviet Union
and its challenge to American supremacy served to focus previously diffuse fears and anxieties over Communism. So did the
arrest of men and women accused of spying for the U.S.S.R.[16]
But the anti-Communist protest of the late 1940's was more
than a simple response to external events. It also sprang from
the goals that American leaders set for postwar foreign policy,
the manner in which they perceived the Soviet challenge to that
policy, and the methods they chose to meet that challenge.

For a variety of reasons—idealism, self-interest, the hubris
of the very powerful—American leaders defined United States
policy in sweeping terms: the creation of a global system of
stability, peace, and prosperity. The Soviet challenge to this new
order was seen as a threat to world peace and to American

American politics and the origins of "McCarthyism"

security, a threat to which the United States was compelled to respond. The character of this response, in turn, helped to create a climate in which anti-Communist politics gained a vastly heightened potency and appeal. In part, this was because the Truman Administration itself couched its policies in a rhetoric of crusading anti-Communism, which stressed American innocence, Soviet depravity, and the necessity for confrontation.[17]

Such views, of course, were scarcely unique to the Truman Administration. Rather they were shared by a broad segment of America's political leadership—liberal and conservative, Democratic and Republican. Both Truman and his conservative critics were influenced to a great extent by the legacy of prewar anti-Communism. Both shared illusions concerning the limits of American power and the nature of Soviet foreign policy. Truman's critics, however, generally proposed more drastic policies and justified them with greater militance than did the Administration. Even Robert Taft, a frequently incisive critic of containment, denounced the Administration for being "soft on Communism," advocated greater assistance for Chiang Kai-shek, and supported General Douglas MacArthur in the controversy over the Korean War. The Truman Administration, committed to an interventionist policy abroad, stressed anti-Communism as a means of winning support from such nationalistic but fiscally cautious conservatives. As a result, most conservatives joined the Administration in a bipartisan anti-Communist consensus, while the rest, including Taft, were left isolated and impotent.[18] A second, and unintended consequence of this tactic, however, was the generation of a new and conservative political climate, resistant to social change at home and to negotiation and compromise abroad.

The new political climate inspired conservative businessmen, organized veterans, patriotic societies, and other zealous anti-Communists and made their efforts appear more plausible and relevant. The Chamber of Commerce, for example, through its Committee on Socialism and Communism, prepared and distributed a series of pamphlets designed to expose Communists in government and labor, to discredit New Deal social legislation, and to help businessmen reassert themselves at the community level.[19] The American Legion was even more active. Led by its Americanism Division and active at both the state and federal levels, the Legion campaigned vigorously to arouse the nation to the perils of Communism. The Legion played an important role in creating and sustaining the Special House Committee on Un-American Activities and in the establishment of "little Dies Committees" in the states. The Legion lobbied hard for new anti-Communist legislation, supporting the Mundt-Nixon Communist registration bill as well as a wide variety of restrictive measures at the state level. Finally, the Legion became deeply involved in the colorful crusade against Communism in Hollywood and in the subsequent spread of blacklisting in the film, radio, and television industries.[20]

The Legion and the Chamber of Commerce were only two among a welter of anti-Communist organizations, which included patriotic societies such as the Daughters of the American Revolution, Catholic groups such as the Knights of Columbus and the Catholic War Veterans, ethnic groups such as the Polish-American Congress, and a host of smaller right-wing organizations. The activities of these groups included lobbying, propaganda, and on occasion picketing and other forms of public protest. The concerns of such groups were amplified by the press. The conservative McCormick, Hearst, and Gannett chains were especially active in this undertaking, though overwrought anti-Communism was not limited to them alone. As early as 1945, for example, *Life* magazine complained that "The 'fellow traveler' is everywhere, in Hollywood, on college faculties, in government bureaus, in publishing companies, in radio offices, even on the editorial staffs of eminently capitalistic journals." [21] From here it was but a short step to the demand that such "fellow travelers" be purged from American life.

This was not, of course, "mass" politics but "interest group" politics, a typical expression of the American political culture and not an aberrational one. The group base of American politics was not aligned, as earlier scholars have suggested, against a mass politics of anti-Communism. Instead, interest groups themselves lay at the heart of the anti-Communist politics of the era.

The aggressive actions of right-wing interest groups were not, moreover, met by countervailing pressures from the left. Instead, the same broad forces that lent strength and legitimacy to the postwar right served to undermine and destroy the postwar left. In 1945 the American left was a relatively large and potentially powerful movement, which included a wide assortment of liberals, socialists, and Communists. Though scarred by the memory of past betrayals and sharply divided among themselves, these leftists nevertheless shared a consensus on two fundamental points: the necessity for radical social change at home and for a conciliatory and pacific foreign policy abroad. The rise of the cold war and the resurgence of conservatism, however, led to bitter divisions within the left over American policy toward the Soviet Union and over the role of Communism in American life. The precarious unity of the popular front was shattered, both by the Communists who repudiated the wartime leadership of Earl Browder and by cold-war liberals who supported the foreign policies of the Truman Administration and sought to purge Communists from labor unions, political parties, and other voluntary associations. The overwhelming rejection of Henry Wallace in the 1948 campaign and the emergence of Americans for Democratic Action (ADA) marked the beginning of a new political era in which the left was in virtual eclipse and in which the distinction between liberals and conservatives became one of method and technique, not fundamental principle. Divided, demoralized, and after 1948 led by men who shared many of the anti-Communist assumptions of the right, the American left was unable to withstand the mounting demands of McCarthyite conservatives.[22]

IV

The political climate of postwar America was thus shaped by the cold war, by the agitation of conservative interest groups, and by the disintegration of liberalism. It remained, however, for politicians to mobilize the support necessary for a politics of anti-Communism. Foremost among such politicians were those Republican and Democratic conservatives who had championed the anti-Communist issues since the thirties and who had maintained all along that Democratic liberalism was leading the country down the road to Communism. After 1945, however, this anti-reformist impulse was joined with the new foreign policy and internal security issues bred by the cold war. Congressional conservatives now charged that the Roosevelt and Truman Administrations were "soft" on Communism abroad and tolerant of subversion and disloyalty at home; and beginning in 1945 they launched a series of investigations into Communist activities designed in part to embarrass the government.[23]

The frequency of such investigations was one measure of the rise of the Communist issue in American politics. There were four investigations during the 79th Congress (1945–47); twenty-two during the Republican 80th Congress (1947–49); twenty-four during the 81st Congress (1949–51); thirty-four during the 82nd Congress (1951–53); and fifty-one, an all-time high, during the Republican 83rd Congress (1953–55). Throughout the forties most of these investigations were conducted by the House Committee on Un-American Activities, led, following the retirement of Martin Dies, by J. Parnell Thomas (Republican-New Jersey) and by John S. Wood (Democrat-Georgia). More

American politics and the origins of "McCarthyism"

important, the focus and character of these investigations changed. Before December 1948 most of HUAC's investigations seemed to be linked to domestic concerns—the committee's primary targets were left-wing New Deal personnel, New Deal agencies such as the Federal Theatre Project and the Office of Price Administration, trade unions whose leadership included Communists, and Hollywood. But after 1948, the year in which Whittaker Chambers accused Alger Hiss first of having been a Communist and then, later, of having spied for the Soviet Union, the committee began increasingly to emphasize the internal security issues of espionage, subversion, and "Communists in government." [24]

The Communist issue was injected into the 1946 elections and was apparently a factor in the Republican triumph, especially among urban Catholics. In 1947–48 the Truman Administration responded to these pressures by justifying its foreign policies with a crusading anti-Communist rhetoric, by instituting a federal loyalty-security program, by prosecuting Communist party leaders under the Smith Act, and in general by stressing its own firm anti-Communist credentials. Indeed, by 1948 the Administration had succeeded, if only temporarily, in using the Communist issue to its own advantage against both the Progressives and the Republicans. Crusades, however, are more easily begun than halted, and by early 1950 those conservative politicians whom Truman had sought to outflank once again held the initiative, now denouncing the Administration for the "loss" of China and demanding a sweeping purge within the government.[25]

The rise of anti-Communism as an issue in national politics was accompanied by the growth of a derivative anti-Communist politics at the state and local levels. In part this was because many of the organizations that had agitated for restrictive measures at the federal level were also active in the states and in the communities. Some of these groups, the Chamber of Commerce and the American Legion, for example, labored not only to arouse others to the menace of Communism, but also to popularize techniques and methods for combating it. The Chamber sponsored anti-Communist seminars for local businessmen, while the American Legion held conferences for state legislators anxious to learn what the federal government and other states were doing to safeguard the Republic. Catholic Church groups and the conservative Hearst press also helped agitate the issue, as did the coterie of staff and witnesses that surrounded the House Committee on Un-American Activities.[26]

More important, state legislatures responded almost slavishly to the force of federal law and precedent and to the anxieties aroused by national leaders. Anti-radical legislation was not, of course, new to most states. Yet what was remarkable about the great outpouring of the late forties was that so many legislatures acted at the same time and in the same way. In 1949, for example, the Maryland legislature passed a Subversive Activities Act, popularly known as the Ober Law. There was little original in the new law, however, for it had been drawn from the Smith Act of 1940, from Truman's Loyalty Program of 1947, and from portions of the Mundt-Nixon bill then pending before Congress. The Ober Law was in turn copied in part or entirely by the states of Mississippi, New Hampshire, Washington, and Pennsylvania. In the case of Pennsylvania, the legislature in 1951 established as the criteria for dismissing state employees not the Ober Law's standard—"reasonable grounds . . . to believe that any person is a subversive person"—but instead "reasonable doubt as to the loyalty of the person involved." The Maryland law had followed the criteria set forth in Truman's March 1947 loyalty order (Ex. Order 9835); the Pennsylvania legislature incorporated a generally unheralded but highly significant change in that criteria, in effect reversing the burden of proof, which Truman had ordered in April 1951 (Ex. Order 10241).[27]

American politics and the origins of "McCarthyism"

During the late forties, nearly thirty states enacted laws seeking to bar from public employment those who advocated the violent overthrow of the government, or who belonged to organizations which so advocated. In only one instance did such a state statute predate the Truman loyalty order; all of them, of course, came after the 1939 Hatch Act, which had provided such restrictions for federal employment. The Attorney General's list, institutionalized by Truman's 1947 loyalty order, was quickly adopted as a test of loyalty by states (including Arizona, New York, Michigan, Texas, Oklahoma), by municipalities (among them Detroit and New York City), and even by private employers (including the Columbia Broadcasting System). Following the passage in September 1950 of the McCarran Internal Security Act, more than a half dozen states rushed to enact so-called Communist Control Laws. Even cities passed municipal ordinances directed against Communists.[28]

Thus state and local anti-Communist legislation, though widespread, is best understood as a reflection, not a cause, of national priorities. Unlike populism, the impact of which was felt first at the local and state level and only later at the national level, the politics of anti-Communism originated at the national level and then spread to the states.[29]

By 1950, then, political leaders had succeeded, through the manipulation of popular myths and stereotypes, in creating a mood conducive to demagogues such as Joseph R. McCarthy. The Wisconsin senator's crude attacks on American policy and policymakers resonated through the political system not because of their uniqueness, but because of their typicality. To call this political impulse "McCarthyism," however, is to exaggerate the senator's importance and to misunderstand the politics that he came to symbolize. McCarthy was the product of anti-Communist politics, not its progenitor. Had he never made that speech

in Wheeling, West Virginia, had his name never become a
household word, what people came to call "McCarthyism"
would nevertheless have characterized American politics at the
mid-century.

THE POLITICS OF RELIGION:

American Catholics and the

Anti-
Communist
Impulse

BY DONALD F.
CROSBY, S.J.

In the mid-1950's it became fashionable to depict American Catholics as part of a mass constituency mobilized by Joe McCarthy in his crusade against Communism. Motivated by anxieties born of rising status, Catholics irrationally joined with Bible belt Protestants in a populistic alliance of the "sticks and slums." The result, in the view of some contemporary observers, was a "radical right" crusade, whose real targets were the institutions and symbols of upper-middle-class America (the eastern universities, the Protestant Church, the metropolitan media), that threatened to destroy the very foundations of American government.[1]

The purpose of this article is not to minimize the influence of Catholics on McCarthyism, nor to argue that such influences were benign or harmless. Rather it is to suggest that Catholic anti-Communism must be analyzed in a broader context—one that includes the historical legacy of Catholic anti-radicalism, the influence of clerical leadership and institutions in shaping Catholic opinion, and the growing coincidence, in the late 1940's, between the views of Catholic leaders and those of American cold-war leaders generally. Viewed in this light, Catholic anti-Communism, though it may have been unwise and extreme, was neither irrational nor radical. Nor, for that matter, was it truly a mass movement—not, at least, in the sense of a catalytic force that wrenched people away from old loyalties and organized them about new issues and leaders. Indeed, what is striking is the degree to which established elites (in this case the leadership of the Roman Catholic Church) played upon historic fears and suspicions in order to arouse the community.

I

Catholic anti-Communism was, of course, rooted deeply in the Church's violent struggle with the secular liberalism of the nineteenth and twentieth centuries, and it received its earliest expression in papal encyclicals such as *Nostis et Nobiscum*

(1849), *Quanta Cura* (1864), and *Diurturnum Illud* (1881).
The popes believed that Communism was essentially atheistic
and irreligious. They objected to the elimination of private property because they viewed property as the basis of orderly society.
Finally, they believed that Communism struck at the heart of
what the Church was about, namely, the world of God and of
the spirit.[2] In the twentieth century much would happen to Communism as new and highly nationalistic forms of Communism
developed and as various Communists adopted new strategies to
fit new circumstances. In the eyes of the popes, however, Communism was always Communism, and papal thought on the subject remained frozen until the time of Pope John XXIII.

The Bolshevik Revolution in Russia, and the bitter persecution of Russian Catholics that later followed, exacerbated the
Church's hostility to Communism. In 1930, Pope Pius XI condemned the Communists for waging an "atheistic" war on the
Church and mounted a worldwide campaign of prayer for the
Catholics in Russia.[3] From this time on, prayers for the "con-
version of Russia" and sermons on the "sorrows of the Russian
people" became staples of American Catholic piety, repeated almost monotonously in Catholic churches from Boston to San
Diego.

During the early 1930's, the reform programs of Franklin D.
Roosevelt's New Deal attracted many leading Catholic liberals,
among them reformers such as Monsignor John A. Ryan and
Dorothy Day.[4] Catholic voters, meanwhile, played a major role
in the electoral triumphs of Roosevelt and the Democratic Party.
By the late thirties, however, many Catholic leaders had become
increasingly worried about the threat of domestic radicalism, and
they came to associate this threat with the Roosevelt Administration. Although few went so far as Father Charles Coughlin or
the *Brooklyn Tablet,* both of whom denounced the New Deal as
the precursor to a Communist take-over, many of the Church's
leaders were anxious over the emergence of depression-bred

The politics of religion

radicalism. In 1938 the American bishops warned against the "spread of subversive teachings" in the United States and called for a "Crusade for Christian Democracy" to instill civic and social virtues in American youth. Though Catholic liberals continued to dispute the conservative equation of the New Deal with Communism, it was nevertheless true, as the leading student of New Deal Catholicism has concluded, that the issue of Communism, "more than anything else, inhibited further progress in Catholic social thought after 1936." [5]

Catholic leaders also took deep offense at the Roosevelt Administration's recognition of the Soviet Union in 1933. Besides seeming to bestow the Administration's blessing upon Marxism, Roosevelt appeared to be ignoring the profound distress the Church's leaders felt over the persecution of the Russian Church. Even *Commonweal,* the most liberal and pro-Roosevelt of all Catholic publications, opposed the President's action, arguing that it was useless to recognize a government opposed to international law and morality. The arch-conservative *Brooklyn Tablet,* expectedly, outdid all Catholic publications in vituperation and organized mass meetings, petition drives, and public demonstrations to protest the government's action.[6]

What the recognition of Russia had begun, the Spanish Civil War brought to a painful climax. Much as Catholics disliked Roosevelt's Russian policy, they found the Spanish war even more troublesome. With the war simplistically depicted by the Catholic press and the European hierarchy as a struggle between the forces of God and the Anti-Christ, American Catholic leaders grew further alarmed over the dangers, real and imaginary, of Communism, dangers that were underscored in 1937 by the papal encyclical *Atheistic Communism.* American Catholic laymen, significantly, were far more divided over the war than the Church's leaders, with substantial minorities opposing Franco or remaining neutral.[7]

By the late thirties, finally, some Catholics had discovered in anti-Communism a means of identifying themselves with the greater American society. As David O'Brien has concluded: "In fighting the red peril the Catholic could dedicate himself to action which was both Catholic and American. Few would disagree that he was proving his worth as an American and demonstrating the compatibility of faith and patriotism." [8] Thus Catholic anti-Communism was reinforced by the secular anti-Communism of the American political culture. Anti-Communism had become a common denominator, the bulwark of both true Americanism and authentic Catholicism. The Catholic leadership, in combining these explosive elements, had mixed a heady brew that would fire the blood of American Catholics for at least the next two decades.

The zeal of the Church's leaders for the cause of anti-Communism diminished only slightly during World War II. In November 1941, on the eve of America's entry into the war, the American bishops condemned Communism and Nazism as "subversive forces, both in control of powerful governments, both bent on world dominance. . . . Neither system understands or permits freedom in its true Christian sense." [9] Throughout the war the news releases emanating from the National Catholic Welfare Conference, an agency of the Catholic bishops whose function was to provide "Catholic" news for diocesan newspapers, maintained a steady barrage of anti-Russian and anti-Communist propaganda. In 1943, when Warner Brothers released the pro-Soviet film *Mission to Moscow,* the Knights of Columbus condemned the work as an attempt to "spread propaganda on behalf of the atheistic, Communist minority in control of Russia." [10]

As the war drew to a close and the Soviet Union moved deep into Eastern Europe, Catholic leaders across the world became increasingly apprehensive about the fate of Catholics in the occupied countries. The rise of Communist regimes in Eastern Europe and in China, and the subsequent persecution of the

The politics of religion

Church in those lands, raised American Catholic anxiety to a fever pitch. Between 1945 and 1950, diocesan weekly newspapers carried articles in nearly every issue detailing the sufferings of Catholics in Soviet-occupied countries. Church leaders were especially critical of the results of the wartime conferences at Teheran and Yalta. Father James Gillis of the *Catholic World,* a Paulist journal, called upon Americans to "remember that since the beginning of our alliance with Stalin, or at the latest since our 'compromise' with him at Yalta, the crimes of Russia are on our soul." The American bishops issued a strong statement declaring that the agreement was not consistent with the "sovereign equality of peace-loving nations . . . We are struck," the prelates lamented, "by the silence of the three great powers on Lithuania, Estonia and Latvia." Still other Catholics worried about what the Yalta agreements would mean for the Church in eastern Germany and the Balkans.[11]

The most vivid symbol of the Church's struggle, however, was Poland, and throughout 1945 Polish American Catholics thronged to their cathedrals and even took to the streets to protest the Soviet occupation of their homeland. Solemn masses were held in Milwaukee, Chicago, and New York in which church leaders lauded Poland as a "Christian Democracy" and called for its "spiritual liberation." In San Francisco, Archbishop John J. Mitty led a "Mass for the Cause of Poland," timed to coincide with the deliberations over the United Nation's Charter.[12] Prominent Catholic clergymen urged President Truman to press for Soviet withdrawal and free elections, while the Knights of Columbus repeatedly denounced the "conspiracy of silence" surrounding news of Poland.[13] United States recognition of the Soviet-sponsored Polish government in the summer of 1945 was, according to Charles Rozmarek of the Polish-American Congress, "a tragic historical blunder," the result of a "shortsighted policy of appeasement" that was "paving the way for world chaos."[14]

THE SPECTER

The Church's resistance to Communist authority in Eastern Europe was symbolized by such men as Archbishop Aloysius Stepinac of Yugoslavia and Joseph Cardinal Mindszenty of Hungary. More important, the arrest and trial of these prominent leaders galvanized American Catholics and supplied them with martyrs to the cause of anti-Communism.

Defiantly opposed to Marshal Joseph Tito's Communist regime, Stepinac was arrested in September 1946, tried on false charges of having collaborated with the Germans and Italians during the war, and sentenced to sixteen years in prison. American Catholics were shocked by the Communists' cavalier treatment of the archbishop, who was widely regarded as one of the leading spokesmen for world Catholicism. The National Council of Catholic Women (NCCW), the official Catholic women's organization in America, broke its policy of avoiding controversial topics by sending a message to Secretary of State James F. Byrnes urging him to intercede personally with the Yugoslav government. Emphasizing Stepinac's "saintly" character, the NCCW resolution denounced the "atheistic communistic forces" of Marshal Tito.[15]

In December 1946, forty thousand people massed at a huge rally in Philadelphia, again objecting to the persecution of the Church in Yugoslavia and demanding the archbishop's release. The crowd jammed the city's Convention Hall and spilled onto the streets outside. Conspicuously present at the gathering were the mayor of the city, leaders of the Catholic War Veterans who had staged the spectacle, and U.S. senator from Pennsylvania, Francis J. Myers.[16] Other Catholic politicians, including Congressmen John McCormack (Democrat, Massachusetts) and John J. Rooney (Democrat, New York), soon joined the crusade to save Stepinac. McCormack called on the Secretary of State to lodge a formal protest with the Yugoslavs, while Rooney sought, unsuccessfully, to push through the House of Representatives a resolution demanding such a protest.[17]

The politics of religion

The most passionate outbursts, however, came from New York City, inspired perhaps by the leadership of Francis Cardinal Spellman. Speaking at a World Peace Rally in New York on October 6, 1946, Spellman asked the prayers of the Catholic faithful for Stepinac, "whose only crime is fidelity to God and country . . . The confidence and conscience of the American people . . . have again been outraged by this latest infamy and affront to human dignity and decency." [18] To emphasize this conviction, Spellman announced a drive for an Archbishop Aloysius Stepinac High School in New York. Responding eagerly to his call, New York Catholics raised $4,000,000 in less than a year, some $2,000,000 more than was needed.[19] At about the same time that the cardinal was dedicating the new school, a group of fifty Catholic students from St. John's University in Brooklyn picketed the Yugoslav consulate in New York City, acting under the auspices of the Committee for the Liberation of Archbishop Stepinac, which claimed to represent thirty-seven organizations of Catholic laymen in New York City.[20]

The greatest of all Catholic martyrs to Communism, however, was Joseph Cardinal Mindszenty, who had fiercely opposed the efforts of the Hungarian government to reduce the authority of the Church. Mindszenty was arrested on December 26, 1948, and tried on grounds of treason, subversion and spying. At the height of the trial he appeared before the court, a gaunt, broken, and dreadfully sick man. Though he meekly "confessed" his guilt on all counts, most Westerners concluded (probably rightly) that his confession had been extorted. The court sentenced him to death, but later commuted the sentence to life imprisonment.[21] Many American Catholics were appalled at Mindszenty's fate; none more so than Cardinal Spellman who knew and admired him deeply. On February 6, 1949, the cardinal, speaking from the pulpit of St. Patrick's Cathedral in New

York for the first time since V-E Day, called on the leaders of the American government to "raise their voices as one and cry out against and work against" the "Satan-inspired Communist crimes." On another occasion he told a group of Catholic boys belonging to the Catholic Youth Organization that Mindszenty was the victim of "Christ-hating Communists" with "anti-Christian minds drenched and drugged in the devil's cauldron of hatreds and inequities." When the cardinal declared February 6, 1949, a day of prayer for Mindszenty, four thousand Catholic Boy Scouts marched down Fifth Avenue to St. Patrick's Cathedral as part of a public demonstration. That same day, three thousand students at Fordham University, the Jesuit college in the Bronx, recited the rosary together on behalf of Mindszenty, and affirmed their support for a group of student leaders who had sent a telegram of protest to President Truman.[22] Later that year, twenty thousand Catholics gathered at Ebbets Field in Brooklyn to recite prayers for the cardinal and to hear speeches condemning the Communists. The principal speaker of the day contended that Mindszenty had been jailed because "he dared to defend Catholic interests against Red tyrants." [23]

The legacy of the Mindszenty crisis was not only a renewal of Catholic protests against Communism, but a new form of Catholic anti-Communism as well. Catholics of extreme right-wing persuasion began to form Mindszenty Circles and Freedom Foundations, dedicated to the destruction of world-wide Communism and modeled along the lines of Communist cells. Meeting in small groups and acting often in secret, they studied Communist literature, plotted political action, kept the memory of the cardinal alive, and looked for the influence of Communism everywhere. Though small in numbers, they bulked large in influence, thanks to the impressive number of priests they attracted to their ranks. Because of their secretive nature little is known about their organization, though they appear to have

The politics of religion

flourished especially well in southern California and seem to have attracted Catholics whose views were extremely right-wing.[24]

By 1950 the worst attacks on the Church in Eastern Europe were over. The Church had either been reduced to impotence or else, as in Poland, existed only through the grace of an uneasy détente with the country's leadership. The American Catholic press, however, continued to act as though the persecutions were continuing unabated, and it reported even small incidents as though they were major crises in the life of the Church. The News Service of the National Catholic Welfare Conference still continued to pour out dispatches sensationally reporting Communist acts of barbarism. As a result, Catholic reaction to Communism and the cold war continued to be played out against a backdrop of constant crises.

II

While Catholic anti-Communism was rooted in the Church's long struggle with radicalism, and although developments abroad remained a primary focus for the Church's leaders, American clerics were also anxious about domestic Communism. This concern was underscored, as early as 1945, by a report prepared by Father John F. Cronin, a liberal priest who had privileged, though unofficial, access to the files of the Federal Bureau of Investigation and the House Committee on Un-American Activities. Entitled *The Problem of American Communism in 1945,* the 148-page report included chapters on Communism in the labor movement, in the media, and among foreign language groups. It also stressed the influence of Communists in government, including the allegation (nearly three years before it was made public) that Alger Hiss was a Communist. Avoiding the simplistic anti-Communism of the extreme right, the report called for a vigorous program of public education combined with the indirect exercise of Church influence among labor unions, ethnic minorities, and other groups in which Catholics were active. Limited in circulation (two hundred copies were prepared for the American bishops) and never officially acted upon, Cronin's report was nevertheless a clear indication of the Church's great and early interest in domestic Communism.[25]

The political leader of Catholic anti-Communism in America was unquestionably Francis Cardinal Spellman. His was basically a simple faith: Communism was evil, Catholicism and America were good, therefore Catholicism and America must join together in combating atheistic Communism. In the late 1930's and the early war years he had enjoyed frequent meetings with President Roosevelt, whom he seemed to admire greatly. Near the end of the war, however, he had seen Roosevelt "give in," so he thought, to the Communists, granting them concessions that were disastrous both to the security of the United States and to those Catholics unfortunate enough to live behind the Iron Curtain. While he worried much about the fate of the Church in the Iron Curtain countries, he was concerned, even obsessed, with the problem of Communist subversion in the United States.[26] As early as October 1946 he warned that the Communists "are today digging deep inroads into our own nation" and are "tirelessly trying to grind into dust the blessed freedoms for which our sons have fought, sacrificed and died." Later the same year he urged the Catholic chaplains of the Army and Navy to "protect America against aggression of enemies within her borders." Unimpressed by the Communist hunt then sweeping the country, he declared in 1947 that "once again while Rome burns . . . the world continues to fiddle. The strings of the fiddle are committees, conferences, conversations, appeasements—to the tune of no action today." Again and again, in the years that followed, he repeated monotonously the same themes: Communist subversion was making "tools and fools" of Americans, anti-Catholic bigotry in America was caused by Commu-

The politics of religion

nists, and America would be unsafe until every Communist was removed from influence in American life.[27] Without question the nation's best-known Catholic prelate, Spellman took every opportunity to pound home the gospel of anti-Communism, exhorting the practice of a brand of anti-Communism that was both truly Catholic and fully American. His language may have been clumsy and repetitive, but no one could claim that his message was obscure.

If Spellman was the political leader of Catholic anti-Communism, then its prophet and philosopher was Bishop Fulton J. Sheen, also of New York City. For nearly twenty years before McCarthy appeared on the scene, Sheen poured fourth a stream of books, articles, pamphlets, sermons, and speeches detailing the theory and practice of Communism, always with special emphasis on its relationship to Roman Catholicism.[28] For Sheen, as for Spellman, Communism was the epitome of both irreligion and un-Americanism. As early as March 1946 he warned of Communist subversion in America and condemned "the fellow travelers in the United States and those whose hearts bleed for Red Fascism." [29] The good Catholic, it followed, was one who gave unstinting support to the efforts of both the Church and the nation to destroy the Red peril.[30] Though his Catholic followers may have used his prodigious mass of works as a pretext for Communist-hunting, Sheen displayed little interest in that effort. It was just as well, perhaps, since his one foray was conspicuously unsuccessful. In a speech before a group of Catholic journalists in March 1946 he announced that a congressional committee had just uncovered a "full-fledged Soviet agent." Pressed for details, he refused to give either the man's name or position in the government, saying, "I am not here to give information, but to stimulate members of the press." One of those so stimulated, a reporter from *The New York Times,* found that neither the FBI nor HUAC knew anything about Sheen's Soviet spy.[31] No one ever found out who the alleged spy was or even if he existed.

The militant anti-Communism preached by Spellman and Sheen was perhaps best exemplified by the zealous, though sometimes crude, activities of the Catholic War Veterans and the Knights of Columbus. As early as 1946, for example, the Catholic War Veterans, who numbered more than two hundred thousand members nationally, demanded that the United States take firm action against Communist regimes in Eastern Europe. They protested Truman's silence over Yugoslavia and condemned the sending of foreign aid to that country. The national commander of the CWV called on local leaders to oppose such aid until "those ignoble puppets of the Kremlin" showed a willingness to "render to God the things that are God's." [32]

In March 1948, the Veterans picketed the Russian freighter *Chukotka,* then moored at a New Jersey dock, on the grounds that it was carrying materials to Russia that could be used to make war against the United States. They carried signs saying "Hitler and Mussolini were amateurs compared to Pal Joey" (a reference to a Broadway musical called *Pal Joey* and to the Soviet Premier Joseph Stalin) and "American goods for American defense." After halting the loading of the vessel for a short period, they picketed a second Russian vessel, and ended their efforts only when assured that the shippers would be investigated.[33] A year later, when a group of fourteen leftist intellectuals from Russia, Poland, and Czechoslovakia came to New York for a Cultural and Scientific Conference for World Peace, the CWV announced that it would picket the meeting, and a Catholic group dedicated to the freeing of Cardinal Mindszenty declared that it would muster fifty thousand demonstrators. The picketers carried crepe-draped flags of the nations behind the Iron Curtain, as well as placards proclaiming "Communists are not welcome here. We don't want you. Get out!" [34]

The politics of religion

Always a potent force in New York City, the Veterans took special pains to oppose the presence of Communists and their "sympathizers," especially in the city's government and educational system. In mid-1947 they pressured Mayor William O'Dwyer to "purge" the city's payroll of all Communists and "fellow travelers." Later that year they demanded that the Board of Education state why it permitted "subversive" groups, such as the American Youth for Democracy, to use school meeting rooms. Other New York Catholic groups also demanded the removal of Communists from the city payroll. The Holy Name Society of the city's police force complained that New York City had more Communists than any other city of comparable size "outside Moscow." Meanwhile, Brooklyn Catholics successfully stopped a local bank from publishing a series of articles on Russia in its monthly publication for schoolchildren.[35]

As alert as the Veterans were to the problem of Communist subversion, the Knights of Columbus, the largest Catholic fraternal organization in the country, matched them in vigilance, energy, and political resourcefulness. Numbering six hundred thousand members, the Knights declared war on subversion almost as soon as World War II ended. In June 1946 its New York State chapters called upon Americans everywhere to reject candidates for office who supported communism or acted as "fellow travelers." The national convention of the Knights later that year proclaimed a four-point program of action designed to combat Communism, insisting especially on an all-out effort against the "infiltration of atheistic Communism into our American life and economy." Not even the entertainment world was safe from subversives; a New York Knights group urged the boycotting of stage and screen entertainment with which Communists or their "sympathizers" had any connection.[36]

All this anti-Communist activity demanded an appropriate system of education, since Communists were often hard to identify, clever as they were at hiding their real work and assuming

THE SPECTER

misleading disguises. Catholic groups therefore drew up detailed and complex programs designed to educate their fellow Catholics about the wiles and machinations of the Communists. The CWV in July 1948 announced the formation of an Officer Candidate School, which would train two men from each state in the workings of subversive groups, as well as in the methods most appropriate to combating them. After completing the course, each man would return to his state and set up similar schools.[37] The next year the Veterans heralded a nationwide campaign to expose Communist fifth columns in America. The drive would feature the presentation of courses in the detection of Communist subversives, the production of films demonstrating the dangers of Communism, and newspaper advertisements publicizing the domestic Communist menace.[38]

The Knights of Columbus, following a slightly different scenario, built their educational programs around the use of the radio and the town-hall meeting. In 1947 they began a series of six broadcasts, carried over 226 stations, entitled "Safeguards for America." Its purpose was to provide "the truth" about the Communists in America. When the *Daily Worker* called the series the "biggest and most vicious scare hoax in the history of radio," a spokesman for the Knights replied confidently that they could not have had better proof that they were "hitting the Commies where it hurts." "Communism is a lie and a lie hates the truth. The six powerful doses of truth about Communism . . . are giving the comrades a headache." [39] In 1948 the Knights initiated a series of town-hall meetings in Washington, D.C. J. Edgar Hoover sent his congratulations, claiming that there was a "definite need" to arouse the citizenry "to those forces which menace the future security of America." [40]

The News Service of the National Catholic Welfare Conference further contributed to the public clamor over Communism by supplying diocesan papers with a seemingly interminable list of dispatches, meticulously and dramatically chronicling every

The politics of religion

investigation, trial, or suspected act of disloyalty. Equally important were the many pamphlets on Communism produced by Catholic instructional groups in the late forties. Some of the most widely read came from the Catholic Information Society of New York, which printed a series of twenty-six pamphlets on Communism written by such notable conservatives as William H. Chamberlain, Eugene Lyons, Suzanne LaFollette, and the recent convert from Communism to Catholicism, Freda Utley.[41] One of the more lurid of such publications was a comic book entitled *Is This Tomorrow?* which showed a Communist mob attacking St. Patrick's Cathedral in New York and nailing Cardinal Spellman to the door.[42]

Catholic anti-Communism was not restricted, however, to the zealous fundamentalism of Cardinal Spellman or the Catholic War Veterans. Liberal Catholics, too, sought to expunge Communism from American life, though they differed sharply with conservatives over the means to this end. The Catholic liberals who published and read *Commonweal,* for example, derived much of their inspiration from the social encyclicals *Rerum Novarum* (1891) and *Quadregesinno Anno* (1931). The answer to Communism, they believed, lay in an expansion of social programs designed to end hunger, disease, and other ills that drove men toward radicalism. They supported the foreign policies of the Truman Administration, especially the effort to contain Communism through foreign aid, and they opposed repressive legislation such as the Mundt-Nixon bill. Such laws, they believed, frustrated the war on Communism because they created a totalitarian atmosphere that was little different from Communism itself.[43]

Liberal Catholics were especially active in the drive to purge Communists from the American labor movement. By 1945 the Church's leaders had organized nearly one hundred "labor schools," which annually trained more than seven thousand

Catholic trade unionists. Originally formed as part of the Church's labor ministry, they rapidly became focal points in the fight against Communism. Although most of these schools were operated by the Jesuits or by local diocesan authorities, their spirit and purpose was best typified by the Association of Catholic Trade Unionists (ACTU). Organized in 1937 as an offshoot of the Catholic Worker movement, the ACTU was a voluntary association of Catholics interested in the problems of unions. Almost from the very beginning it had directed much of its energy toward the fight against Communism. The ACTU helped train anti-Communist labor leaders, sponsored conferences on anti-Communist strategy and tactics, provided legal aid to those seeking to expel Communists from leadership positions in the unions, and published two widely circulated newspapers, *The Labor Leader* and *The Wage Earner*. By 1949, at least in part as a result of ACTU activities, Communist influence had been virtually eliminated from organized labor.[44]

For all their differences, however, both Catholic liberals and conservatives shared a central core of values and beliefs. Both were passionately, even obsessively, opposed to Communism, profoundly convinced that it represented the greatest of all possible dangers to both Church and Republic. Both shared a brand of patriotism that can only be described as strident though the conservatives outdid the liberals in patriotic gore. Both liberals and conservatives found inspiration in the teachings of the Church, though they selected different traditions. Liberals looked to the social encyclicals; the conservatives limited themselves to the Church's anti-Communist polemics. For that matter, the bulk of conservative inspiration came not from Church teachings but from conservative American politics. Neither, finally, doubted the gravity of the Church's confrontation with Communism, though the liberals were quicker to perceive the reduction in tensions that came in the 1950's.

The politics of religion

III

The impact of Catholic anti-Communism on American politics is not easily measured. Public opinion polls seemed to indicate that Catholics were somewhat more concerned over Communism, somewhat less tolerant of civil liberties, and somewhat more disposed to support Joe McCarthy than was the population at large. The differences between Catholics and the general population were not always dramatic, however, and it would be wrong to overstress the role of public opinion among Catholics.[45] Catholic concern over Communism, moreover, did not express itself in the form of a mass or popular demand for a Red-hunt. Indeed, the battle between the "conservatives," who wanted liberal heads to roll, and the "liberals," who wanted the search for Communists carefully circumscribed by law, seems to have taken place on an elite level. Editors, authors, political leaders, directors of fraternal organizations, and leading clergymen fought out the battle largely among themselves.

By 1950 conservatives in the Catholic leadership were predisposed to respond favorably to Senator Joseph R. McCarthy's call to take up arms in the struggle between "our Western Christian world and the atheistic Communist world," a struggle in which the lines were clearly drawn and the final battle near. Many prominent Catholics played important roles in the drama surrounding the McCarthyite right. They were prominent in the entourage that surrounded Senator McCarthy, while Catholic voluntary groups, such as the Catholic War Veterans and the countless Holy Name societies, rallied quickly behind the senator's banner. He was praised, moreover, by important Church leaders, such as Francis Cardinal Spellman of New York.[46] A smaller group of liberal Catholics, though staunchly anti-Communist, were sharply critical of McCarthyism. This group included the editors of *Commonweal,* joined a little later by their counterparts on *America* and the *Catholic Worker,* by social justice advocates such as Bishop Bernard J. Sheil, and by

Democratic politicians such as Senators Dennis Chavez and
Brien McMahon, Congressman Eugene McCarthy, Democratic
National Committee Chairman Stephen Mitchell, and Secretary
of Labor Maurice Tobin.[47]

In 1946 Catholics, especially Polish Americans, contributed
to a sharp Democratic defeat by defecting to the Republicans
over American policy in Eastern Europe. By 1947, as Clark
Clifford shrewdly noted, "the controlling element" for most
American Catholics was their "distrust and fear of Communism." In 1948 the hostility of Catholic anti-Communists was
deflected from the Truman Administration, which had established a popular image of firm anti-Communism through its
sponsorship of a Federal Employee Loyalty Program, the Truman Doctrine, and the Marshall Plan, and onto Henry Wallace
and the Progressives. By 1950, however, the international crisis
represented by the communization of China and the Korean
War, together with the mounting cry of "Communists in the
State Department," led some Catholics to vote against the Administration. In Maryland, for example, the defection of normally Democratic Catholics may have been crucial in the defeat
of Senator Millard Tydings and the election of his McCarthyite
opponent, John Marshall Butler. More important, in 1952 a
record number of Catholics joined in the Eisenhower landslide.
The Catholic vote, normally 65 percent Democratic, declined to
53 percent primarily, according to contemporary analysts, as a
result of the Korean War and the charge of Communists in
government.[48]

The impact of Catholic anti-Communism on American politics was, of course, both more diffuse and more powerful than
this summary would indicate. It was never simply a question of
Catholic support for McCarthy or of Catholic defections to the
GOP or even, for that matter, of "liberalism" versus "conservatism." More important, though also more difficult to document,
was the broad impact of the Church's anti-Communist crusade

The politics of religion

on the general political climate. It seems clear that Catholic spokesmen, both conservative and liberal, played an important role in injecting the Communist issue into American politics. But it is also important to stress that much of the potency of the Church's appeal derived from the congruence between the Church's position and the secular anti-Communism of American society at large. The frequently strident anti-Communism of Catholic leaders resonated and merged with the militant rhetoric of organized veterans, patriotic societies, Republican conservatives, even the Truman Administration itself. The world was crudely divided between "our Western Christian world" and the "atheistic Communist world," the issues were reduced to an apocalyptic struggle between freedom and tyranny, and Americans of all faiths were called upon to do battle for the Lord. In such a climate compromise became equated with appeasement and dissent with heresy. Foreign policy became more rigid, civil liberties were restricted, and politicians took refuge in the fears they had helped to create.

A VIEW FROM THE RIGHT:

Conservative Intellectuals,

the Cold War, and McCarthy

BY RONALD LORA

The atomic destruction of Hiroshima and Nagasaki in August 1945 and the Senate's condemnation of Senator Joseph McCarthy in December 1954 encompassed a conflict-ridden and volatile decade filled with novel international developments: the temporary American monopoly of the atomic bomb, the Soviet entrenchment in Eastern Europe, the crisis in Greece, Turkey, and Western Europe, the Berlin blockade, the victory in China by the armies of Mao Tse-tung, the Soviet explosion of an A-bomb, the Korean War, and massive revolutionary activity throughout the colonial world. At home freedom of thought and expression were constrained. Political partisanship, the near-war atmosphere created by the exploitation of traditional American anti-Communism, and the growth of statism through militarized budgets and the institution of military conscription all combined to produce a climate hostile to a vigorous and open-minded intellectual life.

This essay discusses conservative contributions to the generation of an anti-Communist hysteria in the United States by examining the writings of prominent conservative intellectuals. This is not to suggest that what came to be called "McCarthyism" was simply conservatism on parade. In recent years a sizable literature has emerged which establishes as well the responsibility of liberal spokesmen and politicians for helping to create a feverish anti-Communist sentiment in the nation.[1] And, in a general sense, McCarthyism *did* reflect the ambiguities, the rootlessness, and the insecurities characteristic of the American social structure, although too much has been made of these as causal factors.[2] But McCarthyism also owed its political potency to those conservative intellectuals who supplied ideological support and rationalization for the political right. It is essential, therefore, to investigate how conservative doctrine, with its emphasis on the need for order and conformity in society, coalesced with national and international events to generate such anger among conservative intellectuals that they actively promoted the growth of McCarthyism.[3]

By 1945 American conservativism had developed a set of attitudes that clearly distinguished conservatives from liberals. First, conservatives tended to prefer institutional stability to change, to stress continuities in history, and to seek to conserve as much of the past as was consonant with a harmonious social system. Second, they identified frequently with the wealthier classes, with privilege, and with vested interests. During the New Deal years this was an important, if invidious, distinction. Liberal tolerance, generosity, and cooperation seemed to contrast sharply with conservative selfishness, social insensitivity, and economic exploitation. Third, twentieth-century conservatives identified with programs that supported law and order, states' rights, private enterprise, and a nationalistic foreign policy. Liberals, by contrast, supported programs that sought to regulate business, insure civil rights, increase public power, and extend social welfare. Fourth, modern conservatives defended certain doctrinal positions such as limited government, the inviolable nature of private property, the primacy of empiricism over reason, and the belief that historical change must not be engineered but permitted to unfold organically. They believed, moreover, that a moral consensus was necessary to maintain order, harmony, and social cohesion. Finally, they upheld the doctrine of original sin, believing that man's disagreeable habits were more realistically explained by innate depravity than by environmental theories.[4] This last assumption about human nature informed every significant conservative theory and, in political terms, led logically to programs for the forceful control of what conservatives believed were the irrational and often perverse habits of man.

Throughout most of American history conservatives have labored more strenuously to preserve social harmony than to

A view from the right

liberate the individual. Unsympathetic to the notion of a managed society, which they have variously called the "welfare state," the "planned society," or "socialism," modern American conservatives have sought instead to build a harmonious society by creating a deep-rooted moral and intellectual consensus. In their view, deviant behavior and ideas were heretical and ought to be suppressed, because they posed a threat to social cohesiveness. It was this theoretical postulate, together with the belief in human fallibility, that moved postwar conservatives quickly toward repression of internal dissent.

The conservative view of Communism was a case in point. Deep-seated conservative antagonism toward Communism, muted during the early forties, reemerged in 1944 and 1945 following the wartime conferences at Teheran and Yalta and led conservatives to attack what they viewed as American appeasement of the U.S.S.R. Together with frightened liberals, they created a Munich syndrome so rigidly applied that the United States soon became a challenger of peace as often as a defender. The Truman Administration, of course, had its own reasons for pursuing a vigorously anti-Communist foreign policy. Nevertheless, in the absence of a militant conservative opposition, the Truman Administration would have enjoyed greater room for political and diplomatic maneuver during the early years of the cold war, for it would not have been compelled to repeatedly demonstrate that it was tough on Communism.

Unfortunately, this was not the case. As the cold war intensified after 1945, conservatives increasingly denounced the Democratic Administration for its naïve, even disloyal, policies toward Communism at home and abroad. The conservative intellectuals who articulated this position, and who are the subjects of this essay, included James Burnham, Frank Meyer, John Chamberlain, Whittaker Chambers, Freda Utley, Clarence Manion, Frank Hanighen, William Henry Chamberlain, William F. Buckley, Jr., and other contributors to the conservative journals

THE SPECTER

Human Events, the *American Mercury,* and the *Freeman.* These conservative intellectuals in turn helped to rationalize the programs of a political right, which included Senators Robert Taft, William Knowland, Richard Nixon, Styles Bridges, Pat McCarran, Kenneth Wherry, Homer Ferguson, Karl Mundt, William Jenner, and, after 1950, Joseph McCarthy. The concerns of both conservative intellectuals and politicians were amplified, moreover, by a cadre of right-wing journalists that included Hearst writers George Sokolsky, Westbrook Pegler, Howard Rushmore, and J. B. Matthews, Walter Trohan of the McCormick newspapers, David Lawrence, and Frederick Woltman. Taken as a group they represented for the most part the old Social Darwinian or fundamentalist wing of conservatism associated with the National Association of Manufacturers, the Chamber of Commerce, and, on occasion, the American Legion. They looked to Herbert Hoover as a voice from the past whose warnings about Communism had, in their eyes, been vindicated; and they enthusiastically encouraged the passage of the Smith, Taft-Hartley and McCarran acts.[5]

II

Nothing united cold-war conservative intellectuals more solidly than the philosophical conviction that Soviet Communism was a mortal enormity, behaviorally wrong, and ethically evil. This conservative postulate never changed. What did change was the hysterical intensity of their anti-Communism and their growing belief that this foreign ideology posed a dangerous internal threat to American liberties. Herbert Hoover, who occupied the center of the conservative spectrum, was an accurate representative of conservative thinking on this issue. Thus in June 1941, several days after Nazi Germany attacked the Soviet Union, he described the Communist power as "one of the bloodiest tyrannies and terrors ever erected in history. . . . a militant destroyer of the worship of God," and he recommended

A view from the right

that the United States stand aside and allow Germany and the Soviet Union to destroy each other.[6] When the war ended, the former President portrayed the specters of Communist revolution and creeping socialism as the primary threats to American freedom. And by 1950 he was fond of repeating the Manichean dogma of the right that there was not one world, but two worlds: one was good, the other evil; one world was "militaristic, imperialistic, atheistic, and without compassion." The other world still held to "belief in God, free nations, human dignity, and peace." [7]

Other conservatives agreed. Clare Boothe Luce, an important link between conservative intellectuals and Republican politicians, wrote shortly after the collapse of the Chinese Nationalist regime that the Communist philosophical-religious doctrine of man held simply that he was "an animal without a soul." Man in the Communist view, she declared, was "born to live and die like a pig; you root, and rut, and rot." [8] According to columnist George Sokolsky, Communism was depraved in its very essence. Its rules of life were premised not on love but hate, not on cooperation but confrontation, not on God but on materialistic determinism. Joseph Stalin, in his view, represented the "inevitable product of a wicked idea." [9] In the book that launched his career in 1951, William F. Buckley, Jr., identified the most important duel in the world as a conflict between Christianity and atheism.[10] A year later, Whittaker Chambers wrote that his "witness" to his generation was to testify that in Communism was focused "the concentrated evil of our time." [11]

On the conservative left the poet-historian Peter Viereck characterized the two world powers similarly: "Soviet Russia is the extremest plutocracy in history. The most savage and relentless enemy of all workmen all over the globe is Russia's rich ruling class. The Soviet is the highest fulfillment of the selfish ideals of unlimited monopoly capitalism." On the other hand, America was "history's extremest example of the freedom and well-being of the workingman and his trade-unions. . . . the highest fulfillment of the honorable ideals of socialism (though achieved—significantly—not by socialist means but by a democratic capitalism)." [12] And following the death of Joe McCarthy, William S. Schlamm, then an editor of Buckley's *National Review,* pronounced the conventional conservative judgment on McCarthyism: ". . . at the heart of what McCarthy said and did," wrote Schlamm, "was the very essence of Western civilization." McCarthy "saw the central truth of his age: that his country, his faith, his civilization was at war with communism." An innocent warrior, McCarthy "saw the gargoyles of the Anti-Christ staring and sneering at him from everywhere, and innocently he reached out to crush them . . . and it killed him." [13]

This dichotomous religious vision enabled conservative intellectuals to invest "the crisis of our times" with both historical and metaphysical meaning. Such a vision, in turn, precluded negotiation, for believers could not compromise with issues so fervidly defined as evil. In matters of good and evil, Chambers wrote his son, "evil can only be fought." To this Buckley added that because "truth will not of itself dispel error," the fight against evil must be championed "on every level and at every opportunity." Such absolutist thought poisoned the political climate following World War II and furnished the link uniting the efforts of conservatives to establish a moral and intellectual consensus in American society with James Burnham's advocacy of preventive war against the Soviet Union.[14] Foreign policy, so often discussed in a moralistic framework by cold-war conservatives, had become primary to the politics of the 1940's; and consequently, the conservative predisposition toward moralistic diagnosis and the consensual society became unusually important.[15]

With the moral evil of Communism (not merely Stalinism) established as an absolute, it was difficult for conservatives to understand that hostile Soviet actions were at times provoked

A view from the right

by Western policies. Instead, they believed that Russian policy flowed deterministically from Marxist-Leninist theory. From 1943 until the announcement of the Truman Doctrine, conservative writers warned repeatedly that Soviet expansion would continue, and that peace between the United States and the Soviet Union was an illusion of liberals and fellow travelers. In a 1943 speech on preparations for a postwar peace settlement, Herbert Hoover stressed that Stalin's expansionist objectives should be obvious, and in 1945 he warned that "Communism and Creeping Socialism [were] sweeping over Europe." [16] During 1944 contributors to *Human Events* and the *American Mercury* pointedly admonished American leaders not to be misled by wartime cooperation with Russia. "Moscow has for months now made no secret as to its expansionist plans for Eastern Europe," wrote Felix Morley, co-editor of *Human Events* in January 1944. The American public had been led into a "dangerous oversimplification" as to Russian policy and purpose, he added later that year.[17] No one could predict where the Soviet drive would stop. Less than three months after the Teheran Conference, Frank C. Hanighen, Morley's co-editor, warned that the Russian military and political tide in Eastern Europe had so swelled that "reestablishment of the balance of power may no longer be possible in Europe." [18]

William Henry Chamberlain, the author of several books on Soviet Russia and a frequent contributor to *Human Events* and the *American Mercury,* agreed. The West must prepare for the worst, he wrote in February 1944, for Stalin's Russia would not turn democratic in the foreseeable future. Chamberlain believed, as did conservative writers generally, that Stalin, unlike Western leaders, suffered under no pressures to seek accommodation with the other side. He complained that the Teheran Conference had not guaranteed the independence of Eastern Europe, and he predicted that because "Appeasement, this time of Stalin, [was] once more in the ascendancy," Western leaders had created a second Munich.[19] In early 1944 some twenty publicists, radio broadcasters, and writers (including William Agar, Major George Fielding Eliot, Raymond Leslie Buell, and H. V. Kaltenborn) issued a joint statement calling upon the Soviet Union to honor the Atlantic Charter and to support genuine Polish independence or else risk "estranging millions of Americans whose opinions may be decisive in the development of our foreign policy." [20]

The Yalta Conference seemed to confirm conservative suspicions. Yalta, declared Felix Morley, echoing Chamberlain's earlier view of Teheran, was another Munich. Russia's *de facto* acquisition of nearly one-third of Poland through the use of the Curzon line, wrote Morley, clearly violated the provision of the Atlantic Charter prohibiting territorial changes not in accord with "the freely expressed wishes of the peoples concerned." [21] According to Eugene Lyons, liberals were guilty of appeasement. He granted that Stalin probably held the best cards in Eastern Europe, but he nevertheless concluded that on the Polish question Uncle Sam had "lost his shirt of principles and pawned a large part of his future moral wardrobe as well." [22]

David Dallin, a conservative scholar of Russian affairs, expressed a similar thesis in two widely reviewed books published in 1944 and 1945. In *The Big Three* Dallin lamented the political blindness toward Russia that had been "manifest during the last several years," and elaborately outlined the Soviet tactic of using deceit, ruse, and concealment in foreign affairs. These were, of course, standard conservative themes. Dallin, however, went considerably beyond them in attempting to justify his ideological preconceptions through what he termed was a "realistic appraisal" of a great power conflict. The fate of Hitler and Napoleon, he declared, suggested that no power could possess only half of Europe. "The unwritten law of Europe prescribes that you must take all the rest." What was at stake, then, was all or nothing. Hitler had been driven to Stalingrad, he wrote, not

A view from the right

out of blindness to the dangers of invading Russia, but because of "a logical and inevitable necessity." Peace, in Dallin's view, was scarcely possible. Although he acknowledged that there was still time for the Soviet Union to eliminate Eastern Europe as a source of future conflict by retreating to its national borders, nothing in his book warranted such a hope. Indeed, after surveying a century and a half of Russian-American relations, he concluded that "There is nothing . . . which in itself can be reassuring for the future." [23]

In the summer of 1945 Dallin further warned that Russia would apply the same programs in Asia that she had used in Poland, the Balkans, and Eastern Europe generally. One could not ignore the "inescapable fact" that China was "cast for a role similar to that of Poland." He scoffed at the notion that the Chinese Communists might be independent from Moscow, and he reaffirmed, in a revised edition of *The Real Soviet Russia,* published in 1947, that "a real and durable resolution of the increasing international tensions can come only from Russia, in the shape of an internal transformation." Should this not occur, war was inevitable.[24]

Dallin's major contribution from 1944 to 1947, then, was to fortify conservative assumptions regarding Russia. He provided abundant data on Russia's failures, both practical and moral, and he buttressed the conservative view that Soviet wartime cooperation constituted merely a temporary retreat in a permanent war plan against the free world. He refused to consider whether Western policy could substantially moderate Soviet conduct in international relations, and he placed the responsibility for world peace squarely, if precariously, on Russian shoulders.

Conservative intellectuals were also, unsurprisingly, sharply critical of the Roosevelt and Truman policies toward China. They interpreted the revolutionary turmoil in that country as part of the Communist world conspiracy, and they criticized the United States government for faltering in its support of Chiang Kai-shek.[25] Foremost among such critics was Freda Utley, a passionate ex-Communist who made several trips to China, including a visit, in 1946, to the Communist capital of Yenan. Born in England, Utley had joined the British Communist Party during the late 1920's and had later moved to the Soviet Union. She left Russia in the late thirties after her husband, a Russian, was lost to Stalin's secret police during the great purges. Arriving in the United States in 1939, she became involved in the politics of the extreme right. She worked as a director of the American-China Policy Association and served for two years as the *Reader's Digest* special correspondent in China.

In her book *Last Chance in China,* published in 1947, Utley outlined the need for "a new kind of world hegemony," not an imperialism of brute force, but "a Pax Americana as the only alternative to a Communist totalitarian world or the destruction of civilized life through an atomic war." Peace could come only if the United States used "her few years of 'atom monopoly' to order the world a little nearer to the heart's desire of all mankind." The United States, however, she lamented, seemed interested only in bringing its men home and in forgetting the rest of the world. In China, where Russia threatened American interests, economic considerations, if nothing else, dictated a reversal of this policy. This would become evident, she argued,

> *if mass unemployment comes following the postwar boom, and foreign trade seems a solution for economic crisis and a substitute for the vanished frontier. America's lavish use of her raw material resources has already created some shortages. We are no longer free of the necessity to import vital strategic materials. There may*

A view from the right

*soon be an economic basis for American interest in free
trade and a free world obtainable only through the
exertion of American power.*

To protect American interests, she suggested a program of
large-scale aid to China. Two or three billion dollars would suf-
fice to bolster the Chinese economy and to relieve the worst
poverty in limited areas, but at least ten to fifteen billion dollars
of military aid would be necessary to save China from the Communists.[26] Beyond this explicit though vague faith in the efficacy
of military solutions, she offered few suggestions.

III

Until 1947, then, conservative critics of American foreign
policy had failed to formulate a systematic counteroffensive
strategy for the United States. Utley's *Last Chance in China*
was only the latest manifestation of this period of drift. The
situation changed dramatically, however, with the appearance in
early 1947 of James Burnham's *Struggle for the World*. Burnham, then professor of philosophy at New York University,
operated from two assumptions. First, his reading of Arnold
Toynbee's *Study of History* convinced him that Western civilization had reached the stage that demanded the creation of a universal empire. The two super-powers in pursuit of the empire,
the United States and the Union of the Soviet Socialist Repub-
lics, might be destroyed in the process, "but one of them must
be." [27] Second, the political elite in the Kremlin exercised complete control over international Communism; which Burnham
defined as "a worldwide, conspiratorial movement for the conquest of a monopoly of power in the era of capitalist decline.
Politically it is based upon terror and mass deception; economi-
cally it is, or at least tends to be, collectivist; socially it is totalitarian." Like most cold-war conservatives, Burnham believed
that Communism was a self-conscious and purposeful con-

THE SPECTER

spiracy. The thought that Communism was one among many possible responses to social discontent and that it held attractions for reformers in less developed countries was well beyond his range of social analysis. Social problems furnished a kind of manure to aid its growth, Burnham conceded, but Communism was "independent of the more permanent problem of social conditions." [28] The implacable drive to international expansion and conquest of non-Communist systems flowed inexorably from messianic Communist theory.

It followed from Burnham's analysis that once the Soviet Union obtained the secret of the atomic bomb it would probably use it against the United States. Since no nation could prevent Communism's attempt to conquer the world, the only viable alternative for the United States was to take the initiative in creating a world empire, "set up at least in part through coercion (quite probably including war, but certainly the threat of war), and in which one group of peoples . . . would hold more than its equal share of power." This deductive analysis reflected Burnham's conviction that basic issues such as sovereignty should not be compromised. "They must be *settled*," he emphasized; "That means that on basic issues one side must win and the other must lose." [29]

To thwart the growth of Soviet Communist power, Burnham also demanded the immediate suppression of Communism within the United States,[30] intervention wherever Soviet pressure appeared, the development of a worldwide propaganda campaign to stir Soviet citizens to revolt against their leaders, and the withholding of economic aid to countries sympathetic to Soviet objectives.[31] Should economic and political concessions fail to draw small nations into the new American empire, economic and military force must be employed. Surprisingly, he suggested that Americans join the inhabitants of Great Britain and her dominions in common citizenship and political union.

The Struggle for the World was widely reviewed and hailed

A view from the right

as an important book even by those who disagreed with its contents. The *American Mercury* and *Life* magazine carried condensations of the book; *Life* reprinted those passages that advocated the suppression of domestic Communism and the need for the United States to unilaterally assume the role of world leadership. *Time* magazine suggested that the book, while frightening in its message, was true. *The Struggle for the World* appeared during the very week in which President Truman announced the doctrine of containment, and to the editors of the *Christian Century,* it seemed to provide the intellectual rationale for administration policies.[32] But with his demand for an American world empire and a campaign to create internal revolution within the Soviet Union, Burnham went well beyond the limitations of containment theory and anticipated by five years the Republican Party's commitment to the liberation of enslaved countries.

The growing militancy of anti-Communist intellectuals, such as Burnham, coalesced in the late forties with the conservative critique of New Deal liberalism. Between 1933 and 1945 conservative critics had emphasized five dangers to freedom which they believed were inherent in the New Deal: its fiscal irresponsibility, its incitement of class conflict, its socialistic approach to economic recovery, its rampant centralization of governmental powers, and its substitution of government by men for government by law.[33] Such criticisms were made throughout the thirties and into the forties, but were always limited in their effectiveness by the widespread popular acceptance of the New Deal. Nevertheless, most conservatives continued this traditional attack on welfare economics until shortly before the 1948 election. *Human Events,* for example, regularly attacked President Truman and stressed the dangers of unconstitutional government, civil rights reform, and planned economics.[34] Even Felix Morley, a conservative who was keenly alive to the danger of an emerging American imperialism, exploded repeatedly over domestic welfare

policies, damning Truman's election campaign as "pure socialism and nothing else." [35]

But the political context of 1948, the Soviet-inspired coup
in Czechoslovakia, and the Whittaker Chambers charges against
Alger Hiss all produced important shifts in conservative tactics.
More and more, conservatives stressed the uniqueness of Communism, and not only the threat posed by Soviet expansion but
also the danger of internal subversion.[36] The allegation that the
government was infiltrated by Communists, moreover, served
to link conservatives' fear of the Soviet Union with their antipathy to domestic reform. John T. Flynn, in *The Roosevelt Myth,*
charged that Roosevelt had maneuvered the nation into war
against Japan in order to solve domestic economic problems.
And in a bold display of unsupported generalizations he asserted that Communists were permitted to work within government circles toward the objective of destroying capitalism:

> *It mattered not what the New Dealer touched [Flynn
> wrote], it became a torch to be grabbed, it became an
> instrument for use in his adventures in social engineer-
> ing, and after June, 1941, when Hitler turned on his
> partner Stalin, these bureaus became roosting places for
> droves of Communist termites who utilized their posi-
> tions as far as they dared to advance the interests of
> Soviet Russia and to help 'dispense with the superficial
> paraphernalia of capitalism' in this country under cover
> of the war.*[37]

Edna Lonigan, a former college professor who had served
with the Farm Credit Administration and with the Treasury
Department during the New Deal, outlined for readers of
Human Events the infiltration of the federal government since
1933. The first circle of an emerging Red network was established in the Department of Agriculture from which location it

A view from the right

spread to the Office of Education and to other government agencies, to colleges, and to labor unions. She alleged that the Stalinist members of the network "managed Dumbarton Oaks, UN, UNRRA, our Polish and Spanish policies. They gave Manchuria and Northern Korea to Communism . . . and wrote the infamous instructions under which General Marshall was sent to China. They dismantled German industry, ran the Nuremberg trials and even sought to dictate our economic policy in Japan." Other journalists stressed that there could be no such thing as an "American" Communist Party and drew attention to the influence of foreign-directed totalitarianism in Hollywood.[38]

By attacking domestic reform programs and thus sowing seeds of suspicion, these writers helped to forge a climate of repression long before Senator McCarthy emerged on the scene. Yet, these conservatives were uncertain as to how to handle such a conspiracy. Variously they advocated passage of the Mundt-Nixon bill, the withdrawal of civil rights from Communists, informed "red-baiting," and the strengthening of the federal loyalty program. With James Burnham they believed that a Third World War was already under way, a war fought not with troops locked in armed conflict, but a covert war in which internal agents and fellow travelers played a commanding role.

The conservative infatuation with Communism's allegedly novel powers led, in turn, to a conspiracy theory with few parallels in the history of demonology in America. This conspiratorial view was in part rooted in the conservative doctrine that history is purposive, directed by God, by the laws of nature, or by some vaguely articulated transcendent power. The plan of history was good and, moreover, identical with the interests of American political capitalism. Undermining or threatening influences were conspiratorial (evil) and hence subject to forcible suppression. Nothing was left to chance. Errors of human judgment, historical accidents, misperceptions, and good intentions gone awry were cast aside as irrelevant factors. With these *a priori* assumptions, conservative intellectuals created a Manichean theory of history and politics that anticipated by more than a decade the "protracted conflict" school of historians and political scientists who interpreted Communist political, military, economic, and psychological policies as merely shifting tactics of a comprehensive war against the "free world." [39]

In this intellectual and political atmosphere, midway between the creation of the North Atlantic Treaty Organization in 1949 and the outbreak of the Korean War in June 1950, James Burnham published his second major analysis of American foreign policy. In *The Coming Defeat of Communism,* Burnham conceded that the United States had moved from a policy of appeasement to one of containment. But he also believed that such a policy was still inadequate, lacking in his view the courage to "smash the Communist power." [40] To decisively defeat world Communism, Burnham proposed a "deal" with the Soviet Union, which included: (1) "The liquidation *de facto* of the Communist fifth column" throughout the world; (2) "the cessation of Soviet-directed propaganda in furtherance of Communist world domination"; (3) "the total withdrawal of the Red Army—uniformed or undercover, the MVD, and all other related Soviet institutions, from all territory outside the pre-1939 Soviet borders"; (4) "A free choice of government, after suitable preparation, by the peoples of all the territories and nations which have been submitted to *de facto* Soviet control since 1939." The "suitable preparation" included the fulfillment of the three measures already noted plus "the return of all those . . . imprisoned or sent to slave camps; the return of exiles; a period of education and discussion; and internationally supervised elections." (5) "A sufficient modification of the internal Soviet structure to guard the world against its secret and irresponsible militarization." This would require a forced "opening up of the

Soviet Union to normal intercourse with the rest of the world" and "the prohibition of the manufacture of atomic and other weapons of mass destruction." [41]

Nor was this all. "The terms of this deal," Burnham added, "fall very far short of what we should, and do, desire with respect to Russia." The United States might find it desirable, he continued, to insist on a means of guaranteeing political freedom in Russia, and a free choice of sovereignty by the various nationalities within the Soviet Union. In any case, the five principal points were not negotiable: "They are minimum demands, to be accepted, unilaterally and *in toto.*" Burnham did not shrink from the question of preventive war. Americans were repelled by this idea, he asserted, because of intellectual confusion. Since the Third World War had already commenced, the question of delivering a first strike was merely an expedient, and not a moral, issue. If lives could be saved and a workable world policy could be obtained more easily by a preventive strike, it became "morally obligatory." The United States should say in effect: "We are ready to settle without war. Here are our demands. Meet them, and you may live." [42]

Burnham's callous rhetoric, though extreme, was not untypical of cold-war conservatism. Indeed, his prescriptions were repeated, in only slightly modified form, by powerful conservative politicians. Senator McCarthy, for example, inserted in the *Congressional Record* an editorial of the Ashland (Wisconsin) *Daily Press,* which proposed that the United States "name 100 Russian leaders beginning with Stalin and let us tell the world that they must abdicate or be rubbed out. Then let us get down to business and finish the job, which by our own folly we have allowed to grow so big that it represents the greatest challenge that ever faced America and that ever faced humanity." [43]

Following the outbreak of the Korean War, conservative rhetoric became increasingly more apocalyptic. World War III had now begun in earnest, they contended, and the United States must therefore, at long last, purge traitors and their dupes from American life.[44]

The clearest indication of the new conservative militancy was the substantial support among politicians for the use of atomic weapons in Korea. Politicians who publicly favored atomic warfare, with or without minimal qualifications, included Senators Owen Brewster (Republican, Maine), Ralph E. Flanders (Republican, Vermont), Harry P. Cain (Republican, Washington), Bourke B. Hickenlooper (Republican, Iowa), Edwin C. Johnson (Democrat, Colorado), Henry Cabot Lodge, Jr. (Republican, Massachusetts), Zales N. Ecton (Republican, Montana), Olin D. Johnston (Democrat, South Carolina), and Styles Bridges (Republican, New Hampshire), and Representatives Lloyd Bentsen, Jr. (Democrat, Texas), Overton Brooks (Democrat, Louisiana), and Joseph F. Holt (Republican, California).[45] On at least two occasions General Dwight Eisenhower, first as president of Columbia University and later as President-elect of the United States, supported the use of the atomic bomb against material targets though presumably not against personnel. Harold E. Stassen, then president of the University of Pennsylvania, and General James A. Van Fleet, former commander of the Eighth Army, supported a "limited" use of atomic weapons, while Governor Thomas E. Dewey (Republican, New York), responding to questions during an election-eve telethon in 1952, declared that he "personally would favor using atomic artillery in Korea." [46] This readiness to employ doomsday weapons indicated how completely the times had caught up with Burnham's conservative critiques of 1947 and 1949. The advocates of atomic warfare agreed with President Truman that Korea was a major test of the West's ability to survive Communist aggression, but they surpassed him in their willingness to convert it into a life-or-death conflict.

The emergence of the cold war, the collapse of Nationalist China, and the war in Korea all combined with intense parti-

A view from the right

sanship to undermine the last important remnants of the libertarian right.[47] The libertarian right, exemplified by men such as Herbert Hoover and Robert Taft, had resisted America's entry into World War II and continued in the years that followed to oppose the foreign policies of the Roosevelt and Truman Administrations. They feared the centralization of power and the use of unorthodox fiscal techniques, which had accompanied America's exercise of global power. They therefore resisted foreign military and economic aid, collective security, and the draft. Under the impact of the cold war, however, the libertarian right was transformed.[48]

The most succinct contemporary justification of the transformation of the old right appeared in January 1952 when William F. Buckley, Jr., fresh from the instant success of his *God and Man at Yale,* called for changes in Republican Party policy. He had always considered himself an individualist, even an anarchist, he wrote; and he had believed with Herbert Spencer that the state was "begotten of aggression and by aggression." [49] But the threat posed by Soviet power and aggression made *survival* "the most important issue of the day." In response, libertarians now had "to accept Big Government for the duration—for neither an offensive nor a defensive war can be waged . . . except through the instrument of a totalitarian bureaucracy within our shores." In practice, he declared, Republicans "will have to support large armies and air forces, atomic energy, central intelligence, war production boards, and the attendant centralization of power in Washington—even with Truman at the reins of it all." [50] Buckley's youthful articulation of Republican campaign strategy was a message of suicide for the dwindling libertarian opposition to the Leviathan state, for the preoccupation with national security demanded large budgets and extensive taxing powers.

Buckley's confident assertions obscured the agony and irrita-

tion other conservatives suffered as they moved fitfully from a
quasi-libertarian position toward state directed anti-Communism. Among politicians this was reflected most poignantly in
the senatorial career of Robert A. Taft, the foremost Republican of his generation.[51] Taft's troubled experience with foreign
policy came to a head in 1950 when he was unable to reconcile
his opposition to extensive overseas involvement, his fear of
American imperialism, and his fiscal integrity with his political
partisanship, his anti-Communist militancy regarding Asia, his
belated recognition of the military as well as ideological threat
to American interests posed by the Soviet Union, and his open
support for the anti-Communist investigations of Senator Joseph
McCarthy.

At the outset of World War II, Taft had courageously urged
his country to remain neutral and had opposed lend-lease and
repeal of the "cash-and-carry" provisions of the neutrality act.
During the war he had cautioned against converting the defeat
of the Fascist powers into a crusade for Pax Americana and
warned of the possibility of American imperialism.[52] Afterward
he participated in every debate that surrounded Truman's foreign policies and offered extensive criticism. In 1947 he criticized the President's call for a "Truman Doctrine" in Greece
and Turkey. Truman's request for aid to those two countries,
he felt, would make impossible effective American protest
against similar Soviet policies in her sphere of interest.[53] Believing that the Soviets posed little military threat to Western
Europe, he voted against the NATO alliance of 1949, arguing
that its provocativeness could produce the very aggression it was
designed to prevent. Furthermore, should the Soviet Union undertake further aggression, the United States would find itself
bound to defend its allies everywhere, a task clearly beyond the
capacities of any nation that hoped to remain free.[54] Finally,
when outlining Republican Party policy in April 1949, Taft re-

minded his more aggressive colleagues that excessive economic expansion would engender anti-American sentiment abroad and also dictate a militaristic foreign policy:

> *It is easy to slip into an attitude of imperialism and to entertain the idea that we know what is good for other people better than they know themselves. From there it is an easy step to the point where war becomes an instrument of public policy rather than the last resort to maintain our liberty.*[55]

Yet Taft never questioned the cardinal axiom of cold-war foreign policy: virulent anti-Communism. He "was rabid on the subject of Communism," a friend once noted. "Just the word would make him furious about it." [56] Taft's anti-Communism increasingly influenced his foreign policy and ultimately undermined most of his criticisms of containment. Although he had reservations, he voted for both the Truman Doctrine and the Marshall Plan. And after voting against NATO, he supported Truman's intervention in Korea, supported sending a limited number of ground troops to Europe, defended General Douglas MacArthur's conduct of the Korean War, endorsed McCarthyism, and voted to extend the draft.[57] Though he occasionally still spoke out on principle, increasingly he voted his fears.

In 1951 Taft published *A Foreign Policy for Americans,* a book designed to clarify and publicize his views of world affairs. In it he charged that the Korean and Chinese episodes had demonstrated the ineffectiveness of the United Nations, and he maintained that there was "no choice now except to rely on our armed forces and alliances with those nations willing to fight the advance of Communism." He placed full responsibility for the Korean War and the communization of Eastern Europe and China on the Democratic Party and called for a massive propaganda campaign on behalf of freedom and liberty. He was no

THE SPECTER

longer fearful of provoking the Soviet Union and he embraced the doctrine of liberation by joining James Burnham and others in calling for the infiltration of Communist countries by American secret agents. He called for a thorough house-cleaning in the State Department, condemned the Yalta Conference, belatedly endorsed NATO, and extolled air power as the chief basis for American security.[58]

Thus "Mr. Republican" laid to rest the last lingering traces of his earlier isolationism. That same year Congress passed an amendment to the Mutual Security Act, introduced by Charles Kersten (Republican, Wisconsin), which provided $100,000,000 for subsidizing Army units made up of refugees from Iron Curtain countries. A year later the Republican presidential candidates established party policy for the ensuing campaign by formally supporting "the liberation of the satellite countries." [59]

IV

Conservatives who in this postwar time of crisis had found the general outlines of a liberationist foreign policy agreeable likewise accepted internal repression as its domestic counterpart. They extended their method of moralistic dichotomization to domestic issues and united their rabid anti-Communist bias with an attempt to develop a positive definition of conformity. Both liberation and internal repression were logical expressions of a philosophy that valued moral authority, discipline, tradition, original sin, and an "ordered society." Truth in this philosophy partook of the universal and the absolute. Indeed, conservative literature overflowed with hostility to the pragmatic conception that truth is developmental, that ideas and practices lose and gain in truth value.[60] Given this theoretical postulate, loyalty could be defined and heresy identified. It also became easier to say when censorship was permissible, even obligatory. Conservatives, like others, varied considerably in fixing the precise limits of dissent; but they distinguished themselves by rejecting

A view from the right

the pragmatic doctrines of American liberalism in their search for the conditions of conformity.

Unlike liberals, who in theory would not seek to restrain dissident movements unless they constituted "a clear and present danger," conservatives wanted to proscribe activities that were merely undesirable. They believed, as Wilmore Kendall later put it, that the United States ought to suppress Communism "on the grounds merely that such a movement is undesirable in the United States, and that the proscription of an undesirable movement is clearly within the power of Congress—clearly, and without any complications about impairment of 'freedom of speech' or 'clear and present danger.' " [61] Since Communists stood outside the American consensus, society could legitimately deny them legal protection—not because they were dangerous, but because, as Kendall put it, "from the standpoint of the consensus, their doctrines were wrong and immoral." [62]

This argument, which was used to justify the Hatch Act, the Smith Act, the McCarran Internal Security Act, and the Communist Control Act, reflected a narrow understanding of the fundamental nature of American democratic ideals. It also confirmed a little-discussed but positive relationship between conservative doctrine and political practice. It is hardly accidental, one observer has written, "that conservatives prefer to believe in man's wickedness, that they choose to see man as fallen, untrustworthy, lawless, selfish, and weak." For expressed in political practice, this doctrine may "lie at the root of the conservative inclination to regulate and control man; to ensure that he will not violate the conditions necessary for order; to train him to value duty, obedience, and conformity." [63]

Kendall refused to recognize the extent to which McCarthyism was an attack not on Communism but on the New Deal. Nor did he consider how conservatives often linked liberalism and Communism on programmatic grounds, and how McCarthyism was also an expression of irritation, anger, and frustration at the turn of events in international affairs. But he unerringly documented just how it was that cold-war conservatives wanted to maintain the status quo or, in this instance, to influence historical change. In the interest of social harmony they replaced liberal "social engineering" with a moral and intellectual form of engineering far more coercive and threatening to individual liberties.

Such reasoning informed William F. Buckley, Jr., and L. Brent Bozell's 1954 defense of Senator Joseph McCarthy.[64] The issue for them was not merely conformity but its nature. If it were determined that consent to a certain end was desirable, then society (more specifically, government) might undertake such measures as were necessary to coerce agreement. "Some coercive pressure—i.e., restrictive sanctions of some sort—against dissidents are indispensable to the achievement of *any* conformity," they declared. Whether the means be education, social pressure, laws, or harassment by government committees was less important to the two apologists for McCarthyism than that coercion be used in the name of widely esteemed values. Anti-Communism, they believed, was such a value. Inasmuch as the American people had affirmed anti-Communism before the Wisconsin senator became prominent, McCarthyites were justified in attempting to harden the *"existing* conformity." [65]

But what specifically made the McCarthyites right and the dissenting left-wing intellectuals wrong? With tortuous reasoning, Buckley and Bozell answered that the latter were wrong because "they are confused, they have misread history, and they fail to understand social processes. What is more, they do not feel the faith they so often and so ardently express in democracy. There is only one alternative to this explanation: that they are opposed to the decline of Communist influence at home." In what amounted to a circular argument, Buckley and Bozell added that men such as Frederick Schuman, Harlow Shapley, and Owen Lattimore had become unacceptable not because they

A view from the right

held contrary ideas "but because they expound[ed] a *particular set of ideas and values* which Americans have explored and emphatically rejected, and because the propagation of these ideas fortifies an implacable foreign power bent on the destruction of American independence." Persecution and prosecution of such men and ideas, whether for reasons of duplicity or gullibility—two quite different things—were legitimate responses of consensual societies.[66]

Buckley and Bozell defended their assault on civil liberties with the doctrine that a job in government was a privilege and not a right. Hence the normal legal protections that had evolved through centuries of Anglo-Saxon jurisprudence did not apply. Even the presumption of innocence, one of the legal pillars against lynch law, was cast aside for government employees. It is *"not* the function of a security board to give the employee his 'day in court'," the authors stressed, for justice *"is not the major objective here,"* but rather the protection of the national interest.[67]

The correct approach in defending the national interest, McCarthy's apologists argued, lay in activating the McCarran rider of 1946 (renewed yearly during the McCarthy years), authorizing the Secretary of State *"in his absolute discretion"* to dismiss any employee *"when he shall deem such termination necessary or advisable in the interests of the national security."* Its meaning should be clear. This would have eliminated the adjudication of loyalty and security cases by those lay security boards charged with following normal judicial processes. Moreover, it would have precluded the use of formal hearings, which, in Buckley's opinion, tended "to distract attention from the government's interests." [68]

This tough view was based squarely on the doctrinal belief in the necessity of a moral consensus and on the derivative assumptions about the moral depravity of Communism and its unique capacities to operate for malevolent purposes the technological inventions of the modern world. Given the decisiveness of modern weapons, "conceivably a single individual could shift the [world] balance of power" through effective subversive activity. And so the conclusion: "the new consequences of treason no longer allow us to settle for a security program based on the venerable idea that ten guilty men had better go free than one innocent man be punished." [69]

Buckley and Bozell did not seriously attempt to reconcile their conclusions with democratic theory and practice. Nor did they bother to explain how Italy and France maintained their freedom from Moscow's domination even though both nations had large Communist parties, which permeated the armed forces and helped staff key government posts. Finally, Buckley and Bozell did not substantively advance the inquiry surrounding such questions as "what is loyalty?" except by underscoring that for many conservatives loyalty meant ideological conformity. They voiced the McCarthyite refusal to admit the element of risk in life, the McCarthyite refusal to countenance honest error, the McCarthyite refusal to allow for man's capability for growth —all in the name of absolute national security. It was not surprising, then, that Buckley and Bozell found that the nine individuals who constituted Senator McCarthy's "public cases" could be dismissed legitimately as security risks with little more "evidence" than that adduced in the case of Philip Jessup: *"The essence of Jessup's record is that he was not unsympathetic either to Communists or to their polices from 1939 to 1944."* [70] Whether Jessup, Schuman, Lattimore, and McCarthy's other public cases were Communists, was, in the last instance, immaterial to Buckley, Bozell, and (among politicians) Senators McCarthy, Nixon, Knowland, Taft, Bridges, Wherry, Mundt, Ferguson, Jenner, and Brewster. It mattered only that they were "objectively" on the Communist side, i.e., that they held some ideas that coincided, if vaguely, with those of Communists. Thus the conservative contribution to the handling of internal security

A view from the right

cases was to encourage political purges resembling those of European totalitarian states where mistakes and divergent ideas were equated with criminal acts. The conservative right at once propounded a doctrine of statism and legitimized Gletkin's argument in Arthur Koestler's *Darkness at Noon.*

With important exceptions, such as Peter Viereck and Walter Lippmann, few conservatives during the McCarthy years perceived this. Herbert Hoover saw only "maudlin left 'isms' " endangering America. In a nationwide broadcast of August 1951, he poured out his contempt for the welfare policies of the New Deal and for "the flight from honor" in public life. Liberalism had "turned pink inside." Fortunately, he concluded, Americans now sensed "the frauds on men's minds and morals. Moral indignation is on the march again." Eugene Lyons, expressing the position of the *American Mercury* in January 1953, perceived not the faintest "clamor for repression of unorthodox views"; indeed, "the danger today is not hysteria but complacency." The June 28, 1952, issue of the *Nation,* which documented how men in many fields were hesitant to speak their minds, merely expressed, Lyons wrote, traditional "jitters on the left." [71]

The editors of the *Freeman,* following the dismissal of several counts of the indictment against Owen Lattimore, concluded that legal procedures were not effective in eliminating pro-Communist activity. They jeered at what Justice William O. Douglas called the "black silence of fear" and advocated more "red-baiting" to expose "Communist and pro-Communist infiltration of government departments and private agencies of information and communication." [72] After the hysteria of McCarthyism had subsided, Russell Kirk, perhaps the preeminent "New Conservative" of the 1950's, summed up the McCarthyite case for intellectual conformity. He had not been "much alarmed" over the censorship of books in the State Department's overseas libraries. Believing as most conservatives did that the important changes were those that resulted from reform of the heart and mind,

Kirk defended censorship, even in American educational institutions. Its purpose was to guard moral and intellectual standards against the liberal relativists whose "free market place of ideas" portended lamentable social consequences. Since Kirk believed most individuals incapable of exercising self-censorship, university trustees and administrators had to intervene to protect youthful minds.[73]

V

McCarthyism, then, was born in part of the fear of Communism, which was most intense among conservatives, and of the stress that the right placed on uniformity of thought and action. When cold-war conservatives spoke of freedom in America they usually meant freedom to agree. As apostles of conformity, moreover, they embraced desperate authoritarian arguments. They believed that the United States was locked in an inevitable war with Communism and that a decisive winner must emerge. Coexistence was impossible, for it entailed compromise with an evil that they defined in absolute terms. Because of the special character of the cold war, moreover, any ideology (including liberalism) that concurred, however minutely, with enemy doctrines, had to be attacked. In the interest of national survival, then, the United States had no choice but to prosecute all Communists and proscribe the thought of liberal fellow travelers.

The price conservatives paid for this analysis was high, for it undermined their hopes for limited government and prevented the achievement of the social harmony they had so ardently sought. Indeed, by helping to create and sustain an anti-Communist politics, they contributed to the destruction of competitive capitalism and to the creation of a warfare state dependent on federal spending and deficit financing. Conservatives also lost an opportunity to help construct an effective foreign policy congruent with the needs of a war-torn and revolutionary world. Their apocalyptic vision precluded any analysis of the ways in

A view from the right

which poverty, political oppression, and economic exploitation drove men and governments to solutions inhospitable to those prescribed by the American ethos. Instead of confronting the social problems on which Communism thrived with a sensitivity and concern for justice, all too many American conservatives, unburdened by doubts about the superiority of traditional American values, relied on moral preachments derived from an ideology that rationalized American business and military power.

These conservatives, of course, never won power in America, and indeed were constantly frustrated by what they viewed as the unresponsiveness of these who governed. Their prescriptions went far beyond the Truman Administration's doctrine of containment and its loyalty-security program. They were also disappointed by the "middle of the road" policies pursued by the Eisenhower Administration.[74] Nevertheless, their strident polemics helped to create an anti-Communist politics that limited the arena of permissible debate, shifted the focus of political discussion toward the right, and narrowed the range of options open to policymakers. The resulting cold-war consensus informed American politics at home and abroad for nearly two decades thereafter.

AMERICAN
BUSINESS
AND THE
ORIGINS OF
McCARTHYISM:

The Cold War
Crusade
of the

United States Chamber of Commerce *

of Commerce

BY PETER H. IRONS

McCarthyism did not simply emerge in February 1950 in the wake of Senator Joseph R. McCarthy's charges of Communist infiltration of the State Department. Indeed, McCarthy's charges were essentially a rehash of investigative reports prepared by State Department security officers and "synthesized by congressional investigators two years before" the senator's perfervid speeches, as even his supporters acknowledge.[1] As the personification of a political movement, McCarthy provided simply four years of dramatic and continuously escalating charges detailing treason in high places. But the movement to which the senator lent his name had its roots in a thirty-year-old anti-Communist campaign, a campaign led and coordinated by such disparate organizations as the U.S. Chamber of Commerce, the Catholic Church, the American Legion, and the American Federation of Labor.[2]

This essay will explore the role of the business community in the origins of McCarthyism, particularly the campaign by conservative businessmen for a cold-war crusade. What these businessmen sought was a firm anti-Soviet foreign policy combined with a domestic anti-Communist program aimed primarily at labor unions and animated by hostility toward the social programs of the Roosevelt New Deal.

I

Since 1917 business conservatives had waged a two-pronged attack against domestic radicalism at home and against the Soviet Union abroad. They were in large part responsible for the traumatic "Red Scare" of 1919–20 and, in alliance with conservative leaders in the American Federation of Labor, succeeded in delaying recognition of the Soviet Union for sixteen years. During the 1930's they organized the American Liberty League and launched a vociferous campaign against the New

* The author would like to acknowledge the Louis M. Rabinowitz Foundation's support for his research.

THE SPECTER

Deal.[3] Uneasy over America's wartime alliance with the Soviet Union, they were among the first to demand that the Truman Administration get tough with Communists at home and abroad.

The conservatives, of course, were only one voice in a business community which, though united in its commitment to capitalism, contained widely divergent attitudes toward social change and foreign affairs. Business liberals, for example, accepted the main outlines of the New Deal. They tended to look on business and government as partners in a joint effort to stabilize the economy, provide relief for those displaced by the Depression, and shore up the system of banking and currency. During the 1930's many moderate and liberal businessmen participated in the Roosevelt-sponsored Business Advisory Council, and in 1942 some of the most advanced business liberals founded the Committee on Economic Development (CED). In the years that followed, the CED became an important spokesman for business liberals.[4] Frequently representing large, internationally oriented corporations, business liberals also believed in expanded foreign trade and were less inclined to view the Soviet Union with hostility.

Indeed, by the end of World War II, many businessmen along with government economic authorities thought that it was possible and desirable, even necessary, that the United States greatly expand its trade with the Soviet Union. Thus, in March 1944, Assistant Secretary of the Treasury Harry Dexter White in a memo to Treasury Secretary Henry Morgenthau listed future American raw material needs and cited Soviet sources of manganese, chromium, mercury, lead, and other vital minerals. White recommended that the United States negotiate a $5,000,-000,000 credit with Soviet authorities to be repaid in raw materials. The Soviets themselves encouraged American businessmen to anticipate expanded trade after the war if the necessary credits could be arranged. In 1943 and 1944, during meetings with Donald Nelson, the merchandising executive then serving as head of the War Production Board, and with Eric Johnston of the Chamber of Commerce, Premier Joseph Stalin urged both men to press for credits to finance American trade with the Soviet Union.[5]

During 1945 many business publications reported the enthusiasm of the business community for Soviet trade. In January, *Fortune* noted that some seven hundred American companies were paying $250,000 to advertise in a *Catalogue of American Engineering and Industry* prepared especially for the Soviets. And the editors of *Fortune* wondered if "Russia is in many ways not so very different from the U.S. under the New Deal."[6] *Fortune* conceded that the extension of private bank credits to the Soviet Union would necessitate repeal of the restrictive Johnson Act of 1934. It reported that "the American-Russian Chamber of Commerce, behind which stands the Chase National Bank, is preparing a big campaign to effect that repeal."[7]

Reporting the results of a poll of top management conducted at the end of the war, *Fortune* concluded that "Russia's best friend is the businessman." In that poll, businessmen had been asked whether it was to long-term American advantage to encourage trade with the Soviet Union: 91.2 percent agreed, and 87.4 percent urged that the United States extend the $6,000,-000,000 credit requested by Soviet authorities, whether through a government or private banking loan, or both.[8]

Fortune was not alone in its pro-Soviet sentiments and optimistic forecast of American-Soviet trade relations. In March 1945 *Nation's Business,* the organ of the Chamber of Commerce, emphasized that Soviet orders with General Electric, ITT, and Newport News Shipbuilding indicated that the Soviet Union "will be a greater market than ever before for American businessmen."[9] Six months later, the Chamber's publication commended Soviet policy. Soviet authorities, *Nation's Business* reported, were finding "increasing support" in the Eastern European countries, had raised a new generation "almost completely loyal" to the state, were realistic in seeking to establish "security zones against political aggression" around their borders, and would likely "refrain from direct provocation of Communist revolution" in Europe.[10]

II

This widespread business optimism became one of the first casualties of the emerging cold war, shattered by the Truman Administration's decision to subordinate short-term business interests to long-term strategic, ideological and economic goals, by the growing conviction among even liberal businessmen that it was not possible to do business with the Russians, and by the militantly anti-Communist crusade launched by conservative American businessmen. The latter stemmed more from domestic than foreign policy considerations and was designed to cripple trade union strength and liberalism in general by emphasizing the "Red threat" in unions and government and by painting Americans friendly toward the Soviet Union as tools of the Kremlin's "imperialistic" designs.

The initiative in this effort to intensify public fears about Soviet foreign policy objectives and domestic subversion, which intensified after 1946, was assumed by the organized conservative business community. Shocked by the militance of the labor strikes that broke out during the winter of 1945–46, the greatest in the nation's history, businessmen and their right-wing allies in the American Legion and HUAC reiterated the charge that unions were Communist-infiltrated. Anti-union charges by American conservatives had since the 1930's had little popular impact. But the flurry of postwar strikes combined with increasing public antipathy toward the Soviet Union provided the opportunity for the refinement of that strategy: labor union militance represented Kremlin machinations.

Many business spokesmen forcefully made this identification. Thus, in October 1946 Charles E. Wilson affirmed that "the

American business and McCarthyism

problems of the United States can be captiously summed up in two words: Russia abroad and labor at home." [11] And *Nation's Business* maintained in September 1946 that "Whoever stirs up needless strife in American trade unions advances the cause of Communism." Continuing, the Chamber of Commerce publication warned businessmen that the Communist Party had "gained control of at least 20 of the important unions" and that Communists in the union operated a "transmission belt" from the Kremlin direct to the local union. [12]

These were not exceptional or temporary developments, confined to the problem of postwar labor-management conflict. Rather, these efforts constituted the beginning of a concerted attempt on the part of a diverse group of anti-Communist militants—especially in the Catholic Church, the craft unions, and the federal bureaucracy—to alert the nation to the Communist threat. The specific goal of this campaign was to pressure the Truman Administration into instituting a domestic anti-Communist program. For conservative businessmen, however, the campaign was based on an anti-labor animus and offered the opportunity to purge American institutions of liberal and left-wing influence.

In December 1945 a right-wing Denver lawyer and member of the U.S. Chamber of Commerce board of directors, Ward Bannister, proposed that the Chamber mount a propaganda campaign against Communists in the United States. [13] The board acceded to this recommendation and Eric Johnston, then nearing the end of his term as Chamber president, appointed Francis P. Matthews chairman and Emerson P. Schmidt executive secretary of a committee to prepare a report on "the menace of Socialism in Europe, and its effect upon this country." [14] Since 1941 the chairman of the moribund Chamber Committee on Socialism and Communism, Matthews was an insurance executive from Omaha and an active Catholic layman who had been decorated a Papal Chamberlain and was a former national head of the Knights of Columbus. A former economics professor at the University of Minnesota, Schmidt in 1943 accepted the position of director of economic research for the Chamber.

From its inception, the Chamber's anti-Communist program was directed by zealots possessing an apocalyptic view of Communism and an unremitting zeal to defeat the Soviet Union and its American supporters. "The Reds," declared one Chamber leader during the strike wave of 1945–46, "have a lot to do with our current, very serious labor situation." To avoid becoming a Soviet satellite, "we will have to set up some firing squads in every good sized city and town in the country and . . . liquidate the Reds and Pink Benedict Arnolds." [15] Bannister's and Matthews' views on Communism shed further light on the leadership of the Chamber's campaign of 1946–48. Bannister, considered by Matthews the father of the project even though he did not sit on the committee, was a supporter of such reactionary organizations as the Church League of America, the National Economic Council, and the Colorado Committee for Constitutional Rights.[16] The extent of Matthews' anti-Soviet fanaticism was revealed in a speech he later delivered at the Boston Naval Shipyard in August 1950, advocating that the United States "declare our intention to pay . . . the price of instituting a war to compel cooperation for peace." Apotheosizing the United States as "the repository of the Ark of the Covenant" and the "custodians of the Holy Grail," Matthews argued for preventive war. Becoming "an initiator of a war of aggression . . . would win for us a proud and popular title; we would become the first aggressors for peace." [17]

Initially, Matthews's committee had planned only to produce one pamphlet to be widely circulated to "thought-leaders" so that "our influence will be multiplied many-fold through their speeches, writings and conversations." [18] Schmidt first suggested that Matthews ask the conservative economist Ludwig von Mises to prepare the report. Instead, Matthews hired Father

John F. Cronin on a secret basis. At the time, Cronin was assistant director of the Social Action Department of the National Catholic Welfare Conference (NCWC) and had earlier (in November 1945) completed a secret report on Communism in the United States for the Catholic bishops. Cronin had been recommended to Matthews by Monsignor Howard J. Carroll, general secretary of the NCWC, the national administrative organ of the bishops.[19]

In preparing this earlier report, Cronin had profited from close contacts with FBI agents, who had supplied him with secret FBI files and who in turn secured information from him on Communism in the unions. Believing Communism "even more repressive of human liberty and dignity than was Fascism," [20] Father Cronin began his assignment for the Chamber with a fearful prognosis of the Communist danger. "There are reasons to believe," he wrote Matthews in March 1946, "that Soviet armies may be on the march in but a few weeks. Christianity through much of the world is threatened. Within the nation, the Communist fifth column is functioning smoothly, especially within the ranks of government and atomic scientists." [21]

Father Cronin met the September 20 deadline set by the Chamber board, and Matthews secured the board's unanimous approval to issue an initial printing of four hundred thousand copies. Although written by Cronin, Matthews assumed authorship of the 40-page report in order to avert suspicion by those who would have been critical "if they suspected there was any Vatican influence in it." [22]

On October 7, 1946, Matthews held a press conference to publicize the release of the report, entitled "Communist Infiltration in the United States." The reaction of the press to the report was generous in coverage and generally favorable in tone. And, although the major part of the report had emphasized the Communist problem in the unions, Father Cronin's and the

Chamber's major concern, these press reports concentrated on the charges of Communist influence within the government. Thus, *The New York Times* headlined its front page story "Chamber Opens Campaign to Oust Reds in U.S. Posts" and described the report as accusing "the State Department of being influenced by Communist pressure in its policies toward the postwar treatment of Germany, toward the Perón regime in Argentina and our alleged participation in the betrayal of China with regard to Manchuria." [23] The report had indeed criticized American foreign policy, condemning the "harsh peace" imposed upon Germany and the "cynical" betrayal of the Nationalist Chinese at the Yalta Conference owing to the pressure of "strongly pro-Soviet groups" in the Far Eastern section of the State Department.[24]

Issued at the height of the successful Republican campaign to wrest control of Congress from the Democrats by accusing the Democrats of softness toward Communism and the "betrayal" of Eastern Europe at Yalta, the report highlighted the Chamber's commitment to a broad anti-Communist policy. Not confined to foreign policy, the Chamber sought to pressure the Truman Administration to institute a tough anti-Communist program at home. Two of the report's specific recommendations, given prominence in press reports, included: "Because Communist loyalty is primarily given to a foreign power, Communists *and* their followers should be excluded from government service. Congress should appropriate adequate funds for a stringent but fair loyalty test." And, "As an agent of a foreign power, the Communist Party should be forced by law to reveal its membership, funds, and activities." [25]

The response to the report was satisfying to the leadership of the Chamber: by the end of October 1946 more than 200,000 copies had been distributed. Copies were sent to every Catholic bishop in the country and in November to 80,000 Protestant clergymen. During November the Washington office of the Chamber was receiving orders for the report at the rate of 25,000 to 30,000 per day.

The Chamber report supplemented an already powerful campaign, instituted by many conservatives in the Congress, the Administration, and the press, to pressure President Truman to establish a federal employee loyalty program. In the aftermath of the Republican victory in the 1946 congressional elections, this campaign succeeded. Less than two weeks after the election, an executive order creating a President's Temporary Commission on Employee Loyalty had been drafted. Truman formally established the commission by executive order on November 25.[26]

The Chamber's report soon became an issue of controversy within the President's commission, itself divided between hardline and soft-line factions. Specifically, on January 17, 1947, Assistant FBI Director D. M. Ladd appeared before the commission in place of J. Edgar Hoover, who refused to appear in person. According to the notes of Stephen Spingarn, the Treasury alternate to the commission, Ladd "called the commission's attention to the publication of the U.S. Chamber of Commerce dealing with Communist infiltration of the United States, in which the opinion is expressed that Communists in the government have reached a serious stage." [27] The Army representative to the commission, Kenneth Royall, was appalled that the FBI would rely on the Chamber pamphlet, which named no names, as its sole authority for Communist infiltration of the government.[28]

The establishment of a Federal Employee Loyalty Program (by executive order of the President on March 22, 1947) did not, however, terminate the Chamber's anti-Communist activities. Instead, the Chamber was prompted to prepare and issue a second pamphlet called "Communists Within the Government." The initiative for this second publication, according to Emerson

Schmidt of the Chamber, came from Benjamin Mandel, at that
time a member of the State Department's security staff. Mandel,
who had been organization secretary of the Communist Party in
the late 1920's, had become a zealous anti-Communist and
would, both before and after his brief stint with the State Department, serve on the research staff of HUAC.[29] (Earlier
Mandel had supplied Father Cronin with material from the
HUAC files for his November 1945 report on Communism to
the bishops.)

According to Schmidt, Mandel called him shortly after the
initial Chamber report was issued and offered to help in the
preparation of a report on Communists within the government.[30] Schmidt accepted Mandel's offer to collaborate and emphasized that he wanted the report issued as soon as possible to
"put the pressure on the government to take forthright action". [31] Fearing that the President's Temporary Commission on
Employee Loyalty, chaired by A. Devitt Vanech of the Justice
Department, would issue a "whitewash," Schmidt rushed to publish the Cronin-Mandel report the day before the Vanech commission was due to present its report to Truman.[32]

Although Father Cronin's November 1945 secret report to
the Catholic bishops had named Alger Hiss, Lee Pressman, and
John Abt as members of a Communist cell in the federal government during the 1930's and had cited Whittaker Chambers'
allegation that Hiss had headed the cell, the second Chamber
report cited no names. Its most explicit charge was an estimate
that "about 400" Communists "hold positions of importance in
Washington." [33] The report further attributed Communist penetration into the government to those New Deal liberals who had
"dominated the government" since 1933. The tolerance of liberals for Communists resulted in "a heavy influx of Communists and their sympathizers into the war agencies, such as the
OWI, OSS, OPA, FEA, and WLB." Communists within a government agency would set up a patronage system to infiltrate

more Communists into the agency. "Some of the most dangerous appointments in recent years to such departments as State, Treasury, Labor, Commerce, Federal Communications Commission, and Bureau of the Budget were the work of this patronage system," the report concluded.[34] The danger posed by these appointments, the writers of the report emphasized, derived from the deleterious influence of these Communists on American foreign policy: "A real service could be rendered if the secret story of Yalta and Teheran could be made public." [35] These unspecified charges, based on Father Cronin's and Mandel's knowledge of the FBI and HUAC reports naming suspected Communists in government, foreshadowed the charges that Senator McCarthy would make in 1950.

Truman's issuance of Executive Order 9835 in March 1947, establishing the guidelines for the federal employee loyalty program, paralleled the program demanded by the Chamber.[36] Truman's order also acceded to the Chamber's demand that the Attorney General prepare and publish "a certified list of Communist-controlled front organizations" to be used as a basis for screening government employees. Although the Truman Administration had bowed to the pressures of the Chamber and other right-wing groups in establishing the federal employee loyalty program, the President himself and his Attorney General, Tom Clark, resented this pressure and felt that much of it stemmed from collusion between J. Edgar Hoover and right-wing groups such as the Chamber. The day the Chamber released its report on Communists in government, Clark called the president of the Chamber, bitterly complaining that he had not been forewarned of the report's release. The Attorney General specifically asked for the source of the report's information, querying how the Chamber could charge that there were four hundred Communists in government service when the Justice Department only knew of twenty-six.[37]

Sensing victory in the use of anti-Communism, the Chamber

kept up the pressure. Its efforts coincided with congressional consideration of the Taft-Hartley bill, a measure that contained a tough non-Communist affidavit proviso. Thus, a month after publication of "Communists Within the Government," the Chamber published a third pamphlet, entitled "Communists Within the Labor Movement." Authored primarily by Father Cronin, with assistance from right-wing AFL leader John Frey, this pamphlet also exploited foreign policy concerns: "Every time Molotov toughens up on Secretary Byrnes, the local comrades play rough with foremen and executives in plants around the country," the report quoted from *Fortune*.[38] The pamphlet urged that the forthcoming Taft-Hartley Act include guarantees "to allow employers full freedom of speech" to be able to tell their employees that they did "not like to deal with people whose loyalty is to a foreign power." In addition, the Chamber report urged employers to begin publishing papers intended for their employees that "discuss Communist tyranny in Yugoslavia or Poland, or the harsh peace treaties which were imposed upon Italy and other nations at Soviet instigation." [39]

The Chamber's anti-Communist campaign came to a head in March 1947. Then Matthews managed to secure an appointment with President Truman. Following this meeting, and four days after the President had issued Executive Order 9835, Matthews wrote an anti-Communist leader in Europe, Theodore Aubert, that "I have seen President Truman recently, and on one occasion he spent most of the time discussing Communism and outlining his plans and the plans of the administration to check its further progress.' [40]

While Matthews was exerting pressure on Truman, Emerson Schmidt had arranged to appear before HUAC on March 26 (the same day that J. Edgar Hoover testified before that committee for the first time). Now controlled by Republicans, and with J. Parnell Thomas as chairman and Richard Nixon as its most industrious new member, HUAC was probing for an opening to attack the Democrats, the New Deal, the Communists, and liberals in general. As yet, HUAC had not come up with a specific target. Schmidt, for whom the committee reprinted all three Chamber reports in the text of the hearings, suggested that HUAC investigate "the left-wing press, book publishing, radio, the labor movement, the motion-picture industry, youth organizations, other front groups and organizations." [41] When asked by Congressman Nixon which of these institutions "is most susceptible to Communist infiltration" and deserved investigation, Schmidt suggested the labor movement as the "key point for [Communist] penetration." [42] Schmidt advocated "exposure" by HUAC and the FBI as the "main remedy" against Communist influence, but also urged the committee to press for legislation toughening Truman's loyalty order.[43]

Schmidt's appearance before HUAC highlighted the close relations that existed between the diverse groups and individuals working to initiate a cold-war crusade. The Chamber's reports had been prepared by Father Cronin, the anti-Communist authority of the Catholic Church, who had recently met with HUAC member Nixon to urge him to expose Alger Hiss. Cronin's report of November 1945 to the Catholic bishops and his pamphlet for the Chamber had been prepared with the covert help of FBI agents and of Benjamin Mandel.

Matthews and Schmidt were encouraged by the success of their campaign. The day after appearing before HUAC, Schmidt proposed to Matthews that "we ought to sit down with top-notch lawyers and draft a real bill which could be passed in Congress" to implement the Chamber's proposals. The following year the House of Representatives passed the Mundt-Nixon bill. This bill, which the Chamber enthusiastically endorsed, embodied almost all of the Chamber's legislative goals including the establishmen of a subversive activities control board, requirements for labeling mailed material deemed Communist, and denial of government employment to members of organizations listed by the Attorney General as Communist fronts.[44] The bill, which was killed in the Senate, never became law. Parts of the measure, however, were incorporated in an omnibus "internal security" bill adopted by the Congress in September 1950.[45]

By the end of March 1947, the Chamber was well satisfied with the results of its efforts. Reporting to the Chamber's board of directors at the end of March, Matthews emphasized that "The anti-Communist campaign has attained a high pitch, it has developed a momentum and it certainly ought to have all the leadership that can be given to it." Matthews recommended that no further reports be issued (though the Chamber did publish a pamphlet in 1948 entitled "A Program for Community Anti-Communist Action"). The three reports the Chamber had issued within a five-month period had been widely circulated, the initial report having had a circulation of more than two-thirds of a million and the labor pamphlet of more than 100,000. For one, General Electric, engaged in a fierce battle with the left-wing United Electrical Workers union, distributed 2,300 copies of the labor pamphlet.

III

The Chamber of Commerce's contribution to the cold-war crusade was substantial. It had served as the nexus of an alliance of disparate groups: its cold-war propaganda having been written primarily by Father Cronin of the Catholic Church, who had drawn upon information and files supplied by right-wing forces in the labor movement, the FBI, and HUAC. In turn, the Chamber's publications were distributed in the hundreds of thousands by both Catholic and Protestant groups and anti-union businessmen, and even utilized by the FBI in the internal struggle within the President's Temporary Commission on Employee Loyalty over the need for and character of a federal loyalty program. Primarily directed against labor, the Chamber's campaign was a broad-brush attack on liberal and left-wing groups in general and was intended to shape the Truman Administration's domestic internal security program.

The consequences of all this were manifold. The Chamber's crusade contributed to the growing anti-Communist hysteria, which undercut the advocacy by business liberals of good relations and trade with the Soviet Union. By 1947, even the most fervent of business liberals had abandoned their hopes for amicable Soviet-American relations and expanded trade. As *Nation's Business* noted in October 1946, the changing political situation and increasing hostility toward the Soviet Union were affecting businessmen, who were "forgetting their dream of a great Russian market." [46] The new feeling among businessmen, strongest among those from the more conservative small- and medium-sized firms, was expressed in the industry magazine *Steel* in November 1946. Praising President Truman's strong anti-Soviet stance and advocacy of military strength, the editors of *Steel* declared that the Truman policies gave "the firm assurance that maintaining and building our preparations for war will be big business in the United States for at least a considerable period ahead." [47] Most business liberals came to support the narrowly anti-Communist Marshall Plan, a program that also promised trade expansion, but within the new geographical and ideological limits established by the cold war.

The Chamber's campaign also served to intensify the cold war, increasing the pressure on the Truman Administration to pursue a course of militant anti-Communism in foreign affairs. Finally, the Chamber also served to link foreign policy concerns with domestic politics. Its constant reiteration of the charge that American Communists and their sympathizers in unions and other groups represented an acute danger because of their role as "transmission belts" of Soviet policy was effective. As Les K. Adler has written of the Chamber's attack on unions, "a labor strike in Detroit or West Virginia could be perceived as a manifestation of tension over Berlin or Poland and did not have to be dealt with on its individual merits." [48]

The result of all of this, in turn, was a climate conducive to McCarthy and McCarthyism. McCarthy's ostensible foes were Communists in government, and he rarely attacked labor directly. But business conservatives, who supported McCarthy disproportionately, realized that the "chilling effect" of his charges hurt liberals and radicals in labor and other institutions. As a *Fortune* writer noted in 1954, at a time when McCarthy's business support was waning, "with the businessmen particularly, McCarthy appeals to a greater-than-average distaste for the New and Fair Deals." [49] Business liberals, on the other hand, were generally cool to McCarthy. Many of them had helped shape the policies McCarthy attacked, were conscious of the falsity of his charges, and abhorred his methods. Prominent liberal businessmen such as William Benton, Ralph Flanders, and Paul Hoffman were important opponents of the Wisconsin senator, though Flanders and Hoffman did not actively attack McCarthy until after the election of Dwight Eisenhower.[50]

The irony of the split within the business community in the period preceding McCarthy's emergence to national prominence is that the differences between business liberals and conservatives were more of method and style than fundamental goals. Both sought a stable world order that promised finally to yield to American hegemony. But the willingness of the liberals to entertain the thought that trade with the Soviet Union could be accommodated with this goal soon became a casualty of the antipathy of the conservatives toward the New Deal and labor unions. In this conflict, pragmatism lost out to passion, and Senator McCarthy ultimately benefited from the cold-war atmosphere the conservative business community helped to produce.

American business and McCarthyism

A VIEW FROM THE LEFT:

From the Popular Front

to Cold War Liberalism

BY NORMAN MARKOWITZ

In the 1930's, cocktail party radicals often maintained that a Communist was a liberal with a wife and two children. By the early 1950's, however, both the joke and the whole American left had gone sour. Against the background of the Korean War, Senator Joseph McCarthy sought to identify New Deal liberals with a gigantic Communist conspiracy that had enslaved China and Eastern Europe. Hounded by the McCarthyites and the Truman Administration, beleaguered Communists defended their political beliefs and activities by quoting Thomas Jefferson and the Bill of Rights to congressional investigators. At the same time, anti-Communist liberals, who usually opposed the McCarthyites' methods though not their general aims, acted in ways that compromised the defense of traditional civil liberties in America.[1]

In the last years of the Truman Administration, organizations like the Congress for Cultural Freedom and the Americans for Democratic Action, along with journals like the *New Leader* and *Commentary,* performed the "sober duty" of supporting the overseas extension of American power to thwart radical social revolutions. At home, cold-war liberals defended the search for federal loyalty and security safeguards while ostensibly avoiding the blunt and crude repression advocated by the right. By the 1950's, what Arthur Schlesinger, Jr., had earlier hailed as the emerging "free left," a left rejecting the naïve optimism and large hopes of earlier American reformers in order to accept the responsibilities of world power, had become dominant.[2] The "new liberalism" extolled by Schlesinger and spawned by the cold war had transformed liberals into defenders rather than critics of established authority. It is the contention of this essay

A View From the Left: From the Popular Front to Cold War Liberalism originally appeared in different form in THE RISE AND FALL OF THE PEOPLE'S CENTURY: HENRY A. WALLACE AND AMERICAN LIBERALISM, 1941–1948, by Norman Markowitz (New York: The Free Press, A Division of Macmillan Publishing Co., Inc., 1973). Copyright © 1973 by Norman A. Markowitz.

THE SPECTER

that the postwar liberal retreat into what Schlesinger called the vital center was an act of cowardice and opportunism, a "failure of radical nerve," and that this retreat dramatically displayed the inner contradictions of American liberalism.[3]

Laissez-faire liberalism developed out of the scientific, commercial, and industrial revolutions as the ideology of the bourgeoisie, the class which rose to power through those revolutions. Its central doctrines—individual freedom and equality before the law—served to protect property and entrepreneurial rights from aristocratic and monarchical restrictions and to create a cash and contract world highly receptive to competition and innovation. Modern liberalism, or "social liberalism" as it will be called in this essay, was a response to the rise of industrial society and world empire in the late nineteenth century. Abandoning the precepts of laissez-faire, which had dominated early liberalism, the social liberals in Europe and America had united around the doctrine of the positive state, a state whose power they sought to harness in order to make the existing system work more responsibly for the general welfare. But social liberals were also divided among themselves into two distinct, though not mutually exclusive, groups—the corporate reformers who sought to use state power to consolidate private economic power and the humanitarian reformers who hoped to use the state to redistribute wealth and power, to liberate men, and to eradicate social injustice.[4] But the latter, who are the subject of this essay, never really resolved the contradictions between humanitarian ends and capitalist means. Instead, they placed their faith in a "neutral" state, in a beneficent technology, and in organizing people into interest groups to use the state against business predators. They identified strongly with the New Deal, the CIO, the popular front, and the civil rights movement. But the society that emerged after World War II, at least partially as a result of their efforts, bore little resemblance to the ideals for which they had struggled. The posi-

A view from the left

tive state, operated not by humanitarian reformers but by corporate elites, was used to extend American influence abroad and repress dissent at home.[5] Confronted by this reality and unable to resolve the contradictions it embodied, liberals either became apologists for the industrial state or else began to abandon their faith in the state, technology, and the people.

At the time, of course, neither the internal contradictions nor the imminent collapse of social liberalism were readily apparent. Indeed, for a brief period it seemed as though social liberalism might transform American society. In the midst of depression and war during the 1930's and 1940's, social liberals joined Communists to support the Roosevelt Administration's attempts at social reform and its fight against Fascism. With the exception of the Hitler-Stalin Pact period (1939–41), a vigorous popular front of social liberals and Communists played an important role in American life between 1935 and 1948, serving as the left-wing of the New Deal coalition.[6]

Most scholars and commentators have been unsympathetic toward the American popular front. Eugene Lyons, writing in 1941, established what became the most common post-World War II view, portraying the 1930's as a Red Decade in which liberals were the naïve dupes of conspiratorial Communists and the pawns of Russian power. Arthur Schlesinger, Jr., writing in 1949, compared popular-front liberals of the 1940's with northern "Doughface" Democrats who had defended the southern slaveholders before the Civil War. In the 1950's the anti-Communist liberals and radicals of the *New Leader* and *Partisan Review* echoed Sidney Hook's attack on the popular fronters as "totalitarian liberals." [7]

The popular front, as Irving Howe and Lewis Coser have noted, however, was above all else a mood, a climate of opinion that packaged both hope and fear in the sentimental sloganeering of modern advertising.[8] The popular-front spirit can best be seen in the ballads of Woody Guthrie, especially in the populist nationalism of "This Land Is Your Land"; in the film documentaries of Pare Lorenz; in the radio scripts of Norman Corwin; and in the sentimental, life-affirming novels of John Steinbeck, especially in *The Grapes of Wrath.* In Steinbeck's story of the indomitable Joad family's struggle against prejudice and oppression, the popular front's faith in the righteous people overcoming the vested interests was powerfully expressed. The New Deal state, through its sanitary migrant camps, was portrayed as the people's friend, the agent of social justice.[9]

During the late 1930's much of the energy and attention of the popular front was focused on the Spanish Civil War. Thus, American anti-Fascists fought under Communist leadership in the Abraham Lincoln Brigade, and the American League Against War and Fascism won at least nominal support from mass organizations whose membership numbered in the millions.[10] The mood of the popular front in this period was perhaps best captured by Ernest Hemingway in *For Whom the Bell Tolls,* the story of Robert Jordan, the scion of an old stock Republican family, who chose to sacrifice his life in Spain to help block the advance of Fascism. In a time when radical change seemed to be possible and when barbarians threatened civilization itself, decent men had to choose and to act courageously against evil so that a better world would be born.[11]

The popular front's call for commitment and self-sacrifice during a time of change and trouble gave men the opportunity to overcome sectarian differences and struggle for common goals. World War II—which made America and Russia allies, made Communists more numerous and respectable than ever before, and made anti-Fascism a major war aim—provided the popular front with a new lease on life. During the war, the *New Republic* and the *Nation,* the major organs of liberal opinion, consistently supported a policy of Soviet-American cooperation to win both the war and the peace. Vice-President Henry Wallace, the leading wartime spokesman for social liberal aims,

A view from the left

emerged as the Roosevelt Administration's chief defender of long-range Soviet-American cooperation. Advocating a new international order in which the injustices that had created depression, Fascism, and war would be eliminated, Wallace became the leading wartime defender of what Freda Kirchwey, the publisher of the *Nation,* called a "New Deal for the world." [12]

In essence, social liberals believed that the planning and social welfare of the New Deal, institutionalized by a United Nations organization and made workable by Soviet-American cooperation, could merge with the revolutionary aspirations of oppressed peoples abroad to create a just and lasting peace. The creation of a world New Deal would in turn help to reinvigorate the New Deal at home. The wartime expansion of state power and the success of production planning, social liberals believed, had given the lie to the old conservative argument that planning was unfeasible and that a cooperative society was against human nature. Thus if power was kept out of reactionary hands, Americans might truly build a brave new world following the war.[13]

These ideas were prevalent in the liberal journals throughout the war and were forcefully argued by Max Lerner, Bruce Bliven, and George Soule in a 1943 article entitled "America in the Postwar World." Believing that Fascists saw postwar Allied disunity as their great hope for survival, these writers maintained that "serious trouble" in U.S.-Soviet relations was "likely to develop only if our own domestic and foreign policies are so inept that they give rise to widespread discontent at home and abroad. . . ." Looking with hope and confidence to a coming social revolution in Nazi-occupied Europe, they saw Russia as a positive force in the development of the peoples' revolution in Europe. If the revolution succeeded, the workers in America would follow it, realizing that "political conservatism goes with nationalism and that the two militate heavily against a peaceful

world. . . ." Finally, they concluded that in a world revolution-
ized by the war, "we can save ourselves much needless suffer-
ing if we will accept the situation and consciously work with the
tides of history to make our country, in an old but by no means
discredited phrase, a land fit for heroes to live in." [14]

The result, Bliven and other social liberals argued, would be
a transformation of American society, a transformation confidently hailed by Henry Wallace as an approaching "Century
of the Common Man." The latter was a curious blend of
humanitarian reform and progressive capitalism, a combination
that expressed the essence (and the contradictions) of social
liberalism. Popular-front liberals strongly advocated the extension of New Deal regulatory and antitrust policies designed to
make capitalism progressive. At the same time, they sought cooperation from those capitalists who were already progressive,
contending that a world New Deal would create an interdepend-
ent international marketplace and with it full employment in the
United States, enormous new markets for American business,
and great avenues for "non-imperialist" investments.[15]

In their struggle for an expanded New Deal, wartime liberals were also willing to work with Communists, whom they
both romanticized as selfless organizers of the left and feared
as ruthless power seekers. In a 1943 *New Republic* article,
veteran liberal journalist George West perceptively noted that
liberals had always had contempt for Communist tactics of conspiracy and deceit, because those stratagems "had sacrificed
the most precious thing in American democracy—the simple,
honest, evangelical goodness of our earlier reform movement."
Still, West maintained, the Communists' destructive tactics were
understandable given the Soviet revolutionary model and the
reality of substantial repression in the United States. To West
and to most social liberals, the war was rapidly changing the
minds of many Americans. Soviet-American cooperation might

A view from the left

yet bring with it a true popular front in America, West thought, in which liberals and Communists would stand together on a basis of mutual trust.[16]

The Communists, who comprised the other half of the popular front, were also beset by illusions and contradictions. In 1936, Communist leader Earl Browder had defined the front's purpose: not to create socialism but the conditions for socialism. This the American party failed to do. Thus, whereas other Communist parties had retained their organizational base and strengthened themselves through the popular-front tactic, American Communists had built their mass organizations through identification with the New Deal. Working with and in a sense for Roosevelt, they substituted a loose kind of populist nationalism for a socialist analysis and strategy for America. In the late 1930's, for example, Communists opened meetings with "The Star-Spangled Banner," announced that Communism was the Americanism of the twentieth century, and adopted Thomas Jefferson and Abraham Lincoln as hero symbols. In 1938, Communist election circulars in Wisconsin actually read "Elect Genuine New Dealers and Liberals . . . Vote for Fred Bassett Blair, Communist Candidate for U.S. Senator." [17]

When the 1937 recession shook popular confidence in the administration, Communists were thrown on the defensive along with the rest of the New Deal left. The following year the Hitler-Stalin Pact and the onset of World War II shattered the first popular front, as most social liberals eventually supported pro-Allied interventionist policies, while the Communists, reduced to the slogan of "The Yanks Are Not Coming," sought unsuccessfully to build the American Peace Mobilization into a large left isolationist movement.[18]

The German invasion of Russia, however, saved the Communists from complete isolation outside of the labor movement. Greatly strengthened by the war-induced expansion of the trade union movement and the alliance with Russia, by 1945 the

Communists had used the popular-front tactic to create a movement of some eighty thousand members, with major influence
in the CIO and a myriad of reform-oriented organizations. Working through the CIO's vaunted Political Action Committee and
such offshoots as the National Citizens Political Action Committee (NC-PAC) and the Independent Citizens Committee of
the Arts, Sciences and Professions (ICCASP), they played a
significant role in electing Roosevelt and many left New Dealers
in 1944. The American party's objectives, moreover, did not
differ substantially from those of their wartime popular-front allies, the social liberals. These aims included victory over Fascism, continued cooperation with the Soviet Union following the
war, and the strengthening of labor, civil rights, and social action groups. Only through what would later be popularly known
as peaceful co-existence, American Communist leaders had concluded, could their party have a future.[19]

While Browder's wartime policies brought the Communists
to the pinnacle of power, those policies also increased the bond
between the party's mass organizations and the New Deal.
Pushing the win-the-war policy of both the Roosevelt Administration and the Soviet Union, Browder was less critical of big
business than most social liberals. Indeed, Browder and the
Communists were among the most lukewarm and conservative
backers of Henry Wallace when he sought renomination as Vice
President in 1944.[20]

During the 1930's and then World War II, the popular-front
left made many vital contributions to American life. Its writers and artists explored the life of the common people, sang
their songs, and to an extent brought their stories and aspirations onto the American stage and into the motion pictures. The
popular-front left created civil rights groups like the National
Negro Congress, the Civil Rights Congress, and the Southern
Conference for Human Welfare at the same time that its representatives worked with more conservative groups, such as the

A view from the left

NAACP, to publicize the plight of Black America. The popular-front left also fought discrimination against ethnic and national minorities in all aspects of American life. Above all else, the popular-front left provided the leadership in organizing the mass production unions and in helping to consolidate the New Deal's majority coalition. These achievements were certainly more significant than any made by social liberals alone before or since.[21]

Yet, the popular-front left developed neither an independent base of power nor mutual trust within its ranks. Instead, it was always beset by bitter backstage rivalries and was always subsumed within the New Deal coalition. As a result, the popular front was extremely vulnerable—neither its liberal nor its Communist members were prepared to effectively challenge the Truman Administration's conduct of foreign and domestic policy. The liberals, because they had never resolved the contradictions implicit in their advocacy of humanitarian ends through capitalist means, could not pose real alternatives to the corporate capitalism of the New Deal. The Communists, because their mass organizations remained tied to the New Deal and their small party tied to the Soviet Union, had failed thereby to create an independent base within the New Deal coalition.[22]

II

While the Communists and the social liberals who comprised the popular-front left shared many common goals and a commitment to direct political action within the limits of New Deal politics, the anti-popular-front liberals were united only in their opposition to Communism. Their ranks included the philosopher John Dewey, who had rejected Communism in the 1930's on the pragmatic grounds that the Communists' *a priori* approach to all problems destroyed free thought and that the Communists' call for revolutionary class war could only pro-

duce Fascist reaction in the United States.[23] With Dewey stood
ex-Communists like Jay Lovestone and Max Schactman, the
American Socialist Party and its leader, Norman Thomas, and
such trade unionists as ILGWU leader David Dubinsky. In essence, the anti-popular-front left was composed of diverse radicals and liberals who were competitors for power and prestige
with the popular fronters. Outsiders at war with the orthodox
American Communist Party, the anti-Communists sought to become insiders by attacking the popular front as a creature of
Stalinism.[24]

From the outset, the anti-Communist left was founded on a
reactive politics. When popular fronters organized a League for
Democracy and Intellectual Freedom, the anti-Communists in
1939 created a rival organization chaired by John Dewey, the
Committee for Cultural Freedom, which responded to the deep-
ening world crisis by equating Hitler with Stalin.[25] During World
War II, the *Partisan Review* condemned all the combatants
while American Trotskyists advocated a policy of "revolutionary
defeatism," calling upon the workers of all countries to rise
against their rulers and transform the struggle into an international class war.[26] The Norman Thomas Socialists throughout
the 1930's and 1940's steadily attacked the popular front without, however, offering a realistic alternative to it. Indeed, the
New Leader, the unofficial organ of the Socialists, was usually
more venomous than the conservative press in its attacks on
Communists and the popular front.[27]

Through the 1930's and 1940's, diverse anti-Communist leftists freely compared Stalinism with Fascism and used the phrase
"totalitarian liberal" to attack prominent supporters of the
popular front. Socialist leader Norman Thomas was perhaps the
most persistent champion on the left of the Communist-Fascist
equation. In 1944 he noted privately that "Stalin . . . rather
than Hitler has pioneered in all the techniques of a cruel and
amoral totalitarianism." In a letter to protesting popular fronters

in December 1947 he defended his anti-Communism with the comment that "the difference between a Fascist and a Communist totalitarianism is comparatively small." [28]

During World War II, the Union for Democratic Action (UDA), founded in 1941 by internationalist liberals and former socialists who had broken with Norman Thomas's isolationism, was clearly the leading anti-Communist liberal organization in America. The founder and honorary chairman of the UDA was Reinhold Niebuhr, the noted Protestant theologian. Its most important patron was Eleanor Roosevelt and its chief executive was James Loeb. Although the UDA specifically excluded Communists from membership, it did not stress anti-Communism during the war and even included prominent popular-front liberals, such as Frank Kingdon, in its leadership. Anti-Comunism was not an issue around which to expand a liberal constituency during World War II, and James Loeb was always interested in increasing UDA's size and influence. [29]

Almost from UDA's inception, Loeb struggled to transform the relatively small group into a large national organization. Thus, after George Norris, the dean of the Senate liberals, was defeated for re-election in 1942, Loeb scheduled a UDA testimonial dinner for Norris and tried to use the dinner to gain liberal and labor support for transforming UDA into a national liberal lobby. [30] When that failed as a result of opposition by the Roosevelt Administration and the CIO, Loeb turned instead to a policy of cooperation with the CIO-PAC, the most important popular-front group to emerge from the war. Supporting Henry Wallace for renomination at the 1944 Democratic convention with far greater enthusiasm than the Communists, Loeb hoped for a national political realignment through the growth of labor's power and to an expanded New Deal after the war with the same enthusiasm as the popular-front liberals. [31]

Although his goals seemed to differ little from those of Henry Wallace or even Earl Browder, Loeb continued his search for an issue that would bring prestige and power to UDA. Thus, in 1945 he supported a testimonial dinner for Henry Wallace and focused on the fight for full employment legislation. Wallace, however, was too closely connected with the popular-front left to serve as the unifying symbol that Loeb wanted, while the Full Employment bill was emasculated through amendment. Despite these setbacks, Loeb remained undaunted in his search for an issue that would make his dream of an united liberal movement under UDA a reality. The emergence of the cold war and the resulting rise of anti-Communism would finally provide a unifying issue for Loeb and the UDA. They would then seize this opportunity to conquer what was left of the New Deal market.[32]

III

Having lived in the shadow of Franklin Roosevelt and the New Deal, the popular-front left was devastated by Roosevelt's death and by the subsequent rightward trends in foreign and domestic policy under the Truman Administration. One of the first consequences of the growing friction between the United States and the Soviet Union was an attack in the spring of 1945 by French Communist leader Jacques Duclos on Earl Browder's policy of cooperation with the Democrats. Following publication of the famous Duclos letter, Browder and his supporters were purged, the wartime Communist Political Association dissolved, and a rhetorically militant Communist Party reformed under the leadership of William Z. Foster.[33]

Even then, however, the Communists did not fully abandon the New Deal coalition; instead they accused Truman of betraying its goals. They vacillated between poses of militancy and defensiveness in the trade unions and were unable to decide whether or not to support a popular-front third party. The party's almost schizophrenic stance was expressed with unintended humor by Foster's able second-in-command, Eugene

A view from the left

Dennis, who in the same breath condemned Browderism, advocated the nationalization of industry, and came out strongly for "expanded foreign markets so vital to the farmers, the middle classes, and the entire nation." [34]

Foreign markets were expanded mightily after the war, but the rosy postwar world of progressive capitalism and peaceful cooperation with the Soviet Union never developed. In the repression that accompanied the collapse of the popular front, moreover, the Communists paid the heaviest penalties. The progressive coalition that they had sacrificed so much to build crumbled as the Truman Administration moved vigorously to prosecute American Communists under the Smith Act and to identify Communism with disloyalty through the Federal Employee Loyalty Program and the Attorney General's list.[35]

American Communists were overwhelmed by the cold war and its domestic consequences; lacking an independent base of power outside the orbit of New Deal politics, they could not effectively oppose a Democratic administration that made attacks on them a bipartisan issue. Within five years after the end of the war, the Communists had gone down to defeat with the Progressive Party, lost most of their hard-won gains in the trade unions, and were universally proclaimed as the embodiment of all that was evil and un-American.[36]

Those liberals who refused to abandon the popular front suffered a similar, though far less brutal, fate. They had never, of course, fully accepted Communists as real "fellow travelers," allies working from a basis of trust to build a broad coalition for social change. And when the Communists turned to the left with the removal of Browder, the *New Republic* declared contemptuously that "long ago they [the Communists] lost all their following in the United States except for the humorless hard core of fanatics and abdicated a job the country badly needs—intelligent and sustained criticism from a viewpoint well to the left." [37]

THE SPECTER

The popular front had been a mood more than a movement, and the optimistic mood that had waxed so strong in the last years of the war smashed against the blundering reconversion policies of the Truman Administration and the Democratic electoral disaster of 1946. The pessimism that ensued not only killed the popular-front movement, but also showed how completely social liberals had been prisoners of the New Deal coalition and the Roosevelt personality cult. On the defensive after 1945, the popular front could only invoke the increasingly hollow slogans of the past, seeking to sustain fears of Fascism in a Hitlerless world.[38]

Ambivalent toward Communism and unable to break their ties to the New Deal, the major popular-front organizations— the National Citizens Political Action Committee (NC-PAC) and the Independent Citizens Committee of the Arts, Sciences and Professions (ICCASP)—fell back on the Manichean wartime division between good and evil, fascism and democracy, as a unifying ideology and searched desperately for a surrogate Hitler in Spain, Argentina, or China. At the same time, loyal popular fronters faced the cold war-inspired anti-Communist crusade with courageous, though sometimes confused, gestures aimed at both defending the rights of Communists and yet remaining independent of them. This ambivalence toward Communism, which ran throughout the whole history of the popular front, weakened social liberal activists in the face of the cold war and the strident anti-Communist propaganda of their opponents on the left.[39]

The Truman Administration and its anti-Communist liberal allies were able to exploit the weakness of popular-front liberalism. The general economic expansion that followed the war undercut the rationale of those liberals who for nearly a decade and a half had justified their appeals for social reform in terms of recovery from depression. The capitalist system they had hoped to make both successful and humane had revived, but not

A view from the left

on their terms.[40] The Marshall Plan, moreover, seemed to offer a version of the world New Deal that had been so important to popular-front liberalism. Finally, growing numbers of liberals were intimidated by the militant attack on the popular-front left launched by the newly organized Americans for Democratic Action.

IV

When Henry Wallace was dismissed as Secretary of Commerce in late September 1946, for criticizing the Truman Administration's "get tough" policy toward Russia, UDA leader James Loeb issued a statement praising some of Wallace's criticisms of American foreign policy. Loeb noted, however, that Wallace "said little of the policies of the Soviet Union which breed insecurity." Never one to prematurely abandon a symbol, Loeb argued that the UDA, like Wallace during the war, believed in combating Communism through support of progressive democratic movements for economic and social justice.[41]

As the cold war escalated, however, the UDA turned increasingly to the Communist issue in its campaign for the leadership of American liberalism. Thus, when the leading popular-front groups—the CIO-PAC, the NC-PAC, and the ICCASP—formed a joint committee in the spring of 1946 to pool resources for the forthcoming fall elections, Loeb responded with a *New Republic* article calling for a ban on Communist membership in liberal organizations, warning that "no united-front organization will long remain united; it will only become a front." When the popular-front groups, with CIO backing, in September 1946 issued a call to all major liberal organizations for a conference of Progressives, Loeb began to draw up plans for a rival Conference of Democratic Progressives. After the Conference of Progressives was held in Chicago, Loeb attacked the groups sponsoring the meeting as Communist-dominated and even had Eleanor Roosevelt personally intervene with CIO leader Philip Murray to make certain that his organization would not block UDA's expansion plans.[42]

Even before the disastrous 1946 elections, evidence was mounting that the popular-front left could not deal with the growing wave of reaction. In June 1946, in the aftermath of months of major strikes and consumer goods shortages, a *New Republic* poll of prominent liberal leaders found widespread hostility to Truman, but general opposition to the idea of a third party. Even the Conference of Progressives was seen by its major sponsor, CIO leader Philip Murray, as a device for electing liberal Democrats.[43] Calling upon Wallace to "carry on with confidence that you have the support of millions upon millions of Americans who supported Roosevelt," the conference ended on September 29, 1946, amid high hopes that its Continuations Committee might serve as the starting point for a national liberal organization. This was not Murray's plan, however, and without CIO support any national liberal organization in the 1940's was not feasible. Through the fall of 1946, Murray played for time, hoping to use the Conference of Progressives as a lever against the Truman Administration while carefully parrying the maneuvers of NC-PAC leader C. B. "Beanie" Baldwin and others who sought to use the Continuations Committee as a vehicle for organizing a national organization. Indeed, Murray himself had prefigured the growing frustrations within the popular-front left when he had ad-libbed at the conference that "there is no more damn business for an American Communist meddling in our business than there is for any American meddling in the Russian trade union movement." After the conference, Harold Ickes criticized the latter's defense of Henry Wallace's foreign policy position, eventually resigned his chairmanship of the ICCASP, and accused that organization of Communist domination. With the results of the 1946 elections and the defensiveness displayed by Ickes and Murray, the desire to defend the gains of the New Deal rather than to seek the ambitious foreign and domestic goals of the wartime popular front would become widespread among social liberals.[44]

Social liberals had been pessimistic about the 1946 election prospects since the labor disturbances of the spring. Yet few had really expected that the Republicans would carry both houses of Congress or that the CIO-endorsed candidates would fare so badly. Although Truman received the expected condemnation (some noted that his decision not to campaign actively was one of the few realistic acts of his administration), liberal analysis of the election did not go much beyond the *Nation*'s sad comment that the contest showed "that sagging of the spirit in high places and low which marks the end of a great national effort." [45]

In the wake of the elections, liberal bitterness over the defeat spilled over onto the Communists, an increasingly popular target. This was not surprising in view of the smashing success of anti-Communism in the election. For, although the Republican campaign slogan "Had Enough?" appealed to voters primarily on the very real issues of inflation, housing, and consumer goods shortages, GOP charges of Communist influence in the Truman Administration and in the labor movement had also proven effective. After the elections, Representative Jerry Voorhis, who had been defeated by Richard Nixon, blamed "United Front Liberals" for the debacle, while Senator Robert LaFollette, Jr., beaten in the primaries by Joseph McCarthy, warned liberals to "look out" for Communists in their midst. The National Planning Committee of the American Veterans Committee denounced the entry of Communists into its ranks; Marshall Field fired Ralph Ingersoll, the popular front editor of *P.M.,* the leading liberal newspaper in the country; and Philip Murray repeated his condemnation of Communist interference in the trade union movement at the CIO's annual convention. In the fall of 1946, the popular-front left was collapsing, and its component groups thrashed around wildly, seeking someone to blame.[46]

It was in this atmosphere that UDA chairman Reinhold Niebuhr proposed a "provisional statement of principles" for liberals, a statement that proved to be a major turning point in the formation of the Americans for Democratic Action. In a letter to prominent liberals calling for attendance at UDA's January expansion meeting, Niebuhr skillfully adapted the optimistic rhetoric of wartime liberalism to the new cold-war setting, calling for the transformation of liberalism into a "dynamic faith, the faith of free men." "A new wave of the future," he contended, "is being heralded by men to whom democracy is merely a strategic slogan. We are asked to believe that we now face a simple, inexorable choice between imperialist and Fascist reaction and Communist totalitarianism. We are told that rigid adherence to a one-party line is a necessary discipline to insure economic security, that we must blindly accept the foreign policy of Soviet power or align ourselves with the makers of a new war." [47]

There was, however, no one on the popular-front left who could challenge effectively the logic of Niebuhr's contentions— not even Henry Wallace, who merely challenged Niebuhr's presentation of the facts about Soviet and Communist intentions. The popular front had always been a mood, and the real significance of Niebuhr's appeal was that it fit perfectly the now changing mood of many liberals, a mood that sought to recapture the confident hopes of World War II and to defend the New Deal against the rising tide of domestic reaction.[48]

Niebuhr, the apostle of sober choices and the consistent enemy of utopianism, emerged as the major thinker of a "new liberalism" whose main thrust was essentially escapist and conservative. Niebuhr's own philosophy, rooted in the "crisis theology" of European Protestant Orthodoxy, was well suited to the

A view from the left

dour mood of cold-war liberalism. It stressed both the complexities of life and the persistence of sin—a world where man was
neither Prometheus nor the Noble Savage and in which evil was
a reality. "Believe in the cooperative ideal," Niebuhr had written, but "Never trust men." [49] Niebuhr's philosophy of belief
without trust, however, and his constant stress upon limits and
the need to control the messianic drive within men, had not
represented the mainstream of social liberal thought during the
war. For liberals, belief in a world New Deal and an expanded
New Deal at home had produced an optimism that was anything
but Niebuhrian. Although Niebuhr had attacked wartime optimism as escapist, criticizing the "children of light" who held the
vision of a world New Deal aloft without relating it to any
understanding of political power, he had also provided a powerful rationale for the popular-front left's defense of long-range
Soviet-American cooperation.[50] Rejecting the equation of Communism with Fascism that was so essential to later cold-war
thought (including his own), Niebuhr had argued that Communism, born in the messianic quest for perfection, had grown
morally cynical and brutal with the failure of the Russian Revolution. Fascism, on the other hand, had been morally nihilistic
from the outset, had been rooted in the glorification of nation
and race, and had ended ultimately in war against all those who
refused subjugation to its demands. Communism, he had then
reasoned, was more akin to liberalism, which also possessed
a self-defeating universalism and messianism, than to Fascism.
The postwar struggle in the Soviet Union, Niebuhr then thought,
would be between Russian national interest, which would dictate peace and internal reconstruction, and messianic Communism, which would seek to revive the revolutionary impulse. Although never a popular fronter in the 1940's, Niebuhr at times
had portrayed Joseph Stalin as a realist and a nationalist. In the
early postwar years, he even fluctuated between advocating
firm opposition to the Soviets on all fronts and seeking some

THE SPECTER

accommodation with Soviet power as a realistic solution to the European crisis.[51]

Ironically, the popular-front left, which sought such an accommodation as a step to a lasting peace, was more faithful to Niebuhr's thought than the Truman Administration, which unrealistically fought for free elections and open markets in Eastern Europe. Niebuhr, of course, did not take this position. In the postwar years he forcefully condemned the popular-front left.[52]

In early January 1947 representatives from prominent liberal organizations, former New Deal officials, and trade unionists met in Washington to discuss Niebuhr's provisional statement and other issues surrounding UDA's expansion plans. Only a week earlier, popular-front activists had met in New York to merge the NC-PAC with the ICCASP to form the Progressive Citizens of America (PCA). The PCA convocation had been characterized by sharp denunciations of the Truman domestic and foreign policies and had featured a keynote speech by Henry Wallace that contained strong hints of a third party in 1948.[53]

The PCA convention evoked little enthusiasm in the liberal journals, however. The *Nation*'s Freda Kirchway, generally a stalwart popular fronter, expressed the liberal mood perfectly when she questioned whether the Communists would have any luck with a popular-front organization during a time of mounting reaction. Nor did the PCA command anything more than the very nominal support of a few prominent trade unionists. At the later UDA-sponsored meeting, however, old New Dealers and CIO people were in abundance, third party sentiments were largely absent, and hostility to the failures of the Truman Administration was transferred into attacks upon Republicans and Communists. From the very outset, the Americans for Democratic Action was committed to saving the New Deal by defending the Democratic Party from both the right and the left.[54] Chester Bowles expressed the new spirit of cold-war liberalism clearly in an opening address that fiercely condemned both Communist totalitarianism and Republican reaction. So did Arthur Schlesinger, Jr., who portrayed the Communists as a subversive group, warned that the obstacles to the creation of a third party were too great, and concluded that the Democrats remained "the most likely medium for the progressives in the country." Those attending the January meeting agreed to formally dissolve the UDA, adopted a six-point declaration of principles, and established a committee to form the Americans for Democratic Action (ADA).[55]

The declaration of principles featured oblique support for the Truman Administration's foreign policies, combined with a somewhat muted call for the expansion of the New Deal at home. Only on the Communist issue, and the equation of Fascism and Communism, did the ADA show any real enthusiasm. "We reject," their declaration read, "any association with Communists or sympathizers with Communism as completely as we reject any association with Fascists or their sympathizers. Both are hostile to the principles of freedom and democracy on which this Republic has grown great." [56]

From the outset, ADA was what one liberal journalist called "a revolt of the middle." Somewhat uneasy over the Truman Doctrine, the ADA would adopt the Marshall Plan as its own and charge that those who worked for the creation of a third party in 1948 were serving the purposes of international Communism. As early as July 1947 James Loeb wrote prophetically to Hubert Humphrey: "I am more and more convinced that the ADA has an enormous function to perform. Furthermore, if the Democratic politicians show some sense, the third party movement can be cut down to size and the chances in '48 would not be hopeless by any matter of means." [57]

Through the fall of 1947, ADA connected support for the Marshall Plan with increasingly militant opposition to the embryonic Wallace movement. And after the Communists overcame their initial ambivalence over the third party's chances of success and joined the third party movement in November 1947, the ADA stepped up its campaign. As the third party movement neared its climax in mid-December 1947, the ADA issued a foreign policy position paper hailing the Marshall Plan as "a constructive alternative" that prefigured an "independent Europe" free from the possibility of both Soviet and American imperialism and from the "fatal choice between fascist reaction and Communist totalitarianism." [58] When Henry Wallace, sincerely believing that the Truman foreign policy would produce economic collapse in America and war with the Soviet Union, announced his third party candidacy in late December 1947, the ADA issued a statement charging that Wallace's action would only serve the interests of international Communism and girded itself for the coming struggle against the Progressive Party.[59]

V

Henry Wallace and the popular-front liberals hoped that the new party would become the vehicle for a national political realignment and the emergence of a farmer-labor-liberal majority in the 1950's. The Communists, who as usual had more modest ambitions, probably envisioned the creation and development of a small, balance-of-power party such as New York's American Labor Party. Both Communists and non-Communists, then, hoped to reach major segments of the former New Deal coalition, especially organized workers and minority groups, by appealing to the traditional economic issues of the left New Deal and to the added issue of peace. Having been so totally the agent of New Deal politics, it was somehow fitting that the popular-front left made its last great stand in defense of its right to be considered the legitimate heir of Franklin Roosevelt.[60]

The ADA, for their part, still made support of the Democrats a test of loyalty to the New Deal; and after an abortive attempt

A view from the left

to nominate General Dwight Eisenhower, they lined up solidly behind the Truman candidacy. Depicting Wallace as a naïve dupe of the Communists, the ADA maintained that support for the Progressive Party would throw the election to the Republicans and endanger the New Deal. There was, of course, little evidence of conspiracy in the relationship between the Progressive Party and the Communists—the Communists openly supported the party, fought bitterly with the liberals over the party's organization, and attacked Wallace's Keynesian ideas even while endorsing his candidacy.[61] The same is not true for the special relationship between the ADA and the Democrats.

In November 1947 Clark Clifford had advised Truman that "the administration must persuade prominent liberals and progressives—*and no one else*—to move publicly into the fray. They must point out that the core of Wallace's backing is made up of Communists and fellow travelers." During the campaign, William Batt, a prominent ADA member, was chosen to direct the Democratic National Committee's new research division. Staffing this division with ADAers, Batt worked closely with White House aides to counteract the Progressive Party's threat to Truman. During the campaign the ADA led the attack against the Progressives, publishing lists of party petition signers along with their alleged Communist-front connections and consistently portraying Henry Wallace as a pathetic pawn of the Communists.[62]

Contrasting Wallace's refusal to unequivocally repudiate the Communists with Franklin Roosevelt's earlier disavowal of CP support, the ADA warned that the Wallace campaign was designed to destroy the Marshall Plan and could only result in the election of a reactionary Republican administration. Guilt by association constituted the essence of the ADA's attack, a point made forcibly by James Loeb, who charged that "the presence of Mr. Wallace does not alter the fact that the real authority of your party is vested in the hands of men and women, many of whom followed the dictates of totalitarianism in the period of the Nazi-Soviet pact.[63]

Wallace's crushing defeat and Truman's surprising victory destroyed the popular-front left as a serious force in American politics. Looking at Truman's triumph, ADA members felt that they had helped purge the Communists from liberal ranks, and that the Democratic victory presaged a great birth of liberal political action. Indeed, Senator-elect Hubert Humphrey, who had played a major role in the struggle against the Wallaceites in Minnesota, talked in glowing terms about economic planning, full employment, and an economy of abundance as he began his Washington career. Writing in the aftermath of the election, Arthur Schlesinger, Jr., captured this sense of hopefulness in *The Vital Center,* a work whose ringing phrases reassured Truman's supporters on the left that they were in the vanguard of a brave new left of center world.[64]

The creation of a permanent war economy and a partial war psychology, however, led the nation even further to the right after 1948, and cold-war liberals were compelled to adapt their own aims to an increasingly reactionary politics. Thus, NATO became the instrument to protect the Atlantic Community and a future socialist Europe from Soviet aggression, Korea became the war for the United Nations, and Joseph McCarthy became a reckless demagogue who did the bidding of Communism by diverting popular attention from the real enemy without to a bogus enemy within. In the struggles of the 1940's, and the transformation of popular-front to cold-war liberalism, a mindless anti-Communism had triumphed. The resultant politics of the vital center established the parameters within which foreign and domestic policy were debated and set the stage for the enormous domestic and international crises of the 1960's.

A view from the left

LABOR'S
COLD
WAR:

The CIO
and

the Communists

BY DAVID M. OSHINSKY

In 1950, the Congress of Industrial Organizations expelled its Communist-dominated affiliates to the overwhelming approval of America's liberal community. Since that time, scores of historians and journalists have continued to applaud the purges.[1] They were necessary, we are told, to rid the labor movement of devious ideologues who placed the interests of a foreign power above the interests of the union members they represented; to re-affirm the CIO's commitment to trade union democracy; to aid the free world in its "death struggle" against totalitarianism; and to enhance the CIO's credibility as a responsible political force dedicated to the ideals of democracy. In the words of Max Kampelman, whose book, *The Communist Party vs. The CIO,* is clearly the most influential work in the field, "not only was the integrity and survival of the trade union heritage at stake, but more important was the national interest of the United States. For the CIO to have remained aloof from the battle between Communism and democracy would have stopped it from playing any significant role on the American scene." [2]

In recent years, a few historians have begun to question the necessity of these expulsions.[3] While freely admitting that the Communists followed a pro-Soviet line, they insist that this bias did not affect their performance any more that CIO President Philip Murray's pro-New Deal bias affected his performance. Indeed, they argue that the Communists were often excellent "bread and butter" unionists whose affiliates were actually more democratic than their right-wing counterparts. The Communists were punished, they conclude, not because of their subordination of trade union goals to the interests of a foreign power, but because "they were Communists and saw the world in a different way"—a way that could no longer be tolerated in Cold War America. As soon as the CIO national office realized which way the wind was blowing, it not only capitulated to this anti-Communist hysteria, but actively encouraged it within the labor movement.

THE SPECTER

This new interpretation raises some very significant questions. First, to what extent did the Communists' adherence to the Stalinist line hinder their effectiveness as trade union leaders? Was it, in fact, any more damaging to independent trade union action than the right wing's strict allegiance to the Democratic party? Second, what were the motivating forces behind the expulsions? Were CIO leaders simply responding passively to Cold War pressures, or were these pressures willingly exploited in an attempt to rid the federation of a vocal, and often troublesome, minority. Third, what forces were exerting these pressures? How influential, for example, was the business community, or the Truman administration, or the Catholic church, in bringing about these expulsions? The following essay, analyzing the relationship between the pro-Communist and anti-Communist factions within the CIO, will address itself to these crucial points.

I

Shortly before the CIO was formed, the Communist Party abandoned its attempts at dual unionism in favor of "boring from within" existing labor organizations. This new policy, part of a larger CP strategy to unite with other "progressive forces" in a Popular Front against fascism, encouraged party organizers to work within established AFL unions, and wherever possible, to capture them from below. Yet, despite the intensity of their efforts, the Communists were never able to mobilize much support within the Federation. Virtually every affiliate passed a resolution barring them from membership, while the AFL Executive Board amended the national constitution so that "no organization . . . controlled by Communists or advocating the violent overthrow of our institutions shall be allowed representation in any Central Labor Body or State Federation of Labor." [4] By 1937, the Communists could claim control of only a few unskilled affiliates, including Harry Bridges' Pacific Maritime

Federation and "Red Mike" Quill's Transport Workers Union. The formation of the CIO in 1936, however, provided the Communists with an unprecedented opportunity to establish themselves in the new industrial unions. From the very outset, CIO President John L. Lewis made it known that he would accept aid from any group willing to go out and recruit workers. Although Lewis had a long history of red-baiting within his own union, the United Mine Workers, he sympathized with the Communists' belief that the growing class militancy of unorganized and unskilled workers should be encouraged, not crushed. Unlike Sidney Hillman of the Clothing Workers, David Dubinsky of the Ladies Garment Workers, or Philip Murray of the Steel Workers, Lewis felt that a large degree of rank-and-file insurgency—including the type displayed in the bloody strikes at Toledo, Minneapolis, and San Francisco and in the sit-downs at Flint and Cleveland—was vital to a movement employing mass organizational techniques.[5] And Lewis realized that few groups in America could identify with this working class militancy better than the Communists. During the Depression's early years, the CP organized regional councils for the unemployed which sought to radicalize the jobless through massive demonstrations for more relief. These councils were also instrumental in preventing the eviction of rentless tenants and in organizing gas and electric squads to turn on these utilities after they had been shut off by local companies.[6] On the labor front, the most dramatic strikes of this period were led by Stalinists and Trotskyists. As Len DeCaux so well put it: "The Communists brought misery out of hiding in the workers' neighborhoods. They paraded it with angry demands through the main streets to the Public Square, and on to City Hall. They raised particular hell."[7]

While this initial commitment to working class militancy, coupled with a superb sense of organizational discipline, made the Communists top-flight labor recruiters, their effectiveness

THE SPECTER

within the CIO still varied greatly from union to union. In the established affiliates—like Lewis' United Mine Workers or Dubinsky's Ladies Garment Workers' Union—which were well-organized and controlled by strong leaders, the Communists made no headway at all. Indeed, it is one of the great ironies of labor history that at the very time Lewis was recruiting Communists as CIO organizers, his own union had a law on the books barring them from membership. Similarly, the CIO's new unions in steel, textiles, and meatpacking, which began as national organizing committees governed from the top by Murray, Hillman and Van Bittner, proved difficult to penetrate. By 1938, in fact, Hillman and Murray had quietly removed all known Communists from their organizations. The Communists did succeed, however, among the affiliates—such as the Fur and Leather Workers and the Mine, Mill and Smelter Workers— that had a legacy of radicalism, and among several industrial unions, particularly the United Automobile Workers and the United Electrical Workers, whose devotion to the principle of local autonomy precluded any CIO attempt to organize them from above.[8]

Because of their ability to organize at the local level, the Communists were able to build a powerful faction within the CIO. In less than three years, they obtained "complete or partial control" of about 40% of the CIO unions.[9] On the national level, where their influence was sharply curtailed by the opposition of Hillman and Dubinsky, the Communists still placed Len DeCaux as editor of the *CIO News,* Lee Pressman as CIO General Counsel, and a significant number of party supporters in middle and lower level administrative positions. However, since most of their support was at the grass roots, the Communists exerted greater authority within the CIO's local and regional councils. By 1939, pro-Communist forces had taken over the Industrial Union Councils of New York, Illinois, California, Wisconsin and Minnesota.[10]

Labor's cold war

In the CIO's early years, the tenuous relationship between the left-wing and right-wing factions was based on their common desire to organize mass production workers and to unite in a Popular Front against Hitlerism. Temporarily, at least, basic political and ideological differences were cast aside. From a political standpoint, this meant that both sides unanimously endorsed the New Deal's alleged commitment to industrial unionism, its social welfare programs, and its obvious sympathies for the Soviet Union and the "western democracies" in their relations with the Axis powers. The main difference was that the right-wingers truly believed in the social-reformist philosophy of the New Deal and were determined to channel the CIO's political power through the Democratic party in an effort to make their voices heard, while the Communists believed the concept of a government-labor coalition was anathema to the interests of the working class.[11] Only the Stalinist line of class collaboration, coupled with Roosevelt's enormous popularity among industrial workers, kept most Communist trade unionists in the New Deal camp.

Because the Communists in the CIO adhered so rigidly to the Stalinist line, they were often forced into dangerous political situations. A good example occurred in 1939 when the Soviet Union signed a non-aggression pact with Nazi Germany. As one labor historian noted: "The self-effacing affability of the Communists came to an end with the . . . pact. The Communists stopped deferring to the Roosevelt administration and the liberal CIO leadership and began once again to articulate rank-and-file demands." [12] More specifically, the Communists now viewed Roosevelt's foreign policy, as well as his mobilization program, as a thinly-veiled attempt by the "Wall Street interests" to involve the nation in an unwanted, utterly senseless foreign conflict aimed at protecting the imperialist interests of England and France. And they responded with a series of wildcat strikes in the defense industries—most notably at Allis-Chalmers and North American Aviation.

To many right-wing CIO leaders, the Communists' failure to support Roosevelt and his defense program became the excuse for a major campaign to expel them from the CIO. In 1939, David McDonald, secretary-treasurer of the Steel Workers Organizing Committee, warned his followers that ". . . there are people who would like to use the steel workers union to build a classless society. Agents of the Communist party quite naturally would like to turn SWOC into an instrument for their own use. The steel workers do not want to join the Communist party . . . They will not subscribe to any political or economic theory which is anti-union or anti-American." [13] At the 1940 and 1941 UAW conventions, the Reuther brothers rammed through a series of resolutions opposing both the strikes at Allis-Chalmers and North American Aviation and "the brutal dictatorships, and wars of aggression of the totalitarian governments in Germany, Italy, Russia and Japan." [14] Similar results were achieved at the conventions of the Clothing Workers, the Steel Workers and the Rubber Workers. [15]

In this particular case, the matter of dumping the Communists was complicated by the imposing figure of John L. Lewis. Since 1938, the CIO President had consistently taken issue with Roosevelt's foreign and domestic policies; and, after resigning from Labor's Non-partisan League in protest against its subservience to the Democratic party, he made his famous speech endorsing Wendell Willkie for the presidency. It was difficult, therefore, to condemn the Communists for not supporting Roosevelt without also condemning Lewis—a step that few CIO leaders were willing to take. For his part, Lewis believed that an attempt to purge the Communists would destroy the CIO, and he did everything possible to prevent it. [16]

The issue was finally resolved at the CIO's 1940 national

Labor's cold war

convention when the resolutions committee drafted a carefully worded statement that condemned the "Communist menace," but virtually denied its existence within the CIO. The statement was so contradictory that Tom Kennedy, the committee chairman, moved immediately to close debate on the subject. At this point, Philip Murray, Lewis's hand-picked successor, called for a standing vote, and declared the convention's "unanimous approval . . ." [17]

The right-wingers viewed this resolution as a great victory. It was, they believed, the first step in a program to eliminate Communist influence from the CIO. The left-wingers took a more guarded approach. To their thinking, support for the resolution was necessary to prevent a showdown they could not hope to win. Most CIO members, however, could agree on one basic point: the power and prestige of John L. Lewis had kept this internal dissension from assuming the proportions of a civil war.

All attempts to deal with the "Communist problem" were postponed by the German attack on Russia, and America's subsequent entry into the war. As soon as Russia was invaded, the pro-Communist unions discarded their opposition to the defense effort by promising an all-out effort to increase production and to decrease the possibility of labor-management disputes. Yet even after the political differences dividing the two factions were temporarily put aside, disputes arose over the extent to which organized labor should moderate its demands to conform with the war effort. In this case, it was the Communists who became the most ardent defenders of wartime cooperation. While both sides generally endorsed the "no strike" pledge, for example, several prominent Communist union leaders ignored national CIO policy by supporting the Smith-Connolly Act, which advocated the prohibition of strikes in defense industries and jail terms for strikers, as well as Roosevelt's own proposal for a labor conscription act covering all workers between 18 and 65. Indeed,

Harry Bridges told a meeting of Longshoremen in San Francisco that strikes were "treason"; that the government should "refuse to give consideration to the demands of any section of labor on strike"; and that "the strike weapon is overboard, not only for the duration of the war, but after the war too." [18]

This strict adherence to the concept of wartime cooperation took other forms as well. The Communists actively supported contracts calling for speed-ups, incentive pay, and the reintroduction of piecework; they were also particularly adamant in their determination to break "wildcat" strikes at the local level. Since these policies were often in direct conflict with the wishes of the workers, the left-wing leadership was forced to discard the concept of local union autonomy in favor of strict consolidation at the national level. By war's end, the Communist-controlled unions could hardly claim to be more democratic than any of the other CIO affiliates; to the contrary, their wartime "sellout" of the rank-and-file was soon to serve as a pretext for expelling them from the CIO.

II

Shortly after the war ended, America began the troublesome process of "reconversion." Most labor leaders saw the need for a reconversion with modified government supervision; this meant the rigid enforcement of price controls and the scrapping of wage controls. Industry, on the other hand, desired the retention of wage controls and the elimination of price controls. It soon became clear that this dichotomy was reaching alarming proportions. Many businessmen, remembering the strong anti-labor sentiment that gripped America after World War I, envisioned a golden opportunity to severely weaken their labor opponents. And the unions, faced with rising prices, lower real wages, and growing unemployment, felt the need for immediate action before their bargaining powers were destroyed.[19]

The country was soon plagued by a wave of strikes. In the

Labor's cold war

year's time since Japan's capitulation, 4.9 million workers were involved in 4630 work stoppages totaling 119.8 million man days of labor.[20] The following year was even worse; within a six month period the major industries of America—steel, coal, auto and transportation—were shut down. As one strike would end only to be followed by two more, there was a noticeable increase in anti-labor sentiment. A Gallup Poll conducted in December of 1946 on the question "Should Congress in this coming legislative session pass new laws to control labor unions?" indicated sixty-six percent affirmative, twenty-two percent negative, and twelve percent undecided.[21] In January and February of 1947, more than sixty bills and amendments were proposed in Congress to curb the "abuses" of unionism.[22] Three months later, Congress passed the National Labor Relations (Taft-Hartley) Act.

To make matters worse, the onset of the Cold War offered America's conservative, anti-union forces an opportunity to link these labor disturbances to the "international Communist conspiracy." In part, the conservatives were reacting to a new change in the Communist party's post-war line. After five years of open support for President Roosevelt and the war effort, the American Communists were suddenly condemned by Moscow (through the famous Duclos letter) for their conciliatory attitude towards progressive capitalism and their abandonment of the class struggle. In the future, they were told, Communists must work to strengthen the American left and to reconstitute the party's working-class base.[23] Not surprisingly, the conservatives publicized the letter as yet another example of Joseph Stalin's ability to manipulate large sections of the American labor movement. The Hearst-owned *San Antonio Light,* for example, declared that the post-war strikes were part of a "clear and distinct revolutionary pattern . . . timed to serve Russia's political interests," while Charles Wilson, president of General Motors, claimed that the two great problems facing America

THE SPECTER

were "Russia abroad" and "labor at home." And the U.S. Chamber of Commerce, in a pamphlet on Communist influence in America, wrote that "The tremendous power of labor today permits no . . . complacency . . . When a businessman or industrialist finds that nothing he does can please his union, he tends at first to form a sour view of organized labor. But as he becomes more sophisticated, he realizes that his difficulties may not arise from his own workers, who usually understand his problems, but from outside forces controlling his local union. The Communists demands are insatiable because they thrive on trouble." [24]

The Cold War also renewed factional animosities within the labor movement. The American Federation of Labor, long a bastion of conservative, craft-oriented unionism and vigorous anti-Communism, took its industrial rival to task for coddling "dangerous subversives." George Meany, the AFL's secretary-treasurer, noted that recent developments on the labor front "prove the charge the AFL has been hammering at for months and years, that the CIO is Communist-dominated." [25] Indeed, the AFL was so obsessed with the Cold War that the major issue at its 1946 national convention was not labor legislation, or wages, or hours of work, but rather the infiltration of subversives into the State Department. "The entire story of this infiltration has not yet been told," noted Federation officials, "but it is known that members of the Communist party employed in government departments purloined secret state and other papers, many of which were photographed before being returned to the files, and photostats forwarded to Moscow." [26]

The heightening of Soviet-American tensions had an even greater effect upon the CIO. In the years 1945–1950, the infusion of Cold War issues into union politics was so complete that the major factional battles centered almost exclusively around the Marshall Plan, the Henry Wallace campaign, and the Taft-Hartley non-Communist affidavits. For the CIO's right-wing leaders, of course, the Cold War was a tremendous asset. Walter Reuther rose to the UAW's presidency during this period by red-baiting his opponents into submission, while James Carey, ousted president of the United Electrical Workers, recaptured many of his former constituents by organizing a rival union under the banner of rabid anti-Communism. For the CIO's left-wing leaders, however, the Cold War meant either a rapid adjustment to the realities of domestic anti-Communism, or the possibility of virtual extinction. A few left-wingers, like Joe Curran of the National Martitime Union and Mike Quill of the Transport Workers Union, broke off ties with the Communist party in time to save their careers. But a good many of their former colleagues were simply swept away by the force of these Cold War attacks. By 1950, eleven left-wing unions had been expelled from the CIO; and the remaining affiliates were controlled by vehement anti-Communist leaders.[27]

III

As CIO delegates moved into Atlantic City for the 1946 national convention, the "Communist issue" clearly dominated their thoughts. In the wake of the 1946 congressional elections, where Republicans won control of Congress with a campaign stressing New Deal subversion and Soviet aggression, the CIO was in a most precarious position. As the major power base for domestic Communists, it was becoming a prime target for red-baiters, legislative committees and the right wing press. The choice facing CIO leaders seemed ominous indeed. On the one hand, they could turn on the Communists, thereby encouraging a factional dispute which might destroy the federation; on the other, they could ignore them, waiting helplessly as the albatross of treason was hung around their necks.

At the convention, the leadership could not reach immediate agreement upon a suitable course of action. The more vehement anti-Communists headed by Walter Reuther and James Carey, wanted a showdown on the issue; the pro-Communists, headed by Ben Gold of the Fur and Leather Workers, and James Mattles and Julius Emspak of the United Electrical Workers, were trying desperately to avoid one. And somewhere in the middle was CIO President Philip Murray, who wanted some sort of national policy or statement that would publicly confront the issue without alienating either side.

Murrays' primary concern at this time was preserving unity within his organization. Although he was known to harbor strong anti-Communist feelings (just two months before the convention he told an informal gathering that labor "wants no damn Communists meddling in our affairs"), he also refused to give his blessing to the red-baiting assaults of the CIO's right-wing. Moreover, he seemed to respect many of the left-wingers for their ability to run sound trade unions. A few weeks earlier, he had publicly congratulated Matles and Emspak for their "splendid support . . . for all national CIO policies"; and in a particularly revealing private conversation with radio commentator Martin Agronsky, Murray answered a pointed question about Ben Gold's Communist connections by stating: "Mr. Gold is an estimable gentleman. He runs an excellent union along good trade union lines. He is highly regarded by the employers of his industry." [28]

In an attempt to reach some sort of compromise on the issue, Murray appointed a special committee, composed of three left-wing executive board members and three right-wing members, to respond to "the allegations contained in the newsprints [which Murray, himself, termed "wild and wholly irrational"] . . . that this organization of yours and mine, this great trade union movement, is Communistically inclined." For its part, the committee finally decided on a resolution stating that the CIO "resents and rejects efforts of the Communist Party or any other political party and their adherents in the affairs of the CIO." However, no mention was made of the fact that Communists were presently working within the CIO, and Murray was careful to note that the resolution ". . . should not be misconstrued to be a repressive measure, calculated to do things of a repressive nature." [29]

Considering the hostile political climate surrounding the convention, a resolution which condemned Communist interference but took no action against Communists themselves was surprisingly mild. In fact, it was intended to be mild, and for several good reasons. First, the vast majority of CIO leaders feared that a purge of Communists at this time would tear the organization apart. Indeed, it was only after the overwhelming defeat of Henry Wallace in 1948 that most of them realized the CIO could easily survive such a purge. Second, more than a few CIO leaders were concerned about the constitutional issues involved. They knew that if Communists were legally elected by the rank-and-file of a given affiliate, the CIO could only remove them by expelling the union itself; by this process, the CIO stood to lose upwards of a million members. Third, at this time, the rival factions seemed to be in general agreement on the one issue that usually divided them—foreign policy.

In 1946, the CIO was still unanimous in its opposition to President Truman's handling of foreign affairs. The Communists, of course, were highly critical of the new "get tough" policy towards Russia, and advocated a return to a more "progressive thinking" of Franklin Roosevelt. Interestingly enough, most non-Communist CIO leaders supported this position. As good Democrats, they felt that Truman was moving away from his predecessor's policy of cooperation with Russia in favor of Churchill's proposed Anglo-American alliance against Communism. Therefore, the foreign policy resolution passed at the pro-Communist Fur and Leather Workers' convention of 1946, advocating "friendship with the Soviet Union . . . and strenuous opposition to those who seek to destroy the progressive policies of our great President Franklin Roosevelt and to plunge our country and the Soviet Union into a terrible war," [30] was no different from the ones passed by Hillman's Amalgamated Clothing Workers or Murray's United Steel Workers. Shortly before his death, Hillman told the 1946 ACW convention that the American people would not tolerate a hard-line, anti-Soviet foreign policy. "They demonstrated recognition of this fact," he stated, "by the unanimity with which they rejected the Churchill proposal for an Anglo-American alliance, which, of course, would be directed against the Soviet Union . . ." Hillman then concluded: "Of course, we have our basic disagreements on philosophy with our friends from Russia. That did not stop us from initial agreement on policies . . . We agreed that in Russia, it is their business to build the kind of government they feel they want. We expect them to have the same respect for us. That is the understanding, and it stands up." [31]

By 1947, however, as relations between the United States and the Soviet Union continued to decline, America's liberal community began to feel the effects of the Cold War. Already two opposing groups had been formed: the Progressive Citizens of America (PCA), and the Americans for Democratic Action (ADA). The PCA, an outgrowth of an earlier Conference of Progressives attended by Philip Murray and several members of the CIO's Political Action Committee (all of whom soon resigned), was organized primarily to oppose Truman's handling of domestic and foreign policies—especially his failure to perpetuate ". . . the progressive global thinking of Franklin Roosevelt." The ADA, supported by Walter Reuther and David Dubinsky, was also critical of Truman's failings, but excluded Communists from membership. Indeed, as one sympathetic journalist has noted, "it was in large part set up as a counterpoise to PCA—to provide a rallying ground for anti-Communist liberals who rejected all associations with Communists." [32]
Although the CIO Executive Board refused to endorse either

Labor's cold war

organization at its general meeting in February, 1947, and issued a statement "deploring the division in the liberal movement," this attempt to remain apart from the conflict proved of short duration. The reason for this change was quite simple: in the following months, Truman began to win back many disenchanted CIO leaders by his veto of the Taft-Hartley bill and his espousal of the Marshall Plan. While the ADA applauded Truman's efforts, the PCA, with strong Communist backing, bitterly attacked the Marshall Plan, and set out to organize a third party movement around the candidacy of Henry Wallace. By the summer of 1947, the CIO's Communist faction was marching in step to the drums of Gideon's Army.

The repercussions caused by this opposition to the Marshall Plan and support for the Wallace movement were particularly damaging to the left-wingers. Philip Murray, who had been on record many times against the formation of a third party, was so disturbed by these incidents that he told the CIO Executive Board members in July, 1947: "It is high time the CIO leaders stopped apologizing for Communism. If Communism is an issue in your unions, throw it to hell out, and throw its advocates out along with it. When a man accepts office . . . to render service to workers, and then delivers that service to other outside interests, that man is nothing but a damned traitor." Two months later, Murray demanded the resignations of four Communists on his staff, including *CIO News* editor Len DeCaux, and then made plain his support for Truman by inviting General George Marshall to address the CIO's national convention.[33]

Marshall's welcome was among the most tumultuous that labor observers had ever seen. To the blare of a military band, and a tremendous standing ovation, Murray introduced the Secretary of State as "one of the world's greatest champions of peace," a man "whose ideas reflect the opinions and thinkings of the overwhelming multitude of Americans." Marshall then launched into a spirited defense of Truman's foreign policy, concluding with

an ominous warning about "enemies of democracy . . . who
. . . are determined to undermine the confidence of the labor
elements in the stability of our institutions, and the soundness of
our traditions." [34]

Following Marshall's speech, a particularly acrimonious debate ensued over Truman's foreign policy. Those favoring the
President—including Reuther, Carey, Murray and Bittner—
claimed that the Marshall Plan was really a throwback to the
policies of Franklin Roosevelt—policies designed to "find non-
military—indeed, humanitarian—solutions" to Cold War problems. Ironically, not one speaker attempted to defend the Truman Doctrine or to link it in any way to the new program for
European reconstruction. It was as if the Marshall Plan had
blotted out all of Truman's former pronouncements; they had
simply become too irrelevant to merit serious discussion.

The debate also featured some powerful red-baiting attacks;
indeed, Van Bittner prefaced his remarks by noting: "We must
remember one thing; Thank God we live in the U.S.A. We can
criticize our government here without fear of being shot or
placed in a concentration camp." [35] Moreover, when Joseph
Kehoe, president of the American Communications Association,
objected to these attacks, he was publicly challenged by
Murray.

Kehoe: *"I would like to be able to criticize Amer-*
ican foreign policy without being subjected to
loyalty tests and hounded and driven out of
public life. . . Let us not say that where
someone finds one comma wrong that we are
then American traitors and unfit for human
society. That kind of nationalism is what
breeds war, no matter what nation it exists
in, and it is absolutely contrary to the Amer-
ican tradition."

Labor's cold war

> *Murray:* "*May I interrupt you for a moment? I assume you also believe that the heroes of Stalingrad are entitled to take the rostrum and the public platform to expound their views?*"
>
> *Kehoe:* "*I believe in the American principles of free speech everywhere for everybody.*" [36]

The overwhelming majority of delegates then voted for a "compromise" resolution which endorsed the Marshall Plan and urged the president to see that it was implemented "in the best interest of democracy."

> "*We support sound programs for post-war rehabilitation . . . We urge in support of our nation's fight against hunger throughout the world prompt action to provide food and other economic aid for the rehabilitation of these countries. We also urge that under no circumstances should food or any other aid given by our country be used as a means of coercing free but needy people in the exercise of rights of independence and self-government . . .*" [37]

In his remarks following the vote, however, Murray left no doubt as to why he personally supported the Marshall Plan. "There is no question," he stated, "but that in the distribution of relief in this fight . . . the people who absorb the food might very well refrain from becoming a part of any totalitarian government. That is reasonable. . . And if in the distribution of food those things should ensue in Europe, there is not much you and I can do about it if the people make up their minds they don't want Communism when they get plenty of food. That is true . . . That is a fact . . ." [38]

THE SPECTER

IV

The 1947 CIO national convention accurately reflected the
bitter factionalism that was now surfacing within the various affiliates. Perhaps the most important battles took place within
the United Electrical Workers and the United Automobile
Workers. Here, the anti-Communist forces, led by James Carey
and Walter Reuther, were aided for the first time by powerful
outside interests, including the Association of Catholic Trade
Unionists, the Truman administration, and the business community, in their attempt to purge the pro-Communist factions.

From its very inception, the United Electrical Workers (UE)
was ruled by a coalition of pro-Communist forces, led by Secretary-Treasurer Julius Emspak and Director of Organization
James Matles, and non-Communist forces, led by President
James Carey. But, quite clearly, the Emspak-Matles wing controlled the day to day operations of the UE; Carey, as Secretary-Treasurer of the CIO and a participant in a multitude of
social and religious movements outside the union, simply had
no time to exert the power and authority that the presidency
offered. According to his own recollection, when he finally discovered that Matles and Emspak were going to oust him from
office, ". . . it was too late to fight back . . . I discovered that
they were in complete control of the national office; they dominated the executive committee, ran the union paper, and were
strongly entrenched in the locals and districts. All the organizers
were party-liners." [39]
The trouble began after the Hitler-Stalin pact, when the *UE
News,* under Emspak's direction, abandoned its Popular Front
editorial policy and condemned Roosevelt for violating his
former declarations of neutrality. Although Carey was clearly
irritated by the shift, he intervened only after receiving a letter
from a local union asking whether it could legally pass a resolu-

tion barring "Communists, Nazis or Fascists" from positions of authority. Carey used his weekly column in the *UE News* ("Let's Talk It Over") to inform the local union that such a resolution was clearly constitutional. Although his column was not subject to editorial censorship, Emspak wrote a short rejoinder to the column stating that Carey had been asked to postpone discussion of this issue until after a meeting of the union's executive board, but had refused to do so.[40]

The final break came when Germany attacked the Soviet Union in 1941, and the *UE News* again reversed its editorial policy. In his column of July 12, 1941, Carey focused attention on the shift by calling Matles and Emspak "political acrobats in pink tights posing as labor leaders who are a disgrace to the union and insult the intelligence of the membership." [41] In response to this attack, Matles and Emspak mobilized their forces for a convention floor fight on the issue of whether local unions could prevent known Communists from holding office, and sounded out local feeling about the desirability of opposing Carey for the presidency. At the UE's 1941 convention, the pro-Communist forces easily won both battles; they not only passed a resolution stating that "any good-standing member of the Union is entitled to all rights and privileges without discrimination, unless such member be proven guilty of acts against the nation or against the Union . . ." but also elected their own candidate, Albert Fitzgerald, to the union presidency. Interestingly enough, Fitzgerald told the assembled delegates: "I am not a Communist. I am not dominated by Communists. And as a citizen of the United States I despise the philosophy of the Communist party." [42] But it was obvious to all observers that Matles and Emspak, in selecting a respectable Catholic, a good rank-and-file unionist, and a man willing to spout anti-Communist epithets while actually submitting to the party line, had fulfilled their major objective: they had buried the Carey forces.

It should be noted, however, that the pro-Communist victory

was neither an undemocratic, backroom maneuver, nor a blow to the union itself. For months before the convention, both sides had free access to the pages of the *UE News,* and every letter attacking Carey's stand was matched by one supporting it. Furthermore, the year 1941 was marked by a series of excellent contract settlements, as well as the greatest membership gains in the union's short history.[43] Despite his later statements to the contrary, Carey was obviously aware of these facts. Indeed, following his defeat at the convention, he told the delegates: "When somebody says you have a difference of opinion with Jim Matles, I say that I have many differences of opinion with Jim Matles—but I can sit down with him any day and we can work out an agreement. The same thing is true of Julius Emspak and other members of the General Executive Board." Carey then asked the membership to support them "to assure the continuation of the splendid organization we have all played a part in building." [44]

Early in 1947, Carey began a campaign to regain control of the UE by forming a rival faction, the UE Members for Democratic Action (UEMDA). In a letter to the *UE News,* he drew the battle lines: "The issue between me and the present UE leadership," he wrote, "goes solely to the proposition that our great International Union has become known as a transmission belt for the American Communist Party." [45] Within a few weeks, the UEMDA organized dozens of local chapters and began publishing its own newspaper, *The Real UE,* whose masthead was adorned with Philip Murray's now famous quote: "If Communism is an issue in any of your unions, throw it to hell out, and throw its advocates out along with it . . ."

Carey began his assault upon the left-wing leadership at the UE's 1947 national convention. Here, the UEMDA proposed that the delegates reaffirm the CIO's 1946 pledge ". . . rejecting the efforts of the Communist Party or other political parties to interfere in the CIO." Instead, the delegates, by margins of

8–1, passed a series of resolutions which condemned red-baiting, called for the solidarity of all workers ". . . regardless of craft, age, sex, race, creed, or political belief," and ordered the UEMDA to disband. Carey was bitterly disappointed by his poor showing, and claimed that the convention had ". . . castigated the CIO, not only its leadership, but its membership as well." "I am in this fight, and I will remain, in the face of any action to purge the UEMDA," he warned. "We will ultimately win, and get the Communists out of this union." [46]

Despite this setback, the Carey faction achieved some notable successes at the local level. There were several reasons for this, but one of the most significant was the role played by the Association of Catholic Trade Unionists. Formed in 1937 by a group of Catholic clergymen, the ACTU was committed to the organization of industrial workers in accordance with the encyclicals promulgated by Pope Pius XI and Pope Pius XII. In pragmatic terms, this meant vigorous support for all CIO officials who subscribed to the doctrines of labor-management cooperation and anti-Communism, and vigorous opposition to those who did not. As Father John Clancey, a prominent ACTU spokesman, told the United Rubber Workers convention in 1940: "We don't want to be faced with a choice . . . between Fascism and Communism because there is a middle ground. We don't have to turn right or left, but go straight ahead in establishing industrial democracy. There is no reason why workers and management cannot democratically plan the industrial futures of the various industries." [47]

When Carey began his drive to oust the Communists from the UE, he was offered immediate assistance by the ACTU. In some areas, this assistance proved to be of little value, but in others, where the ACTU was well-established, the Carey forces were aided immeasurably. In Pittsburgh, for example, the home base for Father Charles Rice, ACTU's acting president (and a close friend to both Murray and Carey), the local chapter, while not numerically strong, published a weekly paper, *The Pittsburgh Catholic,* and had the full support of the regional archdiocese.

In 1948, the Pittsburgh chapter organized an opposition group, the "Rank-and-File," within Local 601—a huge UE affiliate of almost 17,000 members, the majority of whom were Catholic. Father Rice personally led the assault. First, he had several of the Catholic churches in Pittsburgh print leaflets urging parishioners to throw out the local UE leaders; second, he combined with other dissidents—including a powerful Socialist faction—to run an opposition slate of candidates in the upcoming local election; third, on the eve of the election, he convinced his close friend Representative Francis Walter of the House Committee on Un-American Activities to subpoena the local's leaders to testify about their Communist backgrounds.[48] The UE's national office was so enraged by this power play that it distributed a pamphlet, "The Members Run This Union," which read: "The ACTU is an organization devoted to capturing control of unions to establish its own kind of domination . . . by fomenting division along religious lines . . . Undemocratic and authoritarian in the last degree, the ACTU operates to impose its program and policies upon labor unions by capturing key personnel, and favors the extension of undemocratic methods in trade unions to perpetuate the power of ACTU puppets, and, through them, the domination of the ACTU over the union." [49] It was Father Rice, however, who carried the day. Local 601 voted the pro-Communist forces out of office, providing Carey with one of his most important "grass-roots" victories.

The Carey faction was also aided by the new anti-Communist crackdown in Washington. The Atomic Energy Commission, for example, used its "implied powers" to order all companies working on classified projects not to recognize unions that were labeled as security risks; the UE thereby lost its bargaining rights at the Knolls Atomic Power Laboratory in Schenectady,

New York. Far more serious, however, was section 9(h) of the Taft-Hartley Act, passed in 1947, which provided that no labor union could avail itself of NLRB facilities unless its officers filed non-Communist affidavits. When the UE leadership balked at signing these affidavits, some employers refused to negotiate with the union.[50] This recalcitrance proved very beneficial to Carey and the UEMDA. In several instances they won control of local affiliates who feared that a continuation of this boycott policy would destroy their ability to bargain for better wages and working conditions. One survey, conducted by *Fortune,* estimated the 70,000 UE members either went over to the Carey side, or left the UE entirely to join the United Automobile Workers or the AFL's International Brotherhood of Electrical Workers.[51]

Interestingly enough, the industries largest single employer, General Electric, refused to become involved in the controversy. Indeed, the company was so conservative that it could perceive no real difference between the UE and the UEMDA. "In our opinion," wrote the company, "whether they realize it or not, both are collectivists—believers in government being big and people being little." [52] GE's policy changed drastically, however, after the UE was expelled from the CIO in 1949, and Carey was issued a charter by Philip Murray to form a rival union, the International Union of Electrical, Radio and Machine Workers. This change was due, in large measure, to the fact that GE executives were hauled before congressional committees and told, point blank, that there *was* a difference between "Communist collectivists" and "anti-Communist collectivists." After a thorough grilling by Senator Hubert Humphrey, chairman of a sub-committee investigating "Communist Domination of Unions," GE Vice-President Lemuel Boulware was forced to admit that "a collectivist who is a free agent" was a far better person to deal with than "a collectivist who represents the interests of a foreign power . . . engaged in a systematic conspiracy." [53] By 1953, GE's policy was so pro-Carey that it advocated the discharge of all employees who refused to answer questions concerning their Communist affiliations before congressional committees.

Despite these favorable circumstances, the Carey forces were still unable to oust the Communists at the national level. Each year the UEMDA would go to the UE convention with high hopes for victory, and each year its assaults would be beaten back. (The issue was finally resolved, of course, with the formation of the rival International Union of Electrical Workers in 1949). The reason for this failure was simple: unlike the more successful anti-Communists—including Walter Reuther and Joe Curran of the National Maritime Union—Carey never made any attempt to prove that the Communists were working against the economic interests of the rank-and-file.[54] At no time, for example, did the UEMDA seriously raise the issue of the UE's wartime advocacy of piecework and incentive pay, or its blatant attempts to break strikes at the local level. As one observer aptly concluded: "The great battles at the UE Conventions of 1946, 1947, 1948, and 1949 were . . . concentrated on political issues: 'red-baiting,' foreign policy, the Progressive Party, etc . . . On these issues, the opposition documented the pro-Communism of the UE leadership, but the opposition remained somewhat distant from the immediate and day-to-day concerns of the workers . . . In other words, the UE membership was not uninterested in the issue of anti-Communism. But it refused to make anti-Communism, in and of itself, a primary and decisive criterion for determining loyalty." [55]

The Communists had also been very influential in the formation of the United Automobile Workers Union. They were well-organized and popular with the rank and file, especially after their successful direction of the famous sit-down strikes against General Motors in 1936. And they had taken the lead in founding the Unity Caucus (along with Walter Reuther and the Socialists) which unseated the inept and undemocratic administration of UAW President Homer Martin. Ironically, however, in an attempt to preserve their alliance with other "progressive forces" in the UAW, the Communists purposely backed non-Communist candidates for the union's highest offices. As one recent student noted: "This . . . must seem especially bizarre to those brought up on the notion of Communists, by brilliant organizational techniques, gaining influence far out of proportion to their actual membership in an organization. Yet, here the Communists apparently settled for far less influence than they were entitled to by virtue of their numbers . . ." [56]

As expected, the signing of the Hitler-Stalin pact completely fragmented the Unity Caucus. During this period, the Communists bitterly condemned President Roosevelt's defense mobilization program and began a series of unauthorized walkouts at Allis-Chalmers and North American Aviation. In both of these instances, the UAW's national office worked openly to break the strikes. And, at the union's 1941 national convention, violent debates ensued over how to best punish the local Communist leaders involved. According to most observers, if the convention had been held a few months earlier (before Hitler invaded the Soviet Union in June, 1941, and before the Communists reversed themselves in favor of total wartime cooperation between labor and management) the Communists might well have been purged from the union. As it was, the Reuther forces still managed to put over a resolution barring from union office anyone "who is a member of, or subservient to, any political organization, which owes its allegiance to any foreign government other than the United States . . . directly or indirectly." [57] Quite clearly, the Hitler-Stalin pact had isolated the Communists on a peripheral political issue—an issue which put them "considerably at variance with the rank-and-file sentiment, the first time that had been true since the founding of the union." [58]

THE SPECTER

What kept the Communists from total extinction was the simple fact that the anti-Reuther forces, led by R. J. Thomas and George Addes, needed all the votes they could muster to keep Reuther from gaining the union's presidency. Reuther was very popular because of his ability to articulate rank-and-file demands as well as his ability to fight for them. But for years he had been denied the UAW's top post by a coalition of forces, led by Communists, non-Communist radicals and unaligned union officials who were put off by his driving ambition. Unfortunately for Thomas and Addes, their own desire to protect the various elements within this coalition made them the perfect targets for Reuther's red-baiting attacks. And it was on the strength of these attacks that Reuther finally achieved his elusive goal.

With the onset of the Cold War, Reuther began a campaign to rout the opposition by concentrating on "Stalinist influences" within the union. Undaunted by the fact that the Communists were clearly a minor faction within the majority coalition, he claimed that Addes and his supporters had fellow-traveled with the Reds during the war (over the issues of the no-strike pledge, incentive pay and piecework) and would continue to do so in the future. By allowing this left-wing activity to go unchecked, Reuther contended, Addes and Thomas were playing into the hands of right-wing reactionaries who were out to destroy the union.

In his attempt to unseat the Addes-Thomas Administration, Reuther, like James Carey of the UE, had the valuable support of the Association of Catholic Trade Unionists. During the years 1945–1947, the official UAW publication, *The United Automobile Worker,* was controlled by Addes, so Reuther used the ACTU's Detroit organ, *The Wage Earner,* to publicize his own version of the controversy. And not surprisingly, *The Wage Earner* claimed that both Addes and Thomas were fellow travelers.

Labor's cold war

Communists and Communist followers began to appear in key staff positions (after their administration took office). The UAW's education department became infiltrated. Soon Thomas himself began to talk the language of the Party line. The same man who, four years ago, angrily rejected Communist support at the Buffalo convention, now claims he couldn't help it if the Commies like him . . . Thus gradually R. J. Thomas was knitted into the so-called 'left-wing' of which Addes has been the leader.[59]

It should also be mentioned, however, that even Reuther was occasionally embarrassed by the ACTU's fanatical anti-communism. When, for example, Michigan Governor Kim Sigler told the House Committee on Un-American Activities in 1947 that Thomas, Addes, and UAW Vice-President Richard Leonard were "Communist captives," *The Wage Earner* complimented him for ". . . performing a service to the people of Michigan in exposing a lot of Communist monkey business." [60] Reuther, on the other hand, claimed that the governor's testimony was a conservative attack "upon the entire UAW and the American labor movement." [61] Unlike Carey, who thrived on government support in his attempt to unseat the Matles-Emspak faction, Reuther believed that government intervention in union affairs was both unnecessary and unwise.

Still, despite Reuther's strong denunciations, attacks upon the UAW by outsiders like Governor Sigler greatly benefited his forces by "proving" their contention that Communists and fellow-travelers had to be purged if the union were to survive. In 1946 and 1947, Reuther was afforded several opportunities to reiterate this point. The first such opportunity occurred when UAW Local 248 (which was one of the largest Communist-dominated locals) again went on strike against Allis-Chalmers. Both sides in the dispute were looking for a showdown. Prior

THE SPECTER

to the strike, the company had made clear its refusal to bargain in good faith with "Communists" by unilaterally restricting the privileges of union stewards to investigate grievances on company time, and by refusing to consider a maintenance of membership clause which had been inserted into the previous contract by the War Labor Board in 1943. There was some feeling, however, that the walkout was called by the local leaders to overwhelm, with a strong show of solidarity, an increasing number of right-wing insurgents within the union. On April 29,1946, the local voted to strike by 8,091 to 251.[62]

The strike proved disastrous for the local. The constant beating of pickets by company goons and local police, coupled with the local's poor handling of organizational matters, forced the strikers back to work without a contract. Reuther seized upon this defeat as a perfect example of how Communist influence worked against the interests of the UAW members. According to his own account of the strike:

> *Our failure at Allis-Chalmers was the result of the open interference on the part of the Communist Party in the affairs of the local union involved. This Communist Party interference served to destroy the confidence and loyalty of the workers in the local strike leadership. It gave the vicious management of this company an all too effective weapon to exploit in breaking the strike. Such incidents as the circulation on the picket line of Communist Party petitions on behalf of the party's gubernatorial candidate afforded the company a perfect basis for its propaganda campaign against the union.*[63]

Although Addes replied to Reuther's charge with a countercharge that the strike failed because "some union members [the Reuther group] started red-baiting other union members and it was not long before the employers and a hostile press took up

Labor's cold war

the same story," the defeat of Local 248 by Allis-Chalmers proved very damaging to national UAW leaders like Addes who had wholeheartedly supported the local's efforts.

In 1947, the Reuther forces won another major victory over the issue of Taft-Hartley. The Addes faction, which by now was clearly on the defensive, backed a resolution opposing compliance with the law. Noting that officials of the United Electrical Workers and the United Steel Workers were both refusing to sign the non-Communist affidavits, they warned that the UAW's compliance would put a "stamp of approval" upon the entire act—an act that most CIO leaders referred to as a "slave labor" measure. In rebuttal, the Reuther forces based their arguments on more pragmatic grounds: if UAW officials refused to sign the affidavits, the union would lose the right to petition the NLRB for its services in cases where union raiding was at issue, or where local elections were in dispute. UAW leaders, therefore, should comply with the law under protest and fight the battle in the courts. The delegates voted overwhelmingly to sign the affidavits—a clear signal that Reuther now held the power to purge his opponents.[64]

Having now complied with section 9(h) of the Taft-Hartley Act, the UAW began at once to reap its benefits. Under the Remington-Rand decision of 1947, the NLRB had ruled that any contract signed by an employer with a union advocating noncompliance could be upset if another qualified union sought an election to determine bargaining rights in a particular plant. Using this decision to its own advantage, the UAW started raiding the membership of the Communist-dominated Farm Equipment Workers Union at the Caterpillar Tractor Plant in Peoria, Illinois. In this particular case, the company had refused to bargain with the union until its officials signed non-Communist affidavits, and the union had responded with a strike to force the company's hand. Almost immediately, the UAW and the AFL's International Association of Machinists rushed hundreds of or-

ganizers to the Caterpillar plant to prepare for the new representation election. Since the FE could not get its name on the
ballot, the UAW picked up 14,000 new members. In the end,
the FE was forced to comply with section 9(h) in order to
avoid total extinction.[65]

In analyzing Reuther's final victory (which came about, technically, at the UAW's 1948 national convention), most historians have concluded that the Communists did themselves in by
consistently working against the economic interests of the rank-
and-file. All Reuther did was to hammer away at this obvious
point.[66] While it is quite true that, unlike Carey, Reuther generally avoided peripheral political issues like the Marshall Plan
and concentrated on vital economic matters, the fact remains
that his major opponents in the UAW were neither Communists
nor fellow travelers. And their economic policies, while sometimes sympathetic to the Communist line, were hardly governed
by it. Indeed, a recent analysis of the factional dispute in the
UAW has shown that Addes's position on crucial economic
matters did not differ significantly from Reuther's position.[67]
More to the point, both sides in the battle used the Communists: the Addes faction used them to help keep Reuther from
gaining the union's presidency, and the Reuther faction used
them in an attempt to show the membership that Addes and
Thomas were obviously following the Communist line. Ironically, the Communists themselves were never a really significant
force in the union after 1939; they were simply pawns in a battle between two warring factions. Reuther's victory was due to
the fact that the Cold War made the Communists dangerous
allies, but perfect scapegoats.

V

On the national level, while the pro-Communist faction was
badly shaken by the strong support given to the Administration's foreign and domestic policies in 1947, its final defeat

came the next year with Truman's stunning re-election. From the very outset, the CIO made it clear that it expected every affiliate to work within the Democratic party, and that support for Henry Wallace would be interpreted as a deliberate attempt "to create confusion and division within the labor movement." Some pro-Communists, like Mike Quill, took the warning to heart. "If being for Wallace will split the CIO, the price is too great," he claimed. "I'm a trade unionist first." A few days after his statement, "Red Mike" broke openly with the third party and began criticizing "the crackpots of the Communist Party." Other left-wingers, however, including Matles, Emspak, Gold and Bridges, were not so easily intimidated. They argued that according to the CIO constitution, the national office had no right to interfere in the political activities of the various affiliates. And Bridges declared that he would vote for Truman only if the CIO conducted a referendum to determine whether a majority of the rank-and-file actually supported him over Wallace.[68]

The CIO responded with a campaign to deprive Wallace of mass labor support by portraying him as a fellow traveler and by harassing his followers. In March, 1948, Murray ousted Harry Bridges from his post as CIO Regional Director for Northern California; two months later, he openly advocated the ouster of any regional council that either condemned the Marshall Plan or supported the third party effort. CIO-PAC, which spent slightly over $1,000,000 in "voluntary contributions" to put Truman and other Democratic candidates over the top, cooperated with the ADA in distributing Quill's denunciations of the Communist party, and printed thousands of copies of a "Speaker's Book of Facts," in which the question "Is Henry Wallace being supported by Communists? was to be answered with the statement: "Yes. The Communist Party National Chairman William Z. Foster, who is under indictment for conspiracy, announced on August 3, 1948, that the Party will endorse and will support Wallace." [69] And national CIO leaders took every opportunity to denounce Wallace as an unwitting dupe of the Communists. In an address to National Press Club Luncheon in Washington, Walter Reuther stated: "I think Henry is a lost soul . . . People who are not sympathetic with democracy in America are influencing him. Communists perform the most complete valet service in the world. They write your speeches, they do your thinking for you, they provide you with applause, and they inflate your ego as often as necessary . . . I'm afraid that's the trouble with Henry." [70]

Truman's resounding pluralities in labor areas, coupled with the disappointing Wallace turnout, provided the final impetus for the Communist expulsions. To begin with, the results indicated (at least to the CIO's national leadership) that the vast majority of CIO members identified strongly with the Democratic party, supported Truman's foreign and domestic policies, and rejected the pro-Soviet attitude of the Gold-Bridges-Matles-Emspak faction. This meant, of course, that the left-wingers were guilty of acting against the political interests of their constituents. Moreover, unlike their stand against Roosevelt, the Communists could not claim to be following the wishes of the CIO's president; indeed, their support for the third party was in direct defiance of Murray and national CIO policy. The Communists were trapped; they had gone out on a limb, only to have Harry Truman saw it off.

VI

The actual purges of the left-wing affiliates took place at the 1949 and 1950 national conventions. Here, they were charged with advocating policies which were ". . . consistently directed to the achievements of the purposes . . . of the Communist Party rather than the objectives set forth in the constitution of the CIO." The charges themselves included opposition to the defense program prior to World War II, wartime collaboration with employers, failure to support the Marshall Plan, and opposition to the re-election of Truman in 1948.[71]

The final question, of course, is why the CIO took such drastic action against these unions. Certainly their adherence to the Communist party line was no more blatant than Murray's adherence to the Democratic party line. Their right to express contrary opinions, moreover, was protected by the CIO's doctrine of local autonomy. Yet, the CIO found the process of "expulsion" to be suitable for two reasons. First, quite clearly the emotional anti-Communist climate brought on by the Cold War (and nursed along by Murray, Reuther and Carey) *had* reached a point by 1950 where drastic action was absolutely necessary. As one labor historian recently noted: "Aside from the fact that many CIO leaders were themselves ideologically opposed to Communism, most of them were able to perceive that organizations accused of being either pro-Communist or Communist-dominated would face serious and increasing difficulties in post-war America . . . Given the attitudes which prevailed in this country it would have been extremely difficult for an organization such as the CIO to refuse to take action against known Communists within its ranks." [72] Furthermore, most CIO leaders, having rejected a third party in favor of a labor-liberal alliance channeled through the Democratic party, were forced to move to the right by the vehement anti-Communism of President Truman and his non-labor supporters. The *CIO News* actually put it best by stating that, like the ADA, its new Cold War position would still be ". . . left of center, but not to the extreme left . . . And that's a good place for a labor organization to be." [73]

Second, given the CIO's new ideological shift, the national office was forced to take action because the anti-Communist factions within the various left-wing affiliates were unable to dislodge the Communists from power. In only three of the sixteen

THE SPECTER

pro-Communist unions were the right-wingers successful in gaining control—an indication, perhaps, that despite their pro-Soviet, anti-Truman position, the Communists were still respected for their ability to run effective trade unions. Indeed, several researchers who analyzed these factional battles have concluded that the anti-Communists made little headway because they concentrated on peripheral issues, and failed to demonstrate that the left-wingers had willingly acted against the interests of the rank-and-file.[74] Not surprisingly, then, despite Murray's statement that the expulsions were necessary ". . . to fight Stalin, to fight Moscow, to fight imperialism, to fight aggression here at home," as well as to remove "the dirty, filthy traitors of American trade unionism from the CIO," few serious attempts were made to save the nearly 1,000,000 expelled workers—the vast majority of whom were non-Communist— from these "dirty, filthy traitors." When the smoke had cleared, CIO leaders simply commended themselves on the thoroughness of the operation, and for the irreparable damage done to the cause of domestic Communism. "To put it bluntly. . . ," the *CIO News* boasted, "we have in a year broken the back of the Communist Party in the United States." [75]

With the Communists now gone, the CIO easily replaced the remnants of its Depression ideology with the more respectable rhetoric of Cold War liberalism. Its publications, free at last from the fear of stinging left-wing rebuttals, wrote comfortably about the problems raised by Communist expansion in Europe and Asia, and by leftist influence in the American labor movement. As Paul Jacobs, a willing participant in the purges, later wrote, "an inevitable consequence of the expulsions was to bring all serious political debate inside the CIO to a standstill . . . Unions could now be counted on to give automatic approval to any action undertaken by the government in its struggle against world Communism." [76]

THE POLITICS OF CIVIL LIBERTIES:

The American Civil Liberties Union

During the McCarthy Years

BY MARY S. McAULIFFE

The emergence of the cold war between the United States and the Soviet Union was accompanied by a bitter and contentious debate over domestic Communism and internal security—a debate symbolized for many Americans by Joseph R. McCarthy, the Republican senator from Wisconsin. McCarthy, however, was not the originator of this cold-war crusade. Rather, he was for a brief time the most audacious and most successful practitioner of an American anti-radicalism that had a long tradition stretching back considerably beyond the earlier post-World War I "Red Scare." This tradition, during the years immediately following World War II and before the senator's ascendance to national prominence, had found strengthened expression in the House Committee on Un-American Activities, the Senate Internal Security Subcommittee, and a series of federal and state loyalty oaths and investigations. McCarthy simply exploited an already-existing Communist issue and molded it into a powerful weapon against the left. The senator's crude style and shotgun attacks elicited an emotional vocal reaction from the liberal community. Yet, while liberals raised their voices against the Wisconsin senator and the inquisitorial methods he practiced and symbolized, many also sought to protect themselves by proclaiming their own anti-Communism and by retreating in their defense of the civil liberties that McCarthy and his followers now threatened. Thus they jeopardized the special moral strength of twentieth-century American liberalism, which, stemming from the traditional liberal commitment to the protection of the rights and liberties of the individual, stressed the importance of free thought and equally free expression. Nor, for that matter, was the liberal retreat particularly effective. Indeed, even as liberals zealously proclaimed their own militant anti-Communism, they themselves came under increasingly bitter attack from the far right.

The internal history of the American Civil Liberties Union illustrates the kinds of compromises liberals felt compelled to make in the name of anti-Communism during the McCarthy years. Although the ACLU had made a distinguished contribution to the defense of civil liberties during the quarter of a century since its founding in 1917,[1] it proved to be an uncertain champion of those same liberties during the anxious years that followed the close of World War II. Unsympathetic to Communists and under conservative pressure to prove its anti-Communism, the ACLU wavered in its defense of freedom and contributed instead to the growing national hysteria. As a result, in large part, of the decisions made by its national board of directors, the actual governing and policymaking body of the organization, the ACLU during the McCarthy years sought to reiterate and strengthen its anti-Communist image and, as a consequence, allowed the political issue of Communism to distract it from a single-minded defense of civil liberties.[2]

During the first two decades of its existence, the ACLU had been relatively untroubled by the Communist issue. But in the late thirties, after the Nazi-Soviet pact and following Congressman Martin Dies's attack on the organization as a Communist front, the leaders of the ACLU sought to establish a strongly anti-Communist image that would be free of any taint of suspicion.[3] In early 1940 the board of directors passed a resolution declaring that supporters of totalitarian dictatorships could not serve on the ACLU's governing committees or on its staff. Shortly thereafter, the board requested one of its longtime members, Elizabeth Gurley Flynn, to resign from the board on the grounds that she was a member of the Communist Party and that consequently, as an "apologizer" for totalitarianism, she could not properly participate as an officer in an organization whose sole function was to defend civil liberties. Miss Flynn had only infrequently attended board meetings and posed no personal obstacle to the workings of the ACLU; indeed, the board had earlier reelected her to its membership in full knowledge of her party membership. Those who opposed her continued mem-

The politics of civil liberties

bership on the board, however, did so from a sensitivity to the possible difficulties the ACLU might encounter, both in court and out, unless it was firmly anti-Communist. Those who supported Miss Flynn's request to remain on the board argued that ousting her on sole grounds that she was a Communist Party member sanctioned the criterion of "guilt by association." By a bare majority of ten to nine, the ACLU board of directors finally voted to expel her.[4]

Following World War II, amid the accelerating anxieties of the cold war, the ACLU board of directors sought to further establish its anti-Communist credentials and to insure the anti-Communism of its general membership. In 1949 it adopted a resolution opposing "any form of the police state or the single party state, or any movement in support of them. . . ."[5] In 1951 it incorporated the 1940 resolution into the ACLU's constitution. This action not only legitimized anti-Communist politics but restricted the protests of critics since the constitution could only be amended by a vote of two-thirds or better of the ACLU's membership.[6] In addition, thereafter the ACLU included a statement affirming its opposition to Communism in all the legal briefs it drafted in those cases where Communism was either directly or indirectly an issue.[7]

By late 1952 and early 1953 McCarthy's influence was at its zenith, and many on the ACLU's board of directors believed that it was urgent that the ACLU strengthen its bulwarks even more solidly against attacks from the right.[8] The steps the ACLU had already taken to establish its anti-Communism provided precedent for further action in this direction. Reflecting this concern, and a desire to check "unreasonable" anti-Communism, certain members of the board of directors in late 1952 pressed for a restatement of the ACLU's position on the Communist Party and on related issues such as Fifth Amendment privileges, academic freedom, and employment in the United Nations. In urging the ACLU to reconsider the Communist

THE SPECTER

question, these board members insisted that, in a period of so much political turbulence centering on the Communist issue, the ACLU needed a specific and detailed statement of policy to provide guidelines for its actions.[9] Uppermost in their minds, however, was the necessity for establishing the ACLU's firm anti-Communism and their conviction that Communism did in fact threaten Western security.[10] Led by Norman Thomas, head of the American Socialist Party, by Morris Ernst, one of the ACLU's two general counsels, and by James L. Fly, a former head of the Federal Communications Commission, these board members were determined to place the ACLU on record as implacably anti-Communist.

Others, within the board and especially within the ACLU's affiliates, were equally anxious that the ACLU's traditional interest in the rights of the individual not suffer as a consequence. Osmond K. Fraenkel, an attorney long associated with the ACLU, Arthur Garfield Hays, the ACLU's other general counsel, and Walter Gellhorn, of the Columbia Law School, were leaders of the major opposition group. They did not object to placing the Union on record against Communism, but they feared that the movement behind such a statement might lead to a lessening of the Union's concern for civil liberties. Finally, Corliss Lamont, a professor of philosophy at Columbia University and a long-standing radical, frequently sided with Fraenkel in the controversy but was absolutely opposed to the ACLU taking any position on Communism. The business of a civil liberties union, he insisted, was to protect civil liberties, not to take positions against political views it found unpalatable.[11]

In the spring of 1953 the board of directors, after a series of stormy sessions, appointed a special committee to draft a single resolution for the board's consideration.[12] The special committee finally agreed to recommend a policy statement that largely reflected the thinking of Norman Thomas and Morris Ernst. The first section of the statement asserted that the ACLU "does not hold that all persons who submit to the Communist Party's rigid totalitarian discipline (whether formal members or not), or even all those who are its leaders, are engaged in illegal secret conspiracy or actual subversive acts." The last paragraph of this section, however, listed a set of conditions under which a person's "voluntary choice of association" limited his civil liberties. Thus, by an exceptionally broad definition of the individual's responsibility for his associations, the statement implicitly sanctioned "guilt by association." [13]

Many on the board were not satisfied with the special committee's statement, which came before the board on April 20, 1953. After much discussion, however, the board voted to accept this special committee's entire proposal. Moreover, in contrast to the ACLU's 1940 resolution, which had only barred Communists from leadership positions in the Union and refrained from extending these conditions to the general membership,[14] the board now agreed that membership application forms and promotional material contain the statement that the ACLU welcomed only those "whose devotion to civil liberties is not qualified by adherence to Communist, Fascist, KKK, or other totalitarian doctrine." [15] Technically, this was not a loyalty oath; in fact, however, it moved dangerously close to being one and reflected the belief of some of the board members that Communists could otherwise easily join the ACLU and influence or control its policy.[16]

Fraenkel and others remained unreconciled to portions of the statement, and Lamont opposed the entire proposal. The ACLU's bylaws, however, did provide for a referendum to the corporate membership by petition of ten members of the board of directors, which, in the instance of the Communist statement, was obtained.[17] Enclosed with the referendum were affirmative and negative arguments, written by James L. Fly and Osmond K. Fraenkel respectively, and a statement by Ernest Angell, chairman of the board of directors.[18] Normally, only the affirmative and negative arguments would have accompanied the referendum; Ernest Angell, however, had requested and received permission from the board to include a statement in his capacity as chairman. In his statement Angell pleaded for the corporation's affirmative votes, warning that "if these Statements are rejected, I despair of the Board being able to reach any more generally satisfactory substitute, of comprehensive nature." [19] The board then waited for the corporate membership's response.

The ACLU's corporate membership consisted of the board of directors, which was the actual governing body of the organization, an essentially figurehead national committee, and the boards of the Union's twenty-three local affiliates.[20] Since the board of directors' 1940 resolution on Communism and the expulsion of Elizabeth Gurley Flynn, relations between the national board and some of the ACLU affiliates had not been cordial. The affiliates were on the whole less militantly anti-Communist than the board, and local groups in Boston, New Haven, Philadelphia, northern California, and southern California had criticized the national body for failing to vigorously discharge its obligations in the field of civil liberties. In 1951 the board had responded to this criticism by seeking to curb the power and voice of the affiliates. Backed by Norman Thomas and his supporters, the board added a new provision to the Union's bylaws which stated that the board of directors would follow the dictates of the majority in any national referendum "except where it believes there are vitally important reasons for not doing so—which it shall explain to the corporation members." This new provision did not enhance the board's reputation with the affiliates nor with those, like Lamont, who commented: "What these new provisions meant was that the Board of Directors had constituted itself . . . an inner dictatorship within the ACLU." [21]

The board was nevertheless surprised when the corporate membership voted in October 1953 to reject the Communist policy statement by a vote of 21,271 to 18,995. With the board split on its vote, the affiliates' role in this defeat was decisive. Of the twenty-three affiliates, one abstained and nineteen voted against the board's proposal. Only three voted for the proposal, and these were among the smallest affiliates.[22]

The board of directors, however, in several angry sessions, refused to accept the results of the referendum as final.[23] Lamont won only two votes for his motion that the board accept the majority vote of the corporation "as concluding the matter" and proceed to settle each civil liberties case "as it arises and on its own merits." Fraenkel and Gellhorn moved, also unsuccessfully, that the board apply the substance of the policy statement to its operations until the biennial conference of the corporation, at which point the board would attempt to "reconcile apparent differences of opinion existing between most of the affiliates of the ACLU and the very large preponderance of the members of the Board of Directors and National Committee. . . ." The board decisively defeated this motion, fourteen to seven. Finally, by a vote of fourteen to four (with five abstentions) the board held, in defiance of the referendum, that the substance of the policy statement expressed "in essence the policy of the Union." The board also directed the ACLU executive director to reformulate the form, but not the substance, of the policy statement to take into consideration the changes proposed by various board members and affiliates.[24]

When the ACLU corporation convened three months later, however, the affiliates were determined to complete a reversal of the board's actions. They demanded that the Communist policy statement be withdrawn and rewritten by a special committee representing the board, the national committee, and the affiliates, and that the 1951 provision in the bylaws, which permitted the board to override a national referendum, be eliminated.[25] Despite Norman Thomas's suggestion that the board continue to abide by the Communist policy statement until the special committee had met, the directors responded in part to the corporation's demands and withdrew the statement.[26]

But only a month later, following a televised charge by Senator McCarthy that the ACLU was a Communist front, the board once again became embroiled in debate over its policy toward Communism. Norman Thomas responded to the McCarthy attack by drafting a militant denunciation of Communism, which he urged the board to adopt in spite of its recent pledge to obtain corporate approval before issuing any further policy statements on Communism. Thomas, together with Morris Ernst and James Fly, threatened to resign unless the board passed and released such a statement.[27] Patrick Murphy Malin, the Union's executive director, was reluctant to commit the board to such a position immediately following the confrontation with the ACLU corporate membership, however. In a troubled telephone conversation with John Finerty, one of the board members who opposed the statement, he conjectured that the affiliates would consider it "sharp practice" for the board to make a Communist policy statement before its special redrafting committee reported its new policy statement. Finerty himself objected strongly to Thomas's proposal and wrote Malin: "If there is any further intimation from any group that they will resign if they don't have their way . . . , I shall resign and I shall state publicly that my reason is that McCarthyism in another guise has invaded the Civil Liberties Union." [28]

At the next board meeting, Lewis Galantiere, program director for Radio Free Europe, submitted yet another Communist policy statement, which both Norman Thomas and Ernest Angell had approved. The crux of the Galantiere statement was that the Communist Party in America was a conspiracy rather than a political theory and instrument: "While that movement seeks to give the appearance of being primarily a political instrument of agitation and propaganda," the statement read, "it is actually an international conspiracy to seize power—political, social, economic—wherever it can." Osmond Fraenkel sought to table the motion, but the board adopted it by a vote of eighteen to three. Only Fraenkel, Dorothy Kenyon, and Dorothy Bromley opposed the measure. Others whom Fraenkel counted on "his side" were absent: Arthur Garfield Hays, John Finerty, Walter Gellhorn, Telford Taylor, and Elmer Rice.[29] According to the New York *World-Telegram,* the ACLU's adoption of the "strongest anti-Communist stand in its 35 year history" indicated "a change in its attitude on backing legal appeals of known Reds." [30] And though ACLU director Malin disputed this claim,[31] it seemed clear that the Union was finding it difficult to straddle the conflicting pulls of militant anti-Communism and the defense of civil liberties.

When the special committee representing the board, the national committee, and the affiliates met in July 1954 to redraft the Communist policy statement, however, it soon became evident that in this small group only Norman Thomas favored a militant statement on Communism.[32] Although no one upheld the strict libertarian position advocated earlier by Corliss Lamont, the committee did draft a moderate statement on the Communist Party, which stressed the responsibilities of a civil liberties organization for protecting the freedom of everyone. The report began by expressing its concern over the suppression of basic liberties and safeguards and affirmed that "the abuse by wrongful un-American methods of the rightful national aim to safeguard the security of the country . . . betrays the noblest traditions of our history." The discussion of the Communist Party was brief and stressed the party's dual nature rather than only its conspiratorial aspects. "It [the Communist Party] is both a political agitation movement and a part of the Soviet conspiracy," the statement read. "Insofar as it is the first, its members have all the rights of members of other parties; to the extent that it is the second, its members may in some particulars be restricted by law." [33]

The special committee adopted the entire report unanimously, and the board of directors also unanimously approved it. The board agreed that no further referendum to the ACLU corporation was necessary, as the Biennial Corporate Conference had not provided for one nor had there been requests for one.[34] The long, bitter debate within the ACLU over the Communist issue was finally over, coinciding almost exactly with the Senate's censure of McCarthy and the denouement of the post-World War II "Red Scare." The ACLU's efforts to establish a strong anti-Communist image for itself during the McCarthy years, however, had created a crisis for the Union, both by diverting its time and energy in lengthy intra-organizational debate and by diminishing the strength and consistency of its commitment to civil liberties. Indeed, in a series of controversial, though highly dissimilar, cases, the ACLU seemed to be abandoning its leadership in the struggle for freedom.

The faltering nature of the ACLU's defense of civil liberties was especially revealed by the Union's actions in the case of Corliss Lamont. During the stormy months in the autumn of 1953, while Lamont was fighting the ACLU's proposed anti-Communist policy statement, he also became engaged in a confrontation with Senator McCarthy himself. Lamont's books had been found in United States libraries abroad, along with the works of twenty-two other authors with suspected or acknowledged Communist ties. In late September 1953 McCarthy subpoenaed Lamont to appear before the Senate Committee on Government Operations, then conducting an investigation of the Voice of America. In his appearance before the committee, Lamont did not invoke the Fifth Amendment, "since a contempt case will not hold against an individual who uses the Fifth Amendment correctly." What Lamont sought was a court test "to halt the excesses of Congressional committees," and he saw the way to do so by challenging the McCarthy committee's jurisdiction. Volunteering the information that he was not and never had been a member of the Communist Party and that he was not in any way employed by the United States Government, Lamont cited the First Amendment and denied that the committee had any right to inquire into his personal beliefs and affairs. He refused to answer most of McCarthy's questions and challenged the committee's jurisdiction, arguing that the statutory limitations of the legislation establishing it precluded such an inquest, that the committee was "not a competent tribunal" because of the resignation of all its Democratic Party members, and that any inquiry into personal beliefs and activities lay within the jurisdiction of the judicial, not the legislative, branch.[35]

The board discussed the Lamont case and agreed that the Union could properly enter litigation on behalf of a board member, but it delayed actually making that commitment. One month after the McCarthy committee's hearing a special committee of the board met and decided that the board should make no public statement on the matter until McCarthy's committee or the Senate as a whole cited Lamont for contempt. The only action the ACLU special committee recommended was that the ACLU write a letter, without publicity, to the Committee on Government Operations protesting the specific violations of procedure during the hearing itself. And, when the Union did finally comment on Lamont's hearing, it gave a summation of McCarthy's questions but not the full grounds for Lamont's failure to respond. Lamont's attorney, Philip Wittenberg, immediately wrote the board: "To have this come as the Union's only statement is heartbreaking. Does the Union think that by ostrich-like tactics it can avoid the attacks of McCarthy . . . ?"[36]

The special ACLU committee on the Lamont case met again in December 1953, and this time it turned down Fraenkel's proposal that the ACLU support Lamont.[37] Several days later, however, the ACLU board approved defending Lamont on the grounds that it was improper for the McCarthy committee to question him on his political beliefs and associations simply because he was an author of books used by the government. The board voted to issue a public statement on its position and, "if possible," file a brief supporting Lamont; it also unanimously instructed the office "to use all proper methods to prevent a citation for contempt" against Lamont. At the same time, the board voted to support Harvey O'Connor, an author who had also refused to answer the McCarthy committee's questions on First Amendment grounds. Fraenkel afterward commented that "this is the first clear-cut position taken by the Board in a long time." [38]

The Union's action on the Lamont case was especially revealing because it coincided with a bitter dispute within the organization over Lamont's status as a member of the board of directors. As a result of his vigorous opposition to an anti-Communist policy statement, Lamont had become offensive to a number of board members, who were determined to prevent his renomination to the board, a post he had held for twenty-one years. Norman Thomas, Morris Ernst, James Fly, and Ernest Angell all threatened to resign if Lamont were renominated. Following Lamont's renomination by a special motion on November 2, 1953, one board member, Whitney North Seymour, actually did resign. Another board member, Merlyn Pitzele, declined to stand for reelection because of Lamont's renomination. Finally, at its November 16, 1953, meeting, the board voted to remove Lamont's name from the list of nominees by a vote of thirteen to eight. Fraenkel, who was not present at the meeting, concluded that his removal was "a shabby business which forebodes no good for the independence of the Board from right wing pressure on other issues." [39]

In response, a group from the ACLU chapter in New York City offered to back Lamont for renomination by special petition, a provision in the bylaws. Lamont declined, citing the endless wrangling within the board and his sense of hopelessness in "waging a minority battle here." "I am tired of all this," he told the board. "I believe that I can be more helpful to the cause of civil liberties by giving over my energies directly to the fight against McCarthy and McCarthyism than by endlessly debating my able and eloquent opponents on this Board." [40]

The Union's ambivalence over the Communist issue was also displayed in its response to the case of Owen Lattimore. Lattimore, a leading Western authority on China who had been one of McCarthy's first targets, had been investigated, subsequent to McCarthy's allegations, by a Senate subcommittee chaired by Senator Pat McCarran of Nevada. The Justice Department, at McCarran's insistence but with little substantial evidence, had Lattimore indicted for perjury on grounds that he had lied when he declared under oath that he had never been a sympathizer or promoter of Communism or Communist interests. The ACLU's board of directors cautiously discussed the case for almost two years, debating whether or not to file a brief in Lattimore's behalf and whether or not to issue a public statement. In January 1954 the board finally agreed to answer inquiries with the statement that "Certainly the case involves civil liberties," but that the ACLU would offer no further statements nor take any action until court proceedings clarified the indictment. Finally, in October 1954, Lattimore's attorney, Thurman Arnold, told the ACLU's staff counsel that the Union's approach to the case was "a resumption of the kind of quibbling debate which ignores the fundamental legal and constitutional issues," and asked the Union to stay out of the case. The board agreed not to intervene but, perhaps piqued by Arnold's remarks, finally decided to issue a public statement that important civil liberties issues were involved in the Lattimore case. Osmond Fraenkel expressed his surprise "that there was practically no opposition" from the board members to such a statement. [41]

In the case of Julius and Ethel Rosenberg, convicted of atomic espionage and sentenced to death, the board took a firm position that no civil liberties questions were involved. John

Finerty, who in 1953 became associate defense counsel for the Rosenbergs, strongly disagreed, and over a period of several months Osmond Fraenkel changed his mind and concurred with Finerty. Fraenkel, in studying the record of the Rosenberg trial, concluded that evidence of the Rosenbergs' Communist Party membership was improperly introduced to prejudice the case rather than to establish motive and intent to injure the United States. He also questioned whether the trial was not actually a trial for treason, in view of the several occasions on which the word was used. Since the crime of treason required proof by two witnesses and the crime of atomic espionage only one, Fraenkel believed that this should be a matter of great concern to the ACLU, especially as the conviction carried with it a death sentence. Despite these grave questions concerning the due process of the Rosenberg trial, the ACLU board of directors once again decided, eighteen to four, that the case involved no civil liberties issues and that therefore the Union should not intervene.[42]

In the case of Harry Bridges, the Union procrastinated for four years before publicly acknowledging that a civil liberties issue was involved. Bridges, a naturalized American citizen, had been president of the powerful International Longshoremen's and Warehousemen's Union since its founding in 1937. For years, the administration had been inundated with demands that Bridges be deported on the grounds that he was a Communist. These earlier demands had been investigated and invalidated. In 1949, however, a federal grand jury indicted Bridges for perjury: that at his 1945 citizenship hearing he had falsely denied being or ever having been a Communist. Found guilty in 1950, Bridges appealed the decision. In 1949 the ACLU board had agreed to take no action on the case. In 1950, however, the ACLU's policy committee recommended that the Union enter the case as a friend of the court "on the ground that the continuous hounding of Bridges amounted to a violation of due process of law." The board, however, rejected this recommendation though continuing to appoint special committees to study the case. By late 1952 a special committee reported to the board that since the case was being appealed to the United States Supreme Court, where at that time it was impossible to file a friend-of-the-court brief, the ACLU should take no action in the matter. In the spring of 1953, however, the board finally decided to issue a statement that "the repeated indictment and trial of Bridges on essentially the same charge is a denial of due process." [43]

The ACLU was also reluctant to become involved with the earlier trial and conviction of the eleven Communist Party leaders tried in 1949 under the Smith Act. The Union clearly opposed the Smith Act of 1940—which had made it unlawful to advocate or teach the violent overthrow of the government—primarily on the grounds that it was a dangerous curtailment of freedom of speech and association. For all the certainty of its position, however, the ACLU refused to become involved actively either in the original trial or in the appeals process. It justified this refusal on the ground that to have done so would have involved the ACLU in factual and other non-civil liberties issues. The ACLU did petition the Circuit Court of Appeals to reverse the convictions. [44] It also wrote the Attorney General to oppose the government's request to revoke bail and filed a friend-of-the-court brief before the Supreme Court. In 1951, moreover, after the Supreme Court upheld the convictions, the board approved the Union's future participation in new cases brought under the Smith Act. This activity, however, had been well out of public view, and many interested in the case were not aware that the ACLU had done anything at all. Following the Supreme Court decision upholding the original convictions, Roger Baldwin, in receipt of "queries as to the Union's views, and some disquiet that they have not been given publicity," suggested to one of his correspondents that "some pressure be put on the Board for action." [45]

During the McCarthy years, the ACLU retreated on a number of issues to positions that were more strongly anti-Communist. The Union continued to oppose the exclusion or expulsion of persons from labor unions for political opinions, "even if they are members of the Communist Party." But in late 1950 the board approved a change in policy that recognized the right of unions to disqualify Communists as candidates for union offices.[46] The board also changed its policy on immigration and naturalization, deciding not to challenge the government's refusal of permanent immigrant status or citizenship to Communists.[47] In an even more dramatic reversal of policy, following the outbreak of the Korean War, the ACLU, which had originated as a pacifist organization devoted to defending the rights of conscientious objectors, rescinded its opposition to military conscription.[48]

The ACLU also deemphasized direct involvement in litigation, a characteristic of the organization during the 1920's and 1930's, and focused instead on submitting friend-of-the-court briefs in behalf of defendants. The Union believed that such an approach enabled it to "focus the courts' attention on vital constitutional guarantees rather than to argue the guilt or innocence of a particular individual on a fact basis." Probably more important, however, was the fact that this indirect kind of involvement in the legal processes had the advantage during the McCarthy years of lessening the possibilities for "public confusion over whether defending a person's civil liberties meant identification with his or her political philosophy." [49]

The new cautiousness in the ACLU's activities during the first half of the 1950's may have been partly the by-product of new executive leadership. Roger Baldwin, executive director since the Union's founding, had conducted the ACLU's business with great vigor and had strongly exercised his leadership within the organization. Patrick Murphy Malin, who replaced Baldwin in 1950 following Baldwin's retirement, was a former professor and a different type of individual altogether. Osmond Fraenkel assessed Malin as the better administrator of the two but noted that he lacked Baldwin's personality. Baldwin himself commented to a friend that Malin was "hesitant to act without his Board's approval of every move. . . ." [50]

More important than the change of executive leadership, however, were the pressures that the cold war and the post-World War II "Red Scare" had placed upon American liberalism, to which even the well-established American Civil Liberties Union was susceptible. Under attack from the right, many of the members of the board of directors attempted to establish beyond doubt their organization's anti-Communist credentials and encouraged a policy that limited the extent to which the ACLU defended the rights of American Communists. In effect, the very drive for such a policy and the fear of the anti-Communist right did modify the ACLU's commitment to the civil liberties of those either directly or indirectly connected with Communism. Thus, instead of helping to block and stop McCarthyism, the Union faltered in its defense of civil liberties and contributed, in part, to the national hysteria over Communism.

THE SPECTER

LEGISLATIVE POLITICS AND "McCARTHYISM":

The Internal Security

Act of 1950

BY WILLIAM R. TANNER AND ROBERT GRIFFITH

On September 23, 1950, the United States Congress voted overwhelmingly to override President Harry S. Truman's veto and to pass into law the Internal Security Act of 1950. Sponsored by Senator Patrick A. McCarran (Democrat-Nevada), the new law tightened existing espionage and sabotage laws and extended the statute of limitations. It also authorized the Department of Justice to bar from immigration or to deport "subversive" aliens and to detain indefinitely deportable aliens who could not secure permission to enter another country. The act's two most controversial sections, however, required all Communist organizations and individual members of "communist action" organizations to register with the Attorney General, and authorized, in time of national emergency, the preventive detention of suspected subversives.[1]

The so-called McCarran Act has frequently been associated with Joseph R. McCarthy and with McCarthyism, the political phenomena to which the senator lent his name. Such an association, however, risks confusing cause with effect and thereby blurs an understanding of the nature of America's domestic cold war. McCarthy did not contribute to the passage of the McCarran Act. Indeed, the senator was not even marginally involved in its legislative history. Rather, the McCarran Act was produced by the same forces that allowed McCarthy to become a symbol of an era.

The most deep-seated of these forces was a repressive anti-radical tradition that extended back at least to the Alien and Sedition Acts of the 1790's. Moreover, following the Bolshevik revolution of 1917 and the Red Scare hysteria of post-World War I, radicalism became increasingly identified with Communism and America's anti-radical tradition became increasingly an anti-Communist one. During World War I, and again prior to America's entry into World War II, the government sought, through a variety of techniques, to suppress what federal authorities defined as seditious and subversive behavior.[2]

THE SPECTER

The anti-Communist strain in America's political culture was exacerbated by the cold war—a war which, according to the standards established by American leaders, the United States was losing. The failure of the United States to achieve its post-war goals in Eastern Europe and in China prompted some partisan critics to charge the Democrats with conspiracy and treason. Such charges, encouraged in the first place by the Roosevelt and Truman administrations' broad-gauged definition of America's lofty goals, gained credibility from a series of trials and investigations into espionage and subversion—the *Amerasia* case, the Canadian spy investigations, and the individual trials of Alger Hiss, Judith Coplon, and the Rosenbergs.[3]

The driving force behind what was to become the McCarran Act, however, was bi-factional partisan politics. For years Republican and Democratic conservatives had raised the Red issue in their attacks upon the domestic programs of Franklin D. Roosevelt, seeking to identify the New Deal with Socialism and Communism. In the years following World War II these attacks were renewed against the Truman Administration and expanded to include charges that Democrats were "soft on Communism" abroad and indifferent to the problems of loyalty and security at home. The revival of the House Committee on Un-American Activities in 1945 and midterm election attacks upon "radical" labor leaders and "New Deal radicals" in 1946 were manifestations of this renewal. During the campaign of 1948, Republican partisans harshly condemned the Truman Administration and promised that if elected they would sweep the traitors from office. Thus, Representative Clare E. Hoffman (Republican-Michigan) could declare in August of 1948: "Every informed individual in Washington knows that from the day Mrs. Roosevelt appeared with a group of Communists before the Dies Committee, the New Deal, and more recently, the Truman Administration, has been coddling and encouraging Communists who, in federal positions, thrive on the taxpayer's dollars." One enthusiastic Republican campaigner promised that if Thomas E. Dewey were elected there would be a "mass exodus from Washington" of those whose loyalty and patriotism were in doubt.[4]

Working through HUAC, congressional conservatives pilloried the Democratic administration for its laxness toward Communism. And although most of the committee's attention was directed toward investigation and exposure, a few of its members—particularly Karl E. Mundt (Republican-South Dakota) and Richard M. Nixon (Republican-California)—sought to establish their anti-Communist credentials through the sponsorship of legislation designed to curb the Communist Party of the United States and its "fronts." The Mundt-Nixon bill, first introduced by the South Dakotan in July 1947, was the lineal ancestor to the Internal Security Act of 1950. Reported from the committee in April of 1948, the bill would have required "Communist political organizations" to register the names of their officers and members with the Attorney General. If organization leaders failed to do so, then it became incumbent on individual members to do so. Section Four of the measure also would have made it a crime, punishable by a maximum penalty of $10,000 and ten years, for anyone to participate "in any manner," perform "any act," take part in "any movement," or conspire "to do anything" toward establishing a foreign-controlled dictatorship in the United States.[5]

Opponents of the measure argued that the bill was clearly unconstitutional since the registration requirement—when combined with Section Four—amounted to self-incrimination and hence a violation of the Fifth Amendment. The bill's sweeping language, these critics further contended, threatened First Amendment guarantees of free speech, press and assembly, while the definition of "Communist organizations" was so broad as to bring almost any group supporting policies also advocated by the Communist Party under the law's purview. In spite of such considerations, the bill passed quickly in the House of Representatives, 319–58. The Democratic Party leadership asked for no time during debate to oppose the bill, and only a handful of congressmen spoke out against it: Democrats Adolph Sabath of Illinois, Emanuel Celler of New York, John A. Carroll of Colorado, Chet Holifield of California, Republican Jacob Javits of New York, and American Labor Party members Vito Marcantonio and Harold Isaacson. Only eight Republicans voted against the measure, while 104 Democrats, most of them Southerners, voted for it.[6]

Althougth the Senate Judiciary Committee held hearings on the Mundt-Nixon bill, no action was taken to get it to the Senate floor before Congress adjourned for the fall election campaign. The bill's supporters, nontheless, continued to press their case. Senate Judiciary Committee Chairman Alexander Wiley (Republican-Wisconsin) called for the election of a Republican Congress in order to secure enactment of the Mundt-Nixon bill, and the Republican Platform of 1948 endorsed "new legislation" to expose "the treasonable activities of Communists and defeat their objectives of establishing here a Godless dictatorship controlled from abroad." Republican presidential hopefuls Harold E. Stassen, Thomas E. Dewey, and Senator Robert A. Taft appeared divided on the issue, however. Stassen endorsed the Mundt-Nixon bill because he believed it outlawed the Communist Party. Governor Dewey was somewhat more equivocal. He was against outlawing of the Communist Party, he declared, and was opposed to the registration bill if that was its purpose. He also expressed doubts as to the constitutionality of the measure. Following passage of the bill in May, however, he seemed to endorse the measure, quoting Karl Mundt on the purpose of the legislation and declaring that he, too, favored "keeping the Communist Party everlastingly out in the open so that we can defeat it and all it stands for." Taft's views on the Mundt-Nixon bill were also somewhat ambiguous. On May 8, 1948, he stated that he was opposed to making it "illegal for an American citizen to think Communism or express his opinions, so long as he does not advocate a violent overthrow of the government," and Representative Javits used this statement on May 14 in a speech attacking the Mundt-Nixon bill. It seems clear, however, that Taft himself supported the principle of exposure on which the bill was based. "I don't know what civil rights there are that entitle a man to pretend he is not a Communist, and then spread Communism through labor unions . . . and through the movies and publications." [7]

In 1949, despite Truman's victory, conservatives renewed their demands for a new internal security law. Karl Mundt, now a senator, joined with Homer E. Ferguson (Republican-Michigan and Olin D. Johnston (Democrat-South Carolina) in reintroducing the registration bill, while Richard Nixon offered a companion measure in the House. Senate debate was delayed until the summer of 1950, however, when, following the outset of the Korean War, the Republican Policy Committee placed the Mundt-Nixon bill on its "must list." It was time, declared Senator Mundt, to quit "coddling" Communists at home while American boys were dying in Korea.[8]

II

Although members of the Truman Administration had opposed the Mundt-Nixon bill from the outset, their opposition was conditioned by a politics of anti-Communism to which the Administration, no less than its conservative critics, subscribed. In a speech delivered during the 1946 election campaign, FBI Director J. Edgar Hoover had said that "During the past five years, American Communists have made their deepest inroads upon our national life." He called for a crusade against "Red Fascism" in unions, in schools and colleges, in magazine, newspaper and book publishing, in radio and screen, in fraternal orders—in short, in almost every area of American life. In September 1948 Tom Clark told how, as Attorney General since 1945, he had been fighting Communists and other subversive elements in and out of the government and claimed that President Truman had always said "that even one Communist in the federal government is too many." In May of 1950 Clark's successor, J. Howard McGrath, could warn an audience that "There are today many Communists in America. They are everywhere —in factories, offices, butcher shops, on street corners, in private business—and each carries with him the germs of death for society." At that very moment, he admonished, they were "busy at work—undermining your government, plotting to destroy the liberties of every citizen, and feverishly trying, in whatever they can, to aid the Soviet Union." [9] Such appeals gave the impression that little had been accomplished to curb the Communist "menace" during Truman's tenure in office, contributed to popular anxiety over domestic Communism, and to the growing public conviction that a new law was needed to deal with the threat.

Truman had opposed the registration bill from the beginning and he continued to oppose it throughout its entire legislative history. At one point in 1950 the President promised to "veto any legislation such as the Mundt-Nixon bill which adopted police-state tactics and unduly encroached on individual rights, and would do so regardless of how politically unpopular it was— election year or no election year." Yet here again, members of the Administration sought to justify their opposition on the grounds of expediency rather than principle, often operating from the same assumptions as their critics. Thus in 1948, Attorney General Clark agreed that Communists were dangerous and should be curbed, but opposed the registration proposal because it would be difficult to administer. Similarly Truman, in his 1950 veto message, denounced the McCarran bill because it "would not hurt Communists," but instead "would help them."

Legislative politics and "McCarthyism"

Although the President expressed concern for individual freedom and civil liberties, he was nevertheless convinced that the measure would

> *actually weaken our existing internal security measures and would seriously hamper the Federal Bureau of Investigation and our other security agencies.*
>
> *It would help the Communists in their efforts to create dissension and confusion within our borders.*
>
> *It would help the Communist propagandists throughout the world who are trying to undermine freedom by discrediting as hypocrisy the efforts of the United States on behalf of freedom.*[10]

Administration opposition to the proposed internal security measure was further weakened by the Justice Department, which frequently acted at cross purposes with the White House. Although opposed to the registration proposal, the department had, since 1949, supported a variety of repressive measures, most of which were incorporated into the final version of the McCarran bill.[11] In a sense, then, the divided and defensive stance of the Truman Administration's efforts and its particular strategy of opposition contributed to what White House aides were soon calling McCarran's "chamber of horrors" bill.

III

Liberal opposition to the McCarran bill, like that of the Truman Administration, was relatively defensive, weak, and ineffectual. In 1948 a few liberals, such as former New Dealers Donald R. Richberg and Adolph A. Berle, Jr., had supported the registration proposals on grounds that the Communist Party of the United States was an agent of a foreign power. So, for that matter, did socialist Louis Waldman, counsel for the Amalgamated Clothing Workers, CIO, who in a 1948 appearance before the House Committee on Un-American Activities denounced Communism as "a clear and present danger" to American ideals and institutions.[12] Most liberals opposed the bill, although not primarily on principle. Some argued, as had the Administration, that the registration procedures would be cumbersome and ineffective, that they would drive Communists underground and thus increase the difficulty of surveillance and infiltration by federal authorities. "In my judgment," declared Senator Paul H. Douglas (Democrat-Illinois), "the act will be almost completely ineffective in labeling Communists because of long delays in hearings, appeals, and criminal prosecutions." Douglas, like Senator Herbert H. Lehman (Democrat-New York), believed that the registration provisions would drive "real Communists" underground, make them "martyrs," and brand innocent persons.[13] Others, perhaps a majority, were opposed to the measure primarily because they feared that the bill's sweeping language would encompass not only Communist organizations but also liberal peace groups, labor unions, and civil rights organizations as well. Thus Senator William Langer (Republican-North Dakota) stated that the Mundt-Nixon bill constituted "the greatest threat to American civil liberties since the alien and sedition laws of 1798!" The measure authorized the government "to outlaw associations of citizens whose views and policies" it considered dangerous. "Under these vague powers, trade unions and other organizations which may seek to alter the status quo or oppose this or that government policy, by lawful means, with no evil intent, could be branded as traitorous agents of foreign governments or movements." [14]

Few liberals, however, were willing to defend the civil liberties of Communists *per se*. Indeed, they were often embarrassed by the campaign against the registration bill launched by the left-wing National Committee Against the Mundt-Nixon Bill. "This is a Commy-front outfit . . . ," complained White House aide Stephen J. Spingarn, "though, as usual, *some* good but gullible people are involved. They, of course, will only help pass the bill." Joseph L. Rauh of Americans for Democratic Action warned Harvard law professor Zechariah Chaffee in 1949 not to associate himself with the National Committee. In August 1950 the directors of Freedom House recommended outlawing the Communist Party and all of its "affiliates" in the United States. And, shortly after the passage of the McCarran bill, a handful of liberal senators declared that "under no conditions should loyal and liberal-minded Americans who oppose the act help the Communists or join in organizations with them in their hypocritical attacks against the Mundt-Ferguson-McCarran Act." [15]

IV

During the summer of 1950, following the outbreak of the Korean War, it became apparent that neither the Administration nor its congressional supporters would be able to contain the drive for new legislation. Indeed, in late August, Majority Leader Scott W. Lucas of Illinois, who had earlier labored to prevent consideration of the Mundt-Nixon and other new internal security bills in the Senate, now requested the Justice Department to draft a registration bill which *he* could sponsor.[16] Meanwhile, White House aides, convinced that it would be impossible "to beat something with nothing," advised the President to send a message to Congress on internal security in hopes of preventing more drastic legislation. The result was a message to Congress that called for relatively modest changes in existing laws. Senator Warren G. Magnuson (Democrat-Washington) thereupon introduced a bill (S. 4061) to implement Truman's message. By then, however, it was too late.[17]

On August 17, Senator McCarran reported out of committee an omnibus internal security bill (S. 4037) that incorporated not only the Mundt-Nixon registration proposal but five other

internal security measures as well.[18] A companion measure
(H.R.9490) was reported out of the House Committee on Un-
American Activities by Congressman John S. Wood (Democrat-
Georgia), and on August 29 the House, hastening toward ad-
journment, passed the measure overwhelmingly, 354–20.[19] The
following week it reached the Senate floor.

At this juncture, a handful of Senate liberals led by Paul H.
Douglas and Harley M. Kilgore introduced an emergency detention bill (S.4130) authorizing the President to declare, either
under specific conditions or at his discretion, an "internal security emergency" during which the Attorney General would be
authorized to round up and detain persons who he had "reason
to believe" might engage in sabotage, espionage, or other subversive activities. This new bill, which a White House aide privately labeled "a concentration camp bill," had been first proposed by Senator Magnuson in early July and was co-sponsored
by Senators Kilgore, Douglas, Hubert H. Humphrey (Democrat-
Minnesota), Lehman, Frank P. Graham (Democrat-North
Carolina), Estes Kefauver (Democrat-Tennessee), and William
Benton (Democrat-Connecticut). It had been drafted by Douglas's staff in consultation with the staffs of the other Senate
sponsors and with attorneys from the American Civil Liberties
Union.[20]

White House aide Stephen J. Spingarn was alarmed by the
new bill, which he considered even more drastic and dangerous
than the Mundt-Nixon and McCarran measures. Even some of
the bill's liberal sponsors had strong misgivings. It was, wrote an
aide to Senator Lehman, "a very bad bill," which had "profound
constitutional weaknesses in seeking to set aside the right of
habeas corpus." Nevertheless, Lehman, Humphrey, Douglas,
Kilgore, and other liberal senators urged Truman to support the
measure as "the only possible way of beating the McCarran
bill." The detention measure, Senator Kilgore later wrote,
"seems fundamentally a more practical and sound method of

meeting the substantive problems of espionage and sabotage. . . ." Truman told the senators to go ahead with their strategy, but that he would reserve judgment on the bill until such time as it came to him from Congress.[21]

Rallying behind the preventive detention proposal, the Senate liberals launched a fight in September against the registration bill. Douglas charged that registration would promote a stifling conformity on public issues. The detention bill, by contrast, would focus on potential sabotage and espionage rather than on propaganda and agitation. While not infringing on free speech and association, it would more adequately protect the nation's security. When Senator Ferguson accused Douglas of sponsoring a "concentration camp" bill, the Illinois senator angrily retorted that "Defamation of character is worse than detention. That is something which seems very difficult for certain persons to understand. Defamation is really more injurious than detention." [22]

The detention bill, argued Senator Humphrey, was a "tough bill," much tougher than the McCarran bill, which he scornfully called the "cream-puff special." The detention bill would aid the FBI in rounding up dangerous Communists and in immediately putting them away in camps for the protection of the nation. "By the way," he added, "we do not have any foolish restrictions in our bill providing that it must be proved that a Communist organization is foreign-controlled." Although the new proposal was drastic, it was necessary, the Minnesota senator concluded, because "we are not living in a peaceful world, and . . . when there is a real menace to our internal security we must be able to act with speed and certainty." [23] McCarran, Ferguson, and other conservatives defended the registration bill and attacked the detention plan as a dangerously unconstitutional measure, which was "obnoxious to the organic law of this country." It was, declared McCarran, "a workable blueprint for the establishment of the dictatorship of the proletariat in the United States." [24]

In a series of complicated parliamentary maneuvers, Majority Leader Lucas, now under pressure over the Communist issue in his Illinois reelection campaign,[25] attempted to amend the McCarran bill. Without consulting the liberal sponsors of the Kilgore bill, he first tried to amend the omnibus bill by replacing the registration section with the emergency detention proposal, and then by *adding* the detention proposal to the entire bill. Both amendments were defeated. Then, as originally planned by the sponsors, Kilgore attempted, also unsuccessfully, to substitute his bill (which included the detention provisions and S. 4061, the Magnuson bill) for the pending measure. Finally, Senator Millard E. Tydings (Democrat-Maryland), also locked in a bitter reelection struggle in Maryland, moved that the vote on the second Lucas amendment be reconsidered. The nation needed a bill with "teeth" in it, he asserted. McCarran, Mundt, and Congressman Nixon, after huddling with Lucas and Senator Spessard Holland (Democrat-Florida), now switched their positions and agreed to accept a modified version of the Lucas amendment. Adopted by voice vote, the detention proposal was thus added to the McCarran bill. The entire bill was then rushed to a final vote. Only seven senators voted against it, and many liberals, including Kilgore, Douglas, Humphrey, Benton, Magnuson, Clinton Anderson (Democrat-New Mexico), and Wayne Morse (Republican-Oregon), voted in favor of passage.[26]

In private, many senators expressed misgivings about the bill. "I was amazed," confided one reporter, "in talking privately to a number of conservative senators—both Republicans and Democrats—that they voted with tongue in cheek for it and with a lot of reluctance." Another newsman reported that a group of Democratic senators who were up for reelection in November "had a meeting and agreed that it was a bad measure and should not be supported," but that "those who faced the electorate *this* year would be taking too great a risk if they voted right because of the popular lack of understanding and hysteria over the issue." "I must say," wrote William Benton, "that my vote for the McCarran bill troubled me more than any vote I made during my entire period in the Senate." Hubert Humphrey later wrote to Estes Kefauver that he was "very proud" of the Tennessee senator's vote against the McCarran bill. "I wish I could say the same for myself." [27]

Most senators, however, continued to defend their position as militant anti-Communists. The McCarran Act, wrote Democrat Tom Connally of Texas, would go "a long way toward protecting the nation and its citizens against internal influences threatening the very foundations of our system of government and our way of life." The Communist issue, agreed William Benton, was "much more serious . . . than the public understands. This is no mere question of civil rights. I learned in the State Department that measures are required to control the Communist danger, and some of these measures, including those requested by the President, are incorporated in the McCarran Act." Even Estes Kefauver, one of the bill's few opponents, found it expedient to emphasize his support for the detention bill. "The senator," wrote an aide, "sponsored an amendment to the McCarran bill which would place all known Communists in concentration camps but it was defeated [sic] in the Senate." [28]

V

The Democratic congressional leaders (Lucas, Vice President Alben Barkley, Speaker Sam Rayburn, and House Majority Leader John McCormack), all of whom had joined in the final stampede in favor of the McCarran bill, now unanimously urged Truman to sign the measure. On the other hand, a group of liberal senators, including some like Humphrey and Kilgore who had voted for the bill, now called on the President to exercise his veto. Truman needed little encouragement. He had already decided to veto the bill, although he did promise congressional leaders that he would send over his message promptly, thus foreclosing the possibility of a pocket veto.[29]

The President's message was a lengthy condemnation of the entire McCarran bill. His most severe criticism, however, was directed at the registration provisions, which he charged would cause "no serious damage to the Communists, much damage to the rest of us." Instead of striking at Communists, he concluded, the bill would "interfere with our liberties and help the Communists against whom the bill was aimed." His comments on the detention plan were briefer and more gentle. Conceding that legislation along these lines might be desirable, the President nevertheless concluded that this specific proposal would "very probably prove ineffective" and, further, "would raise serious constitutional questions." [30]

The House voted to override Truman's veto within an hour. The cry "Vote! Vote!" resounded across the chamber and Speaker Sam Rayburn had to insist that the veto message be read before the roll was called. Only 48 members voted to sustain the President's veto, while 248 voted to override. In the Senate, Kilgore, Douglas, Humphrey, Lehman, Kefauver, and Langer led a thirty-hour filibuster to delay the vote in the hope that public pressure might be brought to bear on individual senators. Langer, a Republican from North Dakota, was the only senator to denounce with equal fervor *both* the registration and detention proposals. The bill, he declared, was "the most vicious, most dangerous piece of legislation against the people that has ever been passed by any Senate." Langer held the floor for more than five hours until he finally collapsed from exhaustion and was carried from the chamber. Douglas and Humphrey continued the delaying tactics for several more hours, but, fearing an "adverse reaction," finally allowed a vote to be taken. The Senate promptly voted to override the veto, 57–10. Only a

Legislative politics and "McCarthyism"

small handful of liberals voted to sustain. Every Republican voted to override as did a majority of the Democrats including the entire congressional leadership. The fact that twenty-nine senators, many of them Republicans, were absent was significant, considering the publicity and importance given to the measure. Republican Robert A. Taft, campaigning in Ohio, added more drama by flying back to Washington to cast his vote to override, and then immediately flew back to his home state. The Internal Security Act of 1950 was now law.[31]

VI

The drive for a new law had been led by Republican partisans such as Mundt, Ferguson, and Nixon, joined by conservative Democrats such as McCarran and Olin Johnston. They sought to play upon anxieties aroused by the cold war and upon what they charged was the inability to deal with Communism at home and abroad. The Truman Administration, divided and defensive, was unable to rally strong opposition to the proposed legislation, especially after the outbreak of the Korean conflict. In part this stemmed from the fact that members of the Truman Administration, such as J. Edgar Hoover, Tom Clark, and J. Howard McGrath, no less than its conservative critics, stressed the seriousness of the "Red menace." For if domestic Communism *was* a grave threat to the nation, was not the McCarran Act, with its provisions for registration and detention, a more logical response than the more moderate proposals sponsored by the Administration? The main thrust of the Administration's opposition, moreover, was limited primarily to practical considerations—the McCarran bill was bad primarily because it would be ineffective and difficult to administer. Democratic congressional leaders, who had labored somewhat reluctantly to prevent consideration of the bill, gave up the fight during the summer of 1950 and joined those urging the need for a new law. And, Democratic liberals, transfixed by the politics of anti-

Communism, sought to outbid the Republican right in the sponsorship of repressive legislation.

This configuration of political forces that produced the McCarran Act was the same as that which sustained the career of Senator Joe McCarthy. To call this "McCarthyism," however, risks inverting a causal relationship and seriously distorting the history of the early fifties. That era did not belong to McCarthy, but he to it. Both the senator and the McCarran Act were products of the politics of anti-Communism, which characterized the American polity in the mid-twentieth century.

ELECTORAL POLITICS AND McCARTHYISM:

The 1950

Campaign

BY
RICHARD M.
FRIED

The first half of 1950 marked Joseph R. McCarthy's emergence as the country's foremost spokesman for militant anti-Communism; no less important were the closing months of the year, for they witnessed the Wisconsin senator's first conspicuous participation in partisan warfare. Observers were quick—too quick—to attribute the tone and the results of the 1950 elections to McCarthy's personal influence and to generate inflated perceptions of his political power. "Above all," wrote one political scientist, "the 1950 election was a springboard" for McCarthy. "In every contest where it was a major factor," Marquis Childs asserted, "McCarthyism won." Drew Pearson declared that "the main issue contributing to Truman's setback was the attack led by Senator McCarthy on the State Department and its China policy." [1]

After 1950, McCarthy and his conservative supporters assiduously cultivated his image as a political spoiler. On one occasion, when Democratic colleagues were belaboring him, McCarthy warned that Senator Scott M. Lucas of Illinois, who had once crossed him, "is no longer a member of the Senate," and Millard Tydings of Maryland, who had done likewise, "is no longer with us." [2] In February 1951 when Senator Harley Kilgore demanded substantiation for McCarthy's year-old charges, William Langer told him to seek it in the recent election results. Herman Welker of Idaho remarked that but for McCarthy some seven senators, himself included, would not be holding forth in the upper house; Owen Brewster of Maine interpreted the 1950 election as a "triumph" for McCarthy's charges of Communist infiltration of the State Department.[3]

All of these appraisals overrated McCarthy's potency and inventiveness as a political agitator. They may even, although the evidence is less clear, have exaggerated the force of the Communist issue itself. The politics of anti-Communism was nothing new to America in 1950, and Joe McCarthy's anti-Red

THE SPECTER

posturings were hardly original contributions to the nation's politics.

Anti-Communist appeals had long been part of American political rhetoric, although it was the New Deal that established them permanently in the arsenal of partisan combat. In 1936, for example, Alf Landon's running mate, Colonel Frank Knox, had accused Franklin D. Roosevelt of "leading us toward Moscow." In 1944 Governor John W. Bricker, the GOP vice presidential nominee, claimed that Earl Browder, leader of America's Communists, had been released from jail to line up Communist support for the Democratic Party, which had become "the Hillman-Browder communistic party with Franklin Roosevelt as the front." Governor Thomas E. Dewey, the Republican presidential candidate, asserted that FDR's reelection was "essential" to the Communist cause. "In Russia," he explained, "a Communist is a man who supports his government. In America a Communist is a man who supports the fourth term so our form of government may more easily be changed." During the 1946 campaign, too, Republicans made allegations of Communist infiltration in government. Congressman B. Carroll Reece declared the election a "fight basically between communism and republicanism" and charged that "a group of alien-minded radicals" had seized control of the Democratic Party. Representative Joe Martin called for a Republican Congress to end "the boring from within by subversionists high up in government." [4]

Even supposedly liberal Republicans took up the anti-Communist theme. In his 1948 campaign for the presidential nomination, Harold E. Stassen adopted a hard line, urging that Congress outlaw the Communist Party. In a national radio debate with Stassen four days before the Oregon primary, Governor Dewey questioned whether Americans, "to defeat a totalitarian system which we detest," should "adopt the methods of that system." Instead, he urged that Communism be fought by "keeping the Communist Party everlastingly out in the open so we can defeat it and all it stands for." [5]

Pursuing the "high road" and "unity" following his nomination, Dewey made only passing reference to the Communist issue during the autumn. "There will not be any Communists in the Government after January 20," he promised; unlike the Democrats, his party did not "regard Communist activity as a 'red herring.' " Other Republicans broached the subject with more gusto. Earl Warren, Dewey's running mate, accused the Administration of having "coddled" and "courted" the Communists. "While we spend billions to halt the spread of the Communist conspiracy abroad," the California governor lamented, "we find this same conspiracy reaching its stealthy fingers to grab the framework of our own free institutions and tear them down." Congressman Hugh Scott, chairman of the Republican National Committee, pledged the Dewey Administration to "the greatest housecleaning . . . since St. Patrick cleaned the snakes out of Ireland." [6]

After the bitter and unexpected defeat of 1948, Republican partisans balked at Dewey's moderation and turned to the Communist issue as an inviting expedient for recouping their party's losses. In 1949, even Dewey's Secretary-of-State-presumptive, John Foster Dulles, raised the topic in his Senate race against Herbert H. Lehman. "I know he is no Communist," said Dulles, "but I know also that the Communists are in his corner and that he and not I will get the 500,000 Communist [*i.e.,* American Labor Party] votes that last year went to Henry Wallace in this state." Dewey himself charged that "the only people" who did not want Dulles to win were "the Communists and their supporters." In 1950 House and Senate Republicans and the Republican National Committee, in a "Statement of Principles" framed for the fall campaign, showed a determination to exploit the loyalty issue. They deplored the Democrats' "soft attitude" toward the Communist threat, the employment of Communists and fellow travelers in high federal posts, and the furnishing of "information vital to our security" to "alien agents and persons of questionable loyalty." [7] By 1950, then, Red-baiting had achieved considerable respectability in GOP councils.

But the Republicans had no monopoly on anti-Communism. Such conservative Democrats as Martin Dies, John Rankin, and Eugene Cox had long pummeled the Roosevelt and Truman administrations for alleged Communist proclivities. Indeed, the Truman Administration itself had used anti-Communist appeals to mobilize support for its foreign policies and to combat critics on both the left and the right.[8] During the 1948 campaign, Truman yoked Communists, Progressives, and Republicans in an unlikely troika of adversaries. The Communists, he exclaimed, actually "want a Republican victory" because they knew that result would weaken American resistance to Communism through "another Hoover depression that will undermine the Marshall Plan"; hence, they supported "that Third Party" (which Truman had earlier characterized as "Henry Wallace and his Communists"). He discounted Republican charges of Communism as ungrounded in fact and motivated by callow partisanship—as when he termed the first charges against Alger Hiss a "red herring" in 1948 and when he flippantly dismissed McCarthy as "the greatest asset that the Kremlin has" in 1950.[9] Thus, before McCarthy deplaned in Wheeling to launch the era that bears his name, anti-Communism had already become a staple of partisan politics.

In 1950 the Communist issue first emerged during the spring and summer in the electioneering of conservative Democrats. In Florida, for example, Congressman George Smathers made the question a central part of his campaign against Senator Claude Pepper. Since the later stages of the New Deal, Pepper had been a bellwether of liberalism; in 1944 he had spearheaded the losing effort to keep Henry Wallace on the national ticket. After World War II, Pepper had opposed Truman's policies toward the Soviet Union, which he considered unduly harsh. As the cold war deepened, Pepper retreated somewhat from this position, yet in 1948 he made a quixotic attempt to deny Truman the party's presidential nomination.[10]

Once a Pepper protégé, Smathers in 1950 sought to identify the senator as an extreme leftist, tying him to the Fair Deal and to causes smacking of "socialism." He reminded Floridians of Pepper's previous soft line toward the Soviet Union. "He likes Joe," said Smathers in reference to his foe's 1945 interview with Stalin, "and Joe likes him." To make his case against Florida's "Red Pepper," Smathers attempted each day to name one more Communist front organization with which the senator had been associated. He labeled his adversary "an apologist for Stalin" and an "associate of fellow travelers" and promised to rescue the Sunshine State from "the spiraling spider web of the Red network." Some of Smathers' backers published a pamphlet entitled "The Red Record of Senator Claude Pepper," which itemized these and other charges and pictured the senator in the company of Paul Robeson, the black supporter of pro-Communist causes.[11]

Smathers also emphasized the race issue, on which Pepper, for a Southerner, held unusually temperate views. The challenger persistently linked his foe with proposals to create a Fair Employment Practices Committee; he also attacked the efforts of organized labor to register Florida blacks to vote. Even obscurantist vocabulary reportedly served Smathers when he addressed rural audiences: he allegedly expressed shock that Pepper's sister had gone off to the city to become a "thespian" and asked his listeners if they knew that Pepper had practiced "celibacy" before his marriage.[12]

THE SPECTER

Smathers' aggressive campaign put Pepper on the defensive. "If they can't make a black out of me," the senator noted woefully, "they want to make me a Red." He reiterated his opposition to FECP and his devotion to traditional Southern approaches to race relations. He tried to burlesque the matter of his earlier foreign-policy views; turning up his coat collar, Pepper would sidle across the stage and whisper: "Joe? This is Claude. Got some secrets for ya." [13]

Pepper's exertions were to no avail; on May 2 Smathers handily defeated him. The results demonstrated general opposition to the Truman Administration and a strong conservative tide, but the race issue was especially damaging. Because of it, Pepper lost many white votes, which the turnout in black precincts did not offset.[14] The impact of the "Red" issue is harder to determine. One scholar has placed Pepper among "the early victims of . . . McCarthyism," and Pepper himself likened Smathers's tactics to those of "that poison-purveying, headline-hunting Republican senator from Wisconsin." [15] But McCarthyism played a secondary role in Florida. The race issue upstaged it frequently, and Smathers's other conservative admonitions against "socialism" and the Fair Deal tended to obscure it at times. Pepper himself concluded that "what they really beat us on was the race issue," which was "the one weapon they had for taking away the little fellow from us." Smathers cut heavily into the lower-class support on which Pepper had relied in the past, particularly in northern Florida, the section most receptive to Pepper's stand on economic questions but also the most susceptible to racist fears. Smathers's more conservative economic views also won the allegiance of upper-income voters.[16] Many of Florida's growing colony of Republicans crossed over to vote for Smathers in the Democratic primary.[17] Then, too, Pepper's position on national health insurance earned the bitter and potent opposition of Florida's doctors.[18] Yet, though Pepper's loss

Electoral politics and McCarthyism

resulted from plural causes, and McCarthyism was not the chief of them, some observers erroneously exaggerated the impact of Smathers's Red-baiting.[19]

Pepper's defeat produced a resonance in North Carolina, where a comparable primary contest pitted Frank P. Graham, appointed to the Senate in 1949, against Willis Smith. A former president of the University of North Carolina, Graham epitomized Southern liberalism. His foe, a prominent corporation lawyer, depicted himself as the more conservative candidate and declared his opposition to FEPC, "socialized medicine," the Brannan Plan, deficit spending, Communism, and "all the ideologies foreign to the American form of government." Like Pepper, Graham had to respond somewhat defensively by avowing that he, too, opposed such noxious programs.[20]

Smith hit particularly hard at Graham's racial views, charging that while in 1950 Graham claimed that he did not favor an FEPC, three years earlier, as a member of the President's Committee on Civil Rights, he had advocated such a proposal. (Actually, Graham had inserted in the committee's report a dissent against a compulsory FEPC.)[21] Smith backers also publicized Graham's selection of a black as second alternate for an appointment to the U.S. Military Academy and distributed handbills bearing the young man's picture. Spurious throwaways signed by "Walter Wite" of the "National Society for the Advancement of Colored People" which urged votes for Graham were circulated by the senator's opponents.[22]

Notwithstanding the virulence of these racist appeals, the Smith campaign concentrated on Graham's so-called radicalism, socialism and Communist links. Smith called Graham a "left wing senator" who preferred the socialistic policies of Norman Thomas. Smith's allies ran advertisements making much of Graham's associations with alleged Communist-front groups, notably the Southern Conference on Human Welfare. (The latter, it was recalled, had sponsored unsegregated public meetings for Henry Wallace.) "We don't accuse Dr. Graham of being a Communist," stated one advertisement, which then went on to charge that Graham had belonged to eighteen groups cited as fronts by the House Un-American Activities Committee.[23]

Graham's supporters sought chiefly to capitalize upon the wide personal following he had gathered as a university president. His most loyal admirers, viewing him as a "homespun saint," were shocked by the assault against a man who once, it was noted, as the coach of a baseball team, had instructed his boys not to bunt against an opposing pitcher who had an injured leg. The Raleigh *News and Observer* exclaimed that Smith's ferocious campaign had "out-McCarthied McCarthy." Startled by the Red-baiting, Graham could only comment that surely a man who had been reviled by Andrei Gromyko and the Communist press for his work as a United Nations mediator was no pro-Communist. One of his supporters remarked: "If Stalin or Molotov could cast a ballot on May 27, it would be cast for some other candidate, not for Frank Graham." [24]

Despite the Red-baiting, on May 27 North Carolina gave Graham a 53,000-vote plurality over Smith. Graham's impressive vote total fell short of an absolute majority, however, entitling Smith to ask for a runoff election. (Two minor candidates received 64,000 votes.) Now Graham was at the mercy of events, and they were not kind to him. Smith's June 7 demand for a runoff came two days after the Supreme Court, in the *McLaurin* and *Sweatt* cases, jolted segregated education in the South; a sharp Senate debate over FEPC served as a further irritant.[25] In the second primary, the Smith forces continued to attack Graham's leftist associations, but they then focused increased attention on the race question. While expressing the pious hope that race would not become an issue, Smith warned of "bloc voting" by blacks on his opponent's behalf. An anonymously published handbill asked Tarheel workingmen: "Did You Know Over 28 Percent of the Population of North Carolina

Electoral politics and McCarthyism

Is Colored?" Luridly it described what FEPC might do to white jobholders. More circulars portraying the black alternate to West Point appeared. Another broadside titled "White People Wake Up" asserted that "Frank Graham favors mingling of the races." [26]

The racial "blitz" took its toll: many Graham backers were intimidated into silence or inaction. On June 24 Graham was defeated by a margin of 18,000 votes. His vote total fell off by less than one percent, but Smith had scored an 11.3 percent gain over his showing in the first primary. Most observers believed the race issue was decisive. Jonathan Daniels, the publisher of the Raleigh *News and Observer,* could not see how anyone "would question the fact that this racial feeling was the one single factor in the second primary." Graham's campaign manager concluded that the senator had been "knocked out by a veritable tidal wave of racial hate and prejudice" among lower- and middle-class voters.[27] In his analysis of the campaign, Samuel Lubell also emphasized the force of racism but added that in some middle-class precincts economic conservatism also hurt Graham. In the first primary Graham had fared well in the highly agricultural eastern counties, which contained the largest proportion of blacks in the state, but eighteen counties he had originally carried switched to Smith in the runoff because of the race issue. Only in the western counties, which had a low percentage of black inhabitants, did Graham increase his vote.[28] As in Florida, a racist argument coupled with an emerging conservative voting trend had produced victory. Anti-Communism was a commonly verbalized issue, but it was supplemental to racism rather than basic.

The Communist issue also surfaced in the California primary. Conservative Democratic opponents of the liberal Congresswoman Helen Gahagan Douglas, a candidate for the party's senatorial nomination, accused her of softness on Communism and supported her rival, E. Manchester Boddy. Mrs. Douglas was accused of having aligned herself with the "notorious New York radical" Vito Marcantonio on votes affecting the nation's security (notably on aid to Greece and Turkey and on HUAC appropriations). Boddy warned voters to thwart the attempt by a "small, subversive clique of 'red hots' " seeking to capture the state's Democratic Party. Mrs. Douglas won the primary, but during the autumn dissident conservatives led by George Creel continued to criticize her for an inadequate appreciation of the Communist menace.[29]

In the Idaho senatorial primary, candidates in both parties attacked Senator Glen Taylor for Communist propensities. Taylor, who had opposed Truman's foreign policies and had run with Wallace as a Progressive in 1948, was unusually vulnerable to such charges (which he had encountered before). His party bolt made regular Democrats, who had never supported him with any enthusiasm, eager to dump him. Ex-Senator D. Worth Clark, his principal Democratic foe, frequently termed him a "dupe" of the Communists. The several GOP senatorial aspirants, led by Herman Welker, pitched their campaigns in a similar key. The hostile *Idaho Daily Statesman* published installments from "The Red Record of Senator Claude Pepper," noted with relish all its references to Taylor, and labeled him Russia's leading spokesman in the Senate. Barnstorming in his customary cowboy fashion with a western-music band, Taylor tried to strike back at his opponents' use of "smear techniques," but on August 8 he was narrowly defeated by Clark.[30]

Senator Taylor—like other political contestants of 1950—found his fortunes enmeshed with the grim reports of battle from Korea. The Korean crisis heavily punctuated all the anxieties under the heading of anti-Communism and altered political strategies in both parties. Republicans in Congress supported the Korean intervention but promptly began to blame the war on the Administration. "Truman's war" loomed sharply as an issue in the autumn elections. Senator Robert A. Taft, Congressman Leonard Hall, and Republican National Chairman Guy G. Gabrielson were soon calling for the resignation of Secretary of State Dean Acheson. Senator Kenneth Wherry declared that "the blood of our boys in Korea is on his shoulders, and no one else." McCarthy, too, joined the fray. "The Korea deathtrap," he claimed, should be laid at "the doors of the Kremlin and those who sabotaged rearming, including Acheson and the President, if you please." During the campaign, the Korean War enabled more fastidious Republicans to talk about and around the Communist issue without fully embracing McCarthy or his rhetoric.[31]

Despite such rumblings, many Democrats optimistically assumed that the war would breed national unity and that Truman's swift response to aggression would squash charges of softness on Communism. Those intuitions influenced the decision to foreclose the Tydings committee investigation of McCarthy's charges and to defer creation of a special presidential Commission on Internal Security and Individual Rights, which some Democrats had proposed in order to defuse the anxieties McCarthy had tapped. Many Democratic senators, according to reporter William S. White, now "expected the Administration's strong stand on Korea and Formosa . . . to submerge 'the McCarthy issue.' " Even some of McCarthy's supporters were admitting that "his show has been taken off the road." [32]

Democrats who gambled that the Korean War would work to their advantage had miscalculated, for, instead, it heightened the cold-war concerns on which McCarthy battened. Although the crisis momentarily removed McCarthy from the headlines, before summer's end a full-scale Red scare had come into being —fueled by events such as the July arrest of Julius Rosenberg and his arraignment (with his wife) in August, followed shortly by the arrest of Morton Sobell and by Alfred Dean Slack's guilty plea a month later to charges of having spied for the Russians. Pointing to ten spy arrests since February, Guy Gabrielson asked: "Does this look like a 'red herring'?" [33]

THE SPECTER

At various levels political leaders responded to what they sensed was a surging wave of anti-Communism. The town fathers of Birmingham warned local Communists to leave town in forty-eight hours; New Rochelle's Reds were required to register with the police; the sale of Communist literature was banned on the streets of Detroit. Federal officials, motivated in part by the Korean emergency, requested revocation of bail in the cases of Harry Bridges and the Communist "eleven" and had the passport of Paul Robeson lifted. When the Polish liner *Batory* entered New York Harbor, port officials subjected her to a four-hour search to make sure she was not carrying an atomic bomb.[34] Perhaps the strongest reaction came from Congress, which in September passed—over the President's veto—the broad-gauge McCarran Internal Security Act. A number of Democrats who voted for the McCarran bill did so in concurrence with Senate Majority Leader Scott Lucas's observation that "the American people are anxious to have an anti-Communist bill placed on the statute books." [35]

As the political potency of anti-Communism grew, the Democrats abandoned the optimistic assumptions of June. Party leaders perceived that the loyalty issue and McCarthy's allegations required countermeasures. The Democratic National Committee published a "bible" defending the integrity and loyalty of State Department officials against McCarthy's charges. The Committee's Nationalities Division worked hard to neutralize GOP "mudslinging" among various ethnic groups by Republicans who exploited the topics of Communist subversion, Yalta, and Korea. Party spokesmen argued, as in 1948, that the far right and left were playing into each other's hands. According to Attorney General J. Howard McGrath, it was the Democrats, because of their "skillful dynamic foreign and domestic policies," whom the Communists feared most. "Who is fighting the Communists anyhow?" asked Senator Clinton Anderson. "Can it be the people who talk about spy rings in the State Department and then vote against appropriations for military aid?" The Democrats offered their foreign policies as the primary answer to allegations of softness on Communism.[36]

If the Democratic campaign had any unifying theme, it was to identify Republican opponents of the Administration's foreign policies as "isolationists." In his single partisan speech of the autumn, Truman declared isolationism "one of the main issues in this election." The McCarthyite claim that the Democrats were "communistic" he termed "the craziest idea of all." His party had "done more to defeat Communism" than any other group—it had "saved free enterprise," prosecuted Communist leaders, and built up the might of the free world. The Republicans, meanwhile, had been "willing . . . to undermine their own Government at a time of great international peril." The emerging "victory" in Korea, Truman exclaimed, was "the greatest step toward world peace . . . in my lifetime." Other party orators pursued similar arguments. "Are you going to tell Stalin and the Kremlin that the American people are not behind the Truman Administration?" Vice President Alben Barkley asked. Senator Warren Magnuson warned that Republican congressional leaders were ready to "march us down that road to isolationism again." [37]

On balance, however, the Korean fighting aided the Republicans: it provided a topic not so much to be argued as simply mentioned. For a few giddy weeks after the Inchon landing and Pusan breakout in September, as U.N. troops rolled toward the Yalu, Democratic campaign sermons about standing up to Communism rang triumphantly true. "If President Truman blundered in Korea," Alben Barkley exulted, "he certainly blundered us into a great victory." Then, in late October and November, the massive Red Chinese counterattack routed U.N. armies. On the eve of the election Harold Stassen could announce that the past week had brought the heaviest casualties of the war. "The voters know," said Guy Gabrielson, "that Chinese Communist divisions are pouring into North Korea." As speculation mounted that Korea might have to be abandoned, arguments about enlightened internationalism and sober anti-Communism circulated at a discount. By January, 66 percent of the respondents to a poll felt that American troops should pull out of Korea; only 25 percent were willing to stay in. A growing number (50 percent) thought the original commitment had been a mistake. Korea had a palpable, if indeterminate, effect upon the election—a more encompassing one than the narrower issue of Communism-in-government associated with McCarthy.[38]

If defined as the broadcast use of the "Communist" issue, McCarthyism did, however, play a key part in *some* elections. In the California Senate race, Congressman Richard M. Nixon, the Republican nominee, made anti-Communism his principal theme. The Democratic primary had already implanted it in the campaign's rhetoric, and during autumn, conservative Democrats continued to link Helen Douglas to "the Communist Party-liner," Marcantonio. Nixon leaned heavily upon the support of the anti-Douglas Democrats and, aside from refighting the Hiss case, had little to add to their exertions. He claimed to speak for those who recognized "that all Americans must stand together" against the Communist threat just as most Republicans and Democrats in Congress united on national-security matters; in contrast, his opponent ran with "the left-wing clique" that voted against such measures. "Mrs. Douglas," he declared, "has not denied that she has voted with the man she calls a Communist party-liner" more often than any other member of the House. "We stopped counting when those votes totaled 354." Nixon taxed Mrs. Douglas for her hostility to HUAC, but he concentrated more heavily upon her association with Democratic foreign policy "blunders." He challenged her to state "whether she subscribes to the Acheson-Lattimore policy" in Asia or to

Electoral politics and McCarthyism

that of General McArthur; later he characterized her as "committed to the State Department policy of appeasement toward Communism in the Far East." [39]

If the campaign surged too frequently around the effigy of "Communism," it was partly the fault of the Douglas forces. They conceded the salience of the issue, for instance, when they sponsored speeches designed to belittle Nixon's role in the Hiss case and to sell Mrs. Douglas as the more redoubtable anti-Communist. They acknowledged the legitimacy of the Marcantonio roll-call comparison when they noted that Nixon and Marcantonio had both voted against aid to Korea and for cutting Marshall Plan funds. Nixon's supporters replied with the so-called "pink sheets," which detailed hundreds of alleged parallels between Mrs. Douglas's votes and Marcantonio's. Mrs. Douglas lambasted her adversary for his use of "smears" and warned that "McCarthyism has come to California." (She also referred to Nixon and his backers as "young men in dark shirts.") Nixon, however, sought to avoid the label of "McCarthyism," pointing both to the fact that he had had no connection with the McCarthy investigation and to his advocacy of a nonpartisan commission to look into the charges of Communist infiltration. [40]

Despite a vast Democratic edge in registration figures, Mrs. Douglas lost the election by nearly 700,000 votes. She suffered because her running mate, Jimmy Roosevelt, offered a weak challenge to the popular incumbent Governor Earl Warren. But Nixon carried the day primarily with his vigorous anti-Communism. [41] Though he had used some methods that could be called "McCarthyism," it would be imprecise to label him a McCarthyite; while there were and would continue to be parallels, Nixon had seized upon the issue of Communism earlier, could point to more concrete achievements, and usually demonstrated greater restraint than McCarthy. The California campaign would have assumed its ultimate outlines even in the absence of a Joe McCarthy. The Wisconsinite's one speech in California, although

THE SPECTER

reaching a peak in rhetorical extremism ("Ask the basket-cases if they agree that Acheson is an 'outstanding American!' ") made no impress on the contest and was not welcomed by Nixon, who preferred "home talent." [42]

Charges of Communist proclivities had considerable influence upon the defeat of Senator Elbert D. Thomas of Utah. The Republican candidate, Wallace Bennett, promised to show that Thomas was the "darlin [sic] of several un-American organizations." A more mordant attack on Thomas was carried out by pamphleteers. Handbills originating outside the state detailed Thomas's alleged ties to Communist-front groups. The most flagrant of these, the *United States Senate News,* was headlined "Thomas Philosophy Wins Red Approval" and falsely accused Thomas of having presided with Paul Robeson at a Communist-oriented fund-raising dinner. Posted late in the campaign, the *United States Senate News* blanketed the state and, according to one student of the contest, "startled and shocked" Utah voters.[43] Even before the appearance of this tabloid, the Democrats had become sensitive to the damage done by the Communist issue: each of the several national party luminaries who campaigned for Thomas assailed the Republicans for questioning the senator's loyalty. Red-baiting probably was the critical factor in Thomas's defeat.[44]

Elsewhere in the West, Republicans plied the Communist issue, but with indifferent results. In Washington State, the Republican senatorial candidate, W. Walter Williams, charged that the incumbent, Warren Magnuson, had once sponsored a rally of Communists and fellow travelers, but Magnuson quashed the allegation by explaining that his name had been used without permission. Williams also tried, unsuccessfully, to link Magnuson's voting record with those of Senators Pepper and Taylor. Notwithstanding such fireworks, it was more typical of Williams to label his foe a "spender." In any case, Magnuson achieved reelection by a comfortable margin.[45] In Idaho, Herman Welker continued to avow his muscular anti-Communism; his identification with the issue may have contributed to his victory over his Democratic opponent, D. Worth Clark, who, in offering post-election congratulations, urged the victor to "continue his fight against Communism in all its forms." Clark himself was not, however, vulnerable to charges of Communism.[46]

The "Red" issue colored, but did not shape, the campaign in Colorado, where Republican Senator Eugene Millikin accused his challenger, Congressman John Carroll, of "coddling Communists." Millikin hit the Truman Administration's "appease- and encouragement of Communism at home" and made reference to Yalta, the loss of China, and Communists in the State Department. A rightist agitator issued a pamphlet charging that Carroll "plays piggy-back with Stalin's pals," but the author had no connection with the Millikin campaign. Only a secondary weapon in Millikin's arsenal, the Communist issue did not account for his victory.[47]

In several races the impact of "McCarthyism" was diluted by either more general or more local issues. Iowa's Senator Hickenlooper sought to reap benefits from his pro-McCarthy stand as a member of the Tydings subcommittee, but farm policy was a far more decisive factor in his reelection.[48] In Oklahoma the Reverend "Bill" Alexander charged that A. S. "Mike" Monroney, his Democratic senatorial rival, "went East and turned left" while serving in Congress and found Monroney's opposition to Communism lukewarm. Monroney retorted that Alexander, by attacking the Administration's policies in Korea, was "unknowingly repeating the Communist Party line." More often, however, Monroney spoke as a defender of the New Deal, while Alexander campaigned more as a barnstorming evangelist (calling it time to "return some Christian principles to Washington") than as a McCarthyite.[49]

With varying emphases, the Communist issue emerged in several eastern states. John Fine, the GOP gubernatorial aspirant in Pennsylvania, attacked the Truman Administration for hiring those who "flirted with Communism" and charged his opponent, Richardson Dilworth, with courting the votes of "pinks" and subversives. Dilworth responded that "political machines" like his foe's were the instruments that really bred Communism. Fine, he said, was ducking the real issues: "All he wants to talk about is Joe Stalin." Senator Francis Myers joined in to charge that the Republicans were "using Communist tactics and techniques." Myers based his reelection campaign upon his experience and seniority and strongly defended the Korean police action against the assertion of his opponent, Republican Governor James Duff, that the war was "unnecessary." Duff criticized the Truman Administration's extravagance and "socialistic experiments," the Yalta agreements, and the nation's unpreparedness for Korea. His anti-Communist appeals were largely geared to foreign policy; he attacked the Democrats for failing to "appreciate the danger" posed by Russia's rapid rise to world power, but he spent little time on the issue of domestic Communism. Duff's popularity as governor and the Korean debacle greatly outweighed the issue of Communist subversion in his victory over Myers.[50]

In Ohio, too, the "pure" issue of Communist infiltration was a secondary ingredient of the Republican campaign. Organized labor supplied the muscle behind the effort to unseat Senator Taft, and Republicans reciprocated by denouncing the "labor bosses." Taftites maintained that Joseph T. Ferguson, the Democratic candidate, was a mere puppet of the CIO Political Action Committee, which, they claimed, had captured control of the Democratic Party. Taft stigmatized the CIO-PAC as "the Socialist Party in this country, and although it has gotten rid of most of its Communists, it still uses Communist techniques." He harangued Ohio workingmen regarding the Communist origins of the CIO, the socialist programs pushed by its minions, and their "lie and smear campaign" against him. He labeled the

Electoral politics and McCarthyism

Fair Deal socialistic and denounced the "strange pro-Red sympathy of the United States government." Communist aggression in Korea, he asserted, had followed hard upon statements by the Administration that it would not defend the area. "We practically invited them," he exclaimed.[51]

Ferguson's ineptness muddled the issues in Ohio. (A popular epigram summarized his foreign policy views as "Beat Michigan.") Ferguson extravagantly declared his inability to "see how any red-blooded loyal American" could support his foe. Trying to dose Taft with his own medicine, Ferguson condemned his use of "communistic tactics in branding labor union leaders and union members as Communists" and demanded that Taft explain a recently republished photograph picturing him together with onetime Communist notable Earl Browder. Ferguson also noted the congruence between Taft's voting record and that of the ever-unpopular Marcantonio. In November Taft swamped Ferguson, who failed even to get labor's undivided support. If the campaign had any central meaning, it indicated broad resentment of the much-bruited strong-arm tactics of labor. Taft's anti-Communistic rhetoric served chiefly to orchestrate this theme and differed in liturgy from McCarthy's, which seldom emphasized a nexus between Communism and labor.[52]

In Michigan a similar contest developed between Governor G. Mennen Williams and his Republican challenger, Harry F. Kelly. Kelly said Williams was "dominated" by "labor bosses" and such "splinter groups" as the Americans for Democratic Action and the CIO-PAC. "It is a short jump," he reasoned, "from the methods used by the Americans for Democratic Action to capture control of the Democratic Party to the teaching of un-American philosophies in our schools." "None of us," Kelly boasted of his own party, "has any secret ambitions to change the American way of life into some other strange way of life."

Williams answered Kelly in several ways. Having worked to

purge a suspected Communist from his own party's ticket, he could lay some claim to active anti-Communism. On the ADA, which he helped found, he equivocated, now praising its leaders (innocence by association), now minimizing his involvement with it. More hyperbolically, he accused the Reds and Republicans of ganging up on him. "Everywhere when the chips are down," he warned, "Communists team up with the extreme right in an effort to defeat those who follow the middle course." The GOP campaign nearly turned the trick; but, after trailing in the preliminary count, Williams eked out a 1,000-vote margin of victory in a total vote of almost 1,900,000.[53] As in Ohio, Republican Red-baiting did not depend particularly upon McCarthy's formulations of the creed and stressed instead a more anti-labor theme.

The states where the senator from Wisconsin actively stumped provide a more precise gauge of the political force of McCarthyism. He intervened with greatest effect in Maryland, where Millard Tydings, a four-term conservative Democrat who had withstood FDR's "purge" efforts in 1938, was opposed by John Marshall Butler, a political novice. As chairman of the subcommittee whose Democratic majority had termed McCarthy's charges "a fraud and a hoax," Tydings had earned the Wisconsinite's bitter enmity. McCarthy had cried "whitewash" from the probe's very outset, but Tydings discounted the impact of such criticism and ignored intelligence from a variety of sources that indicated that McCarthy's charges had stirred doubts among his constituents. Opposition mobilized in Maryland, and during the primary campaign, senatorial aspirants in both parties flayed Tydings' conduct of the investigation. In September a crude poll of state Democratic Party leaders revealed that 81 percent believed that McCarthy's charges had adversely affected Tydings' prospects.[54] Although Tydings won the primary easily, two unknowns, both of whom had retailed McCarthy's "whitewash" allegations, collected 87,733 votes against his 172,577, and 120,000 Democrats who had chosen a gubernatorial candidate declined to state a senatorial preference.[55]

In the autumn, GOP nominee Butler, employing a tactic later described as raising the "big doubt," asked leading questions regarding Tydings' stewardship of the loyalty inquiry. McCarthy campaigned for Butler and provided files, legwork by his Washington staff, and funds from his political supporters. McCarthy aides and employees of the Washington *Times-Herald* assembled the most notorious piece of literature of the 1950 campaign, the tabloid "From the Record." The pamphlet rehashed a number of McCarthy's charges against Tydings, but the most damaging entry was the famed "composite photo" picturing Earl Browder, the fallen eagle of the Communist Party, cheek-by-jowl with Tydings, who seemed to be savoring Browder's revelation that the persons accused by McCarthy were not, in fact, Communists. The creators of the composite had spliced together a current picture of Browder and a photograph of Tydings listening to the 1938 election returns—a fact that accounted for the senator's rapt expression.[56]

Throughout most of the canvass, Tydings ignored the swirling undercurrents of Maryland politics, pitching his campaign in general terms and emphasizing his seniority and heavy responsibilities. "I hear all the secret information on atomic weapons," he confided in one speech. The major issue, he argued, was the GOP's "narrow isolationism" versus the reasoned anti-Communist policies of his own party.[57] When in the closing weeks of the campaign he confronted his enemies' charges, it was too late.

Tydings suffered under multiple handicaps. The Maryland Democratic Party was riven by a divisive gubernatorial primary battle; the winner, incumbent W. Preston Lane, was unpopular because of the sales tax enacted during his tenure. Conversely, Butler benefited from the wide appeal of his own gubernatorial

THE SPECTER

running mate, Theodore R. McKeldin. Maryland's black voters were alienated by the Southern-style conservatism on civil-rights issues of Tydings and state party leaders. The darkening situation in Korea also hurt Tydings, whose foes, pointing to his position as chairman of the Armed Services Committee, implied that he shared the blame for America's unpreparedness. Most significantly, Republican strength in Maryland had been growing since 1938: indeed, Dewey had carried the state in 1948.[58]

Yet it was the Communist issue that most dramatically and pivotally affected the outcome. Many observers reported widespread desertions from Tydings by Maryland's Catholics—a shift that deeply agitated the senator's colleagues. A study by the statistician Louis H. Bean showed that in three groupings of contiguous counties there was a positive correlation between Catholic population and the decline in support for Tydings.[59] Although the evidence is less than overpowering, Maryland offers the clearest case for the political efficacy of McCarthy's allegations. One reporter maintained that "McCarthyism alone would have been sufficient" to defeat Tydings; another called the senator's inability to "argue away the accusations of 'whitewash' " the "most plausible explanation" for his loss. William S. White found among members of the Senate a consensus that McCarthy, plain and simple, "beat" Tydings. Perhaps the explanation of McCarthy's grim success in Maryland lies in the fact that, unlike the Wisconsinite's other targets, Tydings was a conservative. Though his opposition to McCarthy earned some accretions of liberal support, Tydings had long since lost that group's allegiance. When McCarthy undercut his standing among conservatives, therefore, he was peculiarly vulnerable.[60]

In his home state, McCarthy electioneered vigorously, and his presence etched itself sharply on several contests. Some Wisconsin Republicans had at first hesitated to give full support to McCarthy's anti-Communist crusade. During the campaign, however, they eagerly sought his assistance, and he drew the largest crowds of any Republican orator in the state.[61] His colleague Alexander Wiley, who was running for reelection, had been slow to express outright approval of McCarthy during the spring, but by autumn he had suppressed any ambivalence as he welcomed McCarthy's aid and echoed his indictments of American foreign policy. Thomas Fairchild, Wiley's opponent, and other Democrats proceeded on the tactical assumption that the affinity for McCarthyism, properly exposed, would prove damaging to Wiley. "Are you so desperate," Fairchild queried his foe, "that you had to identify yourself with McCarthy . . . ?" Wiley countered that McCarthy was not the issue, that his colleague's "technique" and "personal affairs" were irrelevant. He also charged that the Democrats had whitewashed McCarthy's discoveries; for himself, he found the Administration at fault for "seventeen years of coddling Communists here at home." On another occasion, he volunteered that "Joe didn't find anything new, but he took all the things we knew before about Communists" and "alerted this country to the danger of Communist penetration." [62]

Walter J. Kohler, Jr., the GOP gubernatorial candidate, balanced his rhetoric even more delicately: a public appearance with McCarthy must not, he cautioned, be construed as an endorsement of the senator. Since the Democrats had not uncovered the truth—such as it might be—behind McCarthy's charges, he was "suspending judgment" until Joe got a fair hearing. For good measure, Kohler declared that he had not "the slightest doubt that there are thousands of Communists in key places of the government. The case of Alger Hiss proves that." Other Wisconsin Republicans hastened with more gusto than Kohler and Wiley to campaign as McCarthyites. Charles Kersten, who had assisted McCarthy in the early stages of his Red hunt, all but welcomed his opponent's charges of "McCarthyism" in the congressional contest on Milwaukee's north side. In a neighboring district, another congressional candidate,

John C. Brophy, backed McCarthy but believed he had not gone far enough.[63]

In November all the Republicans but Brophy emerged victorious. Outwardly, the results might appear to be a mandate for McCarthyism, though some observers expressed reservations. They noted that the Democrats had shown extraordinary strength for a party that not long before had comprised Roosevelt every fourth year and unelectable patronage seekers the other three. The organizational effort that younger Democrats, many of them former La Follette Progressives, had pumped into the party since World War II was beginning to bear dividends. The 1950 Democratic gubernatorial candidate had made a 2 percent gain over his showing in 1948, when Truman led the ticket and carried the state. With 46 percent of the vote, Fairchild had offered the sharpest challenge by any Democratic senatorial hopeful in recent years. While they lost ground in Milwaukee, the Democrats scored gains over their 1948 performance in twenty-three other counties. Moreover, in comparison to 1948, the Democratic vote dropped off in forty-three counties, but the Republican vote declined in sixty.[64]

No precise measurements exist to determine exactly how McCarthy's unique style may have altered the traditional, though eroding, Republican strength on which Wiley drew, but apparently McCarthy's direct involvement brought Wiley little help. Robert Fleming, a Milwaukee *Journal* reporter, found that McCarthy "did not pull votes" in the cities where he spoke: relative to 1948, the Republican vote increased in six of these cities but fell off in nine. McCarthy's well-publicized invasion of Democratic South Milwaukee, heavily populated by Polish Americans, did not elect the McCarthyite running for Congress there nor did it help Wiley appreciably. The 1950 election may provide evidence for the contention of one political scientist that McCarthyism's "impact on the political and cultural life of the state was not particularly great." [65]

Electoral politics and McCarthyism

McCarthy also took a keen interest in the Illinois contest between Senator Scott Lucas and former Congressman Everett Dirksen. Dirksen made much of allegations that the Democrats had tolerated Communistic infiltration of the federal government. A Republican victory would let Stalin "know that there will be a house cleaning of his sympathizers and party-liners such as this country has never seen before," Dirksen promised.[66] In a Chicago address, McCarthy classed Lucas with Tydings and Brien McMahon as a culprit responsible for whitewashing the State Department. A vote for Dirksen, he exclaimed, would be a "prayer for America" as well as a "vote against Dean Acheson" and the "Commicrat [sic] party." [67]

Lucas counterattacked principally on the issue of foreign policy, labeling his rival a "fumbling, confused isolationist" aligned with Colonel Robert R. McCormick's Chicago *Tribune*. He capitalized on Dirksen's about-face on the Marshall Plan, which the ex-congressman had once supported but now repudiated as money poured down a "rathole." In October, as U.N. forces pinched the North Koreans back across the 38th parallel, Lucas acclaimed Truman's Korean policy as "a great victory." After Red Chinese armies tipped the balance, Dirksen riposted: "Where is this peace?" of which the Democrats had boasted? [68]

Dirksen's victory owed less to appeals based on "isolationism" or "McCarthyism," however, than to the issue of crime. Senator Estes Kefauver's special investigating committee had held hearings in Chicago during the autumn which implicated, among others, a Chicago police captain, who thereupon became known as "the world's richest cop." Since that entrepreneur occupied a place on the Democratic ticket, Lucas suffered; the votes in Cook County, which he needed to offset Dirksen's downstate strength, were not forthcoming.[69] Despite the fact that his support for Truman's domestic program had been lukewarm at best, the majority leader was chalked up, somewhat incorrectly, as the foremost casualty suffered by the Fair Deal.[70]

THE SPECTER

In Indiana (as in California), McCarthy's intervention was irrelevant. His speech in Indianapolis had little effect upon the contest between Senator Homer Capehart and Alex Campbell, the Democrat. Aided by his colleague William Jenner, Capehart compounded a splenetic mixture of isolationism and anti-Communism; he charged that "we are still appeasing Russia," termed Dean Acheson "Quisling-like" but at the same time expressed a willingness to give up Berlin to the Russians. He labeled his opponent a "Truman stooge" and member of the President's "red-herring brigade." Campbell, however, was unusually resistent to Red-baiting since he had helped, as a Justice Department official, to prosecute Alger Hiss. (The Republicans were quick to denigrate both Campbell's and the Justice Department's role in the case.) Campbell compared Capehart to McCarthy in his use of "unwarranted smears" and asserted that both Indiana senators had "voted consistently" with Vito Marcantonio. To the Republicans' charge that current prosperity was based upon "the warfare state," Campbell retorted that that phrase had first been employed by the *Daily Worker*. The Indiana campaign encompassed issues broader than the question of Communist subversion: Capehart struck at the whole thrust of New Deal-Fair Deal liberalism ("idiotic experiments with all kinds of isms") and Democratic foreign policies ("a third terrible war in thirty-three years"). Despite his vigorous counterattack, Campbell was unable to neutralize or disassociate himself from the conservative discontent at work in the Hoosier state.[71]

If unnecessary in Indiana and California, McCarthy's efforts proved insufficient in Missouri, where Senator Forrest Donnell faced a strong challenge from Thomas C. Hennings, Jr. In his canvass, Hennings warned of the dangers to freedom posed by "McCarthyism" and upheld Truman's veto of the McCarran Act. Donnell, conducting a temperate campaign, did not espouse McCarthyism, but the Wisconsin senator rectified that oversight with a Jefferson City speech in which he repeated his charges against the State Department and what he had taken to calling the "Commiecrat" party. Alluding to Hennings' instruction that Democrats place anti-McCarthy advertisements in the local papers, McCarthy declared that while the Young Communists had employed such devices against him, this marked the first time Democrats had done so. He also claimed baselessly that Hennings' father had paid for the ads. Unimpressed, Missourians elected Hennings by a substantial margin, making Donnell the only GOP senator to lose his seat in 1950.[72]

In Connecticut McCarthy also failed to realize his aims as a political spoiler. His three oratorical descents upon the state had little *éclat*. Since the state Republican organization had no desire to sponsor McCarthy's presence, a non-party group, the Connecticut Volunteers, invited him to appear. When he spoke in New Haven in October, only one GOP candidate, Senator McMahon's foe, graced the platform. On November 3 in Bridgeport, McCarthy spoke against McMahon and his running mates for the benefit of just 300 listeners; in Hartford, in an auditorium with 5,000 seats, he regaled a mere 800 of the faithful.[73] McCarthy was unable to sway many voters in "the Land of Steady Habits." Though McCarthy assailed him for his role in the Tydings committee's "whitewash," McMahon won reelection easily. While Governor Chester Bowles was defeated, Senator William Benton, another McCarthy target, squeaked through with a narrow victory. Relative to 1944, McMahon did lose support in some counties with high concentrations of Catholics; lacking further data, one might assume that the Communist issue and McCarthy's use of it accounted for this decline, but the effect was negligible.[74]

In the aftermath of the elections, McCarthy received credit for many of the critical losses sustained by the Democrats. According to William S. White, the Wisconsinite's colleagues believed that he had caused Tydings' destruction, that he had "contributed a heavy part, if not perhaps the decisive part," to Lucas' downfall, that Herman Welker "owed much" to him, and that Wallace Bennett was "at least unconsciously and unwittingly a beneficiary" of his. Doris Fleeson wrote that fellow senators scored "an assist" for McCarthy in the defeats of Graham and Pepper. The Senate was most severely jolted by the outcome in Maryland. "The ghost of Senator Tydings hangs over the Senate," a reporter observed in 1951.[75]

Undoubtedly, the Communist issue did trouble American voters in 1950. The McCarthyism that prevailed in the campaign produced, in the view of one onlooker, a "panic in the streets." Although that was an exaggerated assessment, there was an inchoate but nonetheless real electoral malaise, and if any political figure profited from it, it was McCarthy. The 1950 elections had witnessed unusual amounts of scurrility, distortion, and Red-baiting.[76] At times it appeared that every Democrat in Washington voted with Marcantonio (which solidarity did not save the Manhattan radical from the Republican-Democratic-Liberal coalition that finally knocked him out of Congress). So many Democrats seemingly had shared the banquet platform with Paul Robeson that that worthy must never have enjoyed a meal in solitude. If not even Robert Taft, steady helmsman of the right, could resist the photographic embrace of Earl Browder, the latter's allure must have surpassed that of Homer's sirens. Not confined to races for the House and Senate, the Communist issue surfaced in the contest for secretary of state of Indiana, for attorney general in California, for lieutenant governor in Pennsylvania, and in numerous local races.

Too many observers, however, failed to distinguish method from mandate, and overstated the impact of "McCarthyism." The Wisconsin senator was not exclusively responsible for the outpouring of anti-Communist appeals in 1950 or for the underhanded tactics that sometimes accompanied them. Because the label "McCarthyism" seemed apposite and was—too facilely—

Electoral politics and McCarthyism

employed, McCarthy received more credit for the results than he deserved. In some ways it was a typical off-year campaign, lacking the central direction of national presidential candidates who might have emphasized themes of cohesion rather than conflict. Moreover, the election occurred at a time when events —the cold war, Korea, Hiss, and Fuchs—were contributing to a climate conducive to both McCarthy and anti-Communist rhetoric. It also coincided with the maturing of the talents and methods necessary for such tactics: the rise of politics by public relations and mass advertising.[77] It was a year of tabloid campaign newspapers: while the more lurid sorts of campaign literature employed against liberals were labeled "McCarthyism," the senator had not invented this genre. For instance, *The Road Ahead,* John T. Flynn's anti-New Deal pamphlet, had first appeared in 1949; this diatribe against "socialism" enjoyed great vogue as a handout in several 1950 campaigns. Other authors produced more extremist tracts for use in various states.[78]

In their results, the elections did not reveal quite the grassroots appeal that friend and foe attributed to McCarthy. Though McCarthyites won, so did more classic Republican conservatives such as Taft and Millikin—without their bumptious colleague's aid. The liberal wing of the party also scored victories. Governors Dewey and Warren, no McCarthyites, were reelected; Duff, likewise critical of McCarthy, won a Senate seat, and incumbents George Aiken and Charles Tobey, no friends of the Wisconsinite either, returned to office. The victories of the moderates balanced the triumphs of the conservatives, so that the 1950 results strengthened both wings of the party, though not equally.[79] Most significantly, the Republicans' gains of five Senate and twenty-eight House seats conferred control of neither chamber and represented smaller midterm increments than the GOP had achieved in 1946, 1942, or 1938. The Democrats could take solace in the fact that their losses were only slightly more than half the average loss in the last three midterm battles.[80]

In another respect, political pulse-takers had exaggerated the spell that the Communist issue cast over the electorate. Opposition to the Internal Security Act of 1950 did not insure the political defeat that some observers predicted. Of 21 Democratic congressmen who voted against the McCarran Act, only 5 lost (two in quests for Senate seats); conversely, of the 28 Democratic representatives beaten in November, 23 had supported the measure. Only one senatorial opponent of the bill, Herbert H. Lehman, had to face a campaign in 1950. The New York liberal vigorously attacked the law on the hustings; his convincing success at the polls argued that his dissent had proven no liability.[81]

On balance, a closer examination of the 1950 results ought to have tempered the optimism of the McCarthyites and the despondency of their foes.[82] Both groups, however, interpreted the election as a mandate for McCarthy and guided their actions according to their heightened perception of his political potency. The problem for his opponents lay in the fact that their apprehension soon outdistanced reality: McCarthy had profited from the connection of his name to electioneering methods and themes that both antedated and subsumed his own charges and devices.

The press and political elites shared much of the responsibility for the rise of McCarthy's reputation as a political *force de frappe*. Just as "Communism" served many Americans as an easy explanation of the nation's ills, so "McCarthyism" provided the senator's critics with a facile shorthand for alarming political trends. The difficulty was partly one of semantics, but more than choice of words was at fault. Too many observers confounded McCarthy's own anti-Communist exertions with the independent efforts of other GOP politicians. They tended to forget that the tactic of anti-Communism was old, that it was bipartisan, and that McCarthy, however expert, did not exhaust the issue's possibilities. They also assumed a single-issue orientation in campaigns that turned upon plural concerns.

McCarthyism did have an effect upon the 1950 elections, but its force was greatly augmented by momentary world conditions —particularly the jarring incursion by the Red Chinese in Korea. Subsequent to the 1950 elections—admittedly, after many additional developments had altered the situation— public opinion analysts found indications that Communism and McCarthyism were far less salient issues than had originally been presumed.[83] The 1950 campaign took place in an atmosphere unusually conducive to McCarthyism, but also never to be replicated.

Thanks to the unique conditions that prevailed in 1950 and to miscalculations on the part of the press and the politicians, an overstated assessment of McCarthy's electoral influence was born. This exaggeration, by producing an expanded perception of McCarthy's power, ultimately enlarged his power itself.

THE SPECTER

McCARTHY AND McCARTHYISM:

The Cedric Parker Case,

November
1949

BY
MICHAEL
O'BRIEN

In the late 1940's, amidst the growing tensions of the cold war, politicians, Democratic and Republican alike, increasingly seized upon the Communist issue as a means of advancing their political fortunes. Democrats such as George Smathers and Willis Smith and Republicans such as Richard Nixon and Karl Mundt all found advantages in accusing their opponents of pro-Communist sympathies. The career of Joseph R. McCarthy, and the manner in which he came to select the Communist issue as his own is important—both because of its typicality and because of McCarthy's later notoriety. It is important, further, to clear away the considerable confusion that surrounds McCarthy's initial use of the Communist issue.

Like many other Republican campaigners, McCarthy had first used the Communist issue in 1946, when he accused his Democratic senatorial opponent, Howard McMurray, of being "communistically inclined" and a "little megaphone for the Communist-controlled PAC." In April 1947 he appeared in a radio debate on "Town Meeting of the Air" to argue that the Communist Party should be outlawed and in May of that same year he sought, unsuccessfully, to amend the Taft-Hartley bill in order to allow employers to dismiss workers previously expelled from unions because of membership in the Communist Party or because of Communist "sympathies." [1]

But these were relatively isolated incidents, and most commentators have stressed other factors in attempting to explain the immediate circumstances that led McCarthy to adopt anti-Communism as a political issue. The most recent and least reliable account has been suggested by Roy Cohn, who served as McCarthy's brash, young chief assistant in 1953–54.[2] According to Cohn's vague account, "a G-2 officer" took an "FBI report" on subversion and passed it around to various persons. A "small group" became concerned and sought out a senator who would awaken the public to the danger. Just before Thanksgiving 1949 three men approached McCarthy and asked him to publicize the

report. "Literally overnight," Cohn insisted, "the senator decided to make the battle against Communism his issue." He did
so because he was patriotic and worried about Communism subversion, and because the issue presented a dramatic political
opportunity.[3] Although there may be some truth to Cohn's account, his close association with McCarthy and the obvious bias
of his book make one hesitant to accept it without confirmation.
His story is hopelessly vague. The G-2 officer, the small group
that became interested in the report, and the three men who approached McCarthy remain unidentified. No one, moreover, has
substantiated this account.

According to a second, and more widely accepted view,
McCarthy adopted the Communist-in-government issue because
of a suggestion made during a dinner at the Colony Restaurant
in Washington, D.C., on January 7, 1950. The dinner was arranged by Charles Kraus, a member of McCarthy's staff and an
instructor of political science at Washington's Georgetown University. Those invited included McCarthy, Father Edmund A.
Walsh, the scholarly dean of Georgetown University's foreign
service school, and the noted Washington attorney William A.
Roberts. After-dinner conversation focused on McCarthy's political future. He confessed to his three fellow Catholics that he
desperately needed an issue with which to build a record for his
1952 reelection bid. "How about pushing harder for the St.
Lawrence seaway?" suggested Roberts. But McCarthy was not
impressed. The senator then suggested a Townsend-type pension
plan for the elderly, but his friends rejected the idea. The conversation drifted on until Father Walsh remarked: "How about
Communism as an issue?" McCarthy allegedly pounced upon
the suggestion. "The government is full of Communists," he declared; "the thing to do is hammer at them." The priest's suggestion, supporters of this interpretation believed, inspired
McCarthy to seek information on subversives in government. As
a result, a month later at Wheeling, West Virginia, he publicly

initiated his anti-Communist crusade.[4] The dinner did take place, and Communism was no doubt discussed. Perhaps Father Walsh's remarks did inspire McCarthy to some degree. Possibly there was some truth in Cohn's account as well. But McCarthy needed little encouragement to take up the Communist issue, for he had used it, very effectively, three months earlier in a successful, if little noticed, attack on the *Capital Times* (Madison, Wisconsin) and its city editor Cedric Parker.

From 1947 to 1949, the liberal Madison newspaper had repeatedly attacked and exposed McCarthy's record. Its reporters had revealed his "quickie divorces," investigated his financial affairs, publicized his censure by the State Supreme Court in 1941, and initiated the proceedings that led to his censure by the same court in 1949. A few other major newspapers publicized these devastating stories and also criticized his Senate record. This alone, of course, would not have endangered his political career so much had the dominant conservative press found something to credit during his three years in the Senate. Although Republican papers sometimes defended him from critics, rarely did they praise him. By the fall of 1949, all evidence indicated that McCarthy was in serious political trouble, and for this frightful predicament, he could partially blame the liberal Madison daily.[5]

William T. Evjue, editor of the *Capital Times,* liked tough, independent reporters. Reckless, hard-drinking Cedric Parker admirably measured up to this criterion. In his twenty-one years on Evjue's staff, Parker had earned his reputation as a crack reporter by performing such stunts as storming into gambling joints just ahead of raiding policemen. Evjue rewarded Parker by promoting him to city editor in 1948. Parker's renown as a reporter was equaled only by his reputation as a left-wing Madison CIO official who allegedly followed the Communist Party line before World War II. It was the latter aspect of his career that attracted McCarthy.

THE SPECTER

The senator had been scheduled to address the Madison Shrine Club on November 11, 1949. Two days before the speech, he mailed out a nine-page mimeographed "document" to four hundred daily and weekly newspapers and to all the radio stations in Wisconsin, and to the school clerks of Dane County (which included Madison). Attached to each copy was a note from McCarthy which read: "Enclosed is a document which I thought you might be interested in. I intend to discuss this matter in some detail while back in Wisconsin." [6]

In his press release the senator charged that Cedric Parker was a Communist and that the *Capital Times* followed the Communist Party line. He leveled seven specific accusations at Parker. First, he charged that Evjue had once called Parker "the Communist leader in Madison." Second, he declared that Farrell Schnering, a former Communist Party member from Milwaukee, had testified under oath that "The president of the Dane County [Communist] Council is Cedric Parker, a reporter of the *Capital Times,* who has been a sympathizer with the party and a fellow traveler since early in 1935. He joined the party toward the end of 1935." According to McCarthy, Parker had also been identified as a Communist by Kenneth Goff of Delavan, a Young Communist Party member from 1936 through 1939. Parker was also listed as a sponsor of a mass meeting held in June 1938 by the American League for Peace and Democracy, which, McCarthy pointed out, had been labeled an "advocate of treason" by the House Un-American Activities Committee. McCarthy charged that Parker and Eugene Dennis, a Communist leader, had organized and sponsored a statewide conference on Farm and Labor Legislation in April 1934. HUAC, he declared, listed this organization as "Communist controlled." Parker had also attended a meeting of the Wisconsin Conference on Social Legislation, a group listed by the United States Attorney General as a Communist organization. Finally, McCarthy charged that Parker was named by HUAC as "being affiliated" with the Communist-inspired Citizens Committee to Free Earl Browder. The evidence indicated, McCarthy wrote, that Parker was "at one time a member of the Party and was closely affiliated with a number of Communist-front organizations." Nothing in his subsequent writings "would indicate he has in any way changed his attitude toward the Communist Party." [7]

The rest of the press release attempted to "prove" that the *Capital Times* was the "red mouthpiece" for the Communist Party in Wisconsin and that it "never" attacked Communists. This was accomplished mainly by noting the "similar" views of Evjue's newspaper and the Communist *Daily Worker*. McCarthy concluded:

1. *Has the Communist Party with the cooperation of the Capital Times Corp. won a major victory in Wisconsin?*
2. *Is Cedric Parker, city editor of* The Capital Times, *a Communist?*
3. *Is the Capital Times Corp. the red mouthpiece for the Communist Party in Wisconsin?*
4. *What can be done about this situation?* [8]

At his November 11 speaking engagement before three hundred Madison Shriners and their Knights of Columbus guests, McCarthy repeated his charges and added some new twists. He taunted Evjue on his employment of Parker. "I sent Mr. Evjue a wire yesterday," he informed his audience, "and told him 'I have a question to ask you. Were you lying [on March 14, 1941] when you said Parker was Madison's leading Communist?' If so, tell us when he changed." He urged Evjue to start a libel suit "if a single word of what I say is not the truth." His audience should seriously consider whether they desired to support a newspaper with Communist sympathies. "When you can expose a Communist paper," he said, "no businessman should write a check for advertising in it. And anyone who spends a nickel to buy that paper should remember he is helping the Communist cause." Quoting J. Edgar Hoover, the senator claimed that the primary aim of the Communist Party in the United States was to plant party members in important newspapers and radio stations, especially in college towns. The implication was clear. Evjue owned a newspaper and a radio station; the University of Wisconsin was located in Madison. Adopting the posture of a fearless, principled public servant willing to court political danger by attacking a powerful newspaper, McCarthy revealed a soon-to-be characteristic retort: "When the time comes that I quit exposing things because I might bleed a little in return, I promise you, gentlemen, I will resign from the U.S. Senate." Then he lectured his audience on the immorality of Communism, the danger of Communists in college towns, the need for government officials to expose them, and the possibility of a final showdown between Russia and the Western world.[9]

To this barrage, Parker responded, "I am not a member of the Communist Party." He admitted having been a sponsor of the American League for Peace and Democracy, but declared that he did not consider it subversive since "many good Americans were members." He denied any connection with the Browder Committee; "doubted" that he had sponsored the Farm and Labor Legislation Conference; and disclaimed any acquaintance with Goff and Schnering. If he had attended the Conference on Social Legislation, it was only as a reporter. Evjue also defended the anti-Communist credentials of his newspaper, noting correctly the many occasions on which it exposed or criticized Communist activities. The angry editor termed the senator's charges the familiar defense mechanism of reactionary Republican leaders who always placed the label of Communism on those who opposed them.[10]

But in general, for the first time in his career, McCarthy had maneuvered his major nemesis into a defensive position. According to newspaper accounts, Parker refused to answer a direct question as to whether he had "ever" been a member of the Communist Party. Evjue issued the embarrassing statement that Parker "has repeatedly assured the management of the *Capital Times* that he is not a member of the Communist Party." An intelligent reader might ask: Why, if there was no substance to the senator's charges, would Parker "repeatedly" have to assure the "management"? Initially, Evjue was certain that he had the effective answer to the senator's barrage. In 1948, the last time Parker was elected president of the Madison Newspaper Guild, Evjue confidently asserted, he had signed a non-Communist affidavit and filed it with the National Labor Relations Board. But McCarthy was prepared with a devastating reply. During his Madison speech, taking note of Evjue's rebuttal, he pulled from his briefcase a letter from Claude Calkin, affidavit compliance officer for the National Labor Relations Board. "This office has no record of a non-Communist affidavit having been filed by Cedric Milford Parker," the letter stated.[11]

In an elaborate but awkward attempt to defend his fellow worker, Aldric Revell, a reporter for the *Capital Times,* tried to rationalize Evjue's remarks of 1941. Parker had made a speech at the University of Wisconsin in which he called Evjue a "war monger" and a "red baiter." At that time, he said, Parker was a reporter for the *Capital Times* and an influential leader in the Dane County CIO. Sometimes, Revell embarrassingly noted, "the policies followed by Parker at that time were the policies advocated by the Communists." Evjue called Parker a Communist because Parker's "view that the coming war was imperialistic happened to be the view held by Communists at the time." [12]

When first confronted by McCarthy's allegations, Evjue claimed that he could not recall when or if he had called Parker a Communist. During his Madison speech, McCarthy enlightened him by waving aloft a "photostatic copy" of the March 14, 1941, editorial signed by Evjue. The latter refused to comment.[13] Evjue was obviously embarrassed because he had made the charge. In early 1941 the fiery editor became embroiled in an argument with the CIO leadership at the Gisholt Machine Company in Madison. He demanded that the union members at Gisholt categorically repudiate Communism. The union leaders objected to his "dictation" to them. When the local union passed an innocuous resolution opposing "Communism, Nazism, and Fascism," Evjue blasted the leaders in a public letter to Clifford H. Johnson, secretary of the Steel Workers Organizing Committee of Madison. "I am wondering, Mr. Johnson," Evjue angrily asserted, "why are you so fearful of dictation at the hands of the editor of the *Capital Times* and why you accept so easily dictation at the hands of Mr. Cedric Parker, the Communist leader in Madison. . . . Let's get down to cases. Mr. Parker is a Communist and I defy him to publicly deny that statement." [14]

Perhaps Parker was a Communist Party member before the war, or at least a "fellow traveler." Certainly Evjue thought so in 1941, despite his subsequent rationalization for his editorial.[15] Miles McMillin, a reporter for the Madison newspaper, later recalled of Parker: "I think that he was certainly going along a Communist line. . . . I know that, because I talked to him in those days." [16] It was difficult to trace many of McCarthy's undocumented charges; some of them were exaggerated and others were distorted. Parker did associate with Wisconsin Communists and did join organizations in which Communists played prominent roles. Neither Parker nor Evjue attempted to deny that.[17] The important point, however, is not that Parker was or was not a Communist before World War II, but that in November 1949 McCarthy was successful in making Parker *appear* to have been a Communist. As for McCarthy's attack on the *Capital Times,* this aspect of McCarthy's allegations severely misrepresented and distorted the persistent anti-Communist stance of the Madison newspaper. Articles and exposés by the *Capital Times* were partly responsible for ousting Communists from the state CIO in 1946–47. Indeed, Evjue's consistent and vigorous anti-Communist stance partly explains his discomfiture over McCarthy's charges. Evjue, who had made Parker the target of his Red-baiting in 1941, now ironically became the target of McCarthy's Red-baiting because of his employment of that same person, Cedric Parker.

Neither the *Capital Times* nor any of the state's other journals were willing to challenge the assumptions that underlay McCarthy's attack. Largely, it seemed, they shared the senator's belief in the damaging nature of Communist associations. Indeed McCarthy's charges were potent precisely because they drew upon an emerging anti-Communist consensus. In the absence of a challenge to this consensus, however, Evjue and the *Capital Times* were left with only lame excuses and rationalizations.

Besides embarrassing the staff of the *Capital Times* and throwing them on the defensive, the senator's assault gave him much needed publicity. Atfer his Senate victory in 1946, for example, McCarthy received very little news coverage in the *Wisconsin State Journal* (Madison). His initial attack on Parker, however, resulted in the largest single article printed about him from 1947–49 by the conservative newspaper. In all, it carried about 4,000 words on the incident. The *Capital Times* printed 8,000 words on the controversy. The *Milwaukee Journal,* which had been very critical of McCarthy's Senate record, wrote five lengthy articles and an editorial, totaling about 7,500 words. The senator must have been especially pleased with the coverage the controversy received in the Fox River Valley. The two largest circulation newspapers in the area prominently displayed his entire 6,000-word press release, along with numerous articles on the resulting feud. Smaller newspapers printed at least one or two long reviews of the incident. Even *Time* magazine covered

THE SPECTER

235

the story.[18] Senator McCarthy received as much or more publicity during this controversy than for any other action or policy statement during his first three years in the Senate.

More important, it was favorable publicity for the fledgling senator. Newspapers printed the most dramatic captions: "McCarthy Quotes Record to Show How Capital Times Follows Reds," "McCarthy to Welcome Libel Suit on Red Charge," "Sen. McCarthy Points Red Finger at Capital Times," "McCarthy Dares Editors to Debate Red Charges," "Evjue Called Parker a Red, Senator Recalls Date." [19] The senator was undoubtedly pleased by the contents of the articles. Twice the *Milwaukee Journal* printed Evjue's entire editorial of 1941 in which he labeled Parker a Communist.[20] Most articles described McCarthy's charges as "documented" or "from the record." His accusations usually appeared first and took up the initial three quarters of the article. *Time,* which slanted its story in McCarthy's favor, described his opening salvo as a "blistering letter." It noted that Parker "had faithfully followed the Communist line" and that although Evjue called him a Communist in 1941, he promoted him to city editor seven years later.[21] While newspaper accounts made McCarthy appear as the defender of "Christian democracy," the rebuttals of Parker and Evjue seemed vague and evasive.

State journalists recognized the publicity value of McCarthy's attack and its connection with his 1952 reelection bid. McCarthy "has decided to start his campaign early," one columnist wrote, "judging by the newspaper headlines he's trying to create." Another described his offensive as the "opening shot of his campaign for reelection in 1952." Evjue called the charges "the first note to be sounded in his campaign for reelection. . . ." Another anti-McCarthy editor thought that his aim was to get "a lot of publicity . . . in preparation for his 1952 campaign. And here we are suckers enough to give it to him." Aldric Revell urged Evjue not to sue his antagonist because this

McCarthy and McCarthyism

would only give him more publicity. "The Republican newspapers in Wisconsin," he noted prophetically on November 15, 1949, "would love to conduct McCarthy's [1952] campaign for him on the Communist issue and forget all about his voting record." [22]

McCarthy actually began his anti-Communist crusade on November 9, 1949, when he distributed his document on Parker and the *Capital Times*. Two days later, when he repeated and extended his allegations before the Madison Shrine Club, the title of his speech was "Communism as a Threat to World Peace." At that time he told reporters his tour of the state was a "personal campaign against Communism." [23] Throughout November and December he kept the controversy alive and received more publicity as he constantly repeated his charges, challenged Evjue and Parker to start a libel action, and urged Evjue to debate him. [24]

Thus by the late autumn of 1949 McCarthy had discovered the political value of Red-baiting. More importantly, he now extended his anti-Communist attacks to new and more dramatic targets. At a Young Republican gathering in Kenosha on November 15, his major theme was Communist infiltration of the State Department. He specifically attacked John Stewart Service and castigated the State Department, which he charged had a "red tint" and was "honeycombed and run by Communists." [25] On December 3, at a gathering of realtors in Philadelphia, Pennsylvania, McCarthy devoted half of his speech to blaming the "bumbling foreign policy" of the State Department for the precarious position of the country in the cold war. [26] On December 5 he again assailed the State Department during an address to the Marquette University chapter of the Alpha Kappa Psi. "The picture of the current 'war' between the Communist atheistic world and the Christian nations is becoming more and more dangerous," he said, "not every month or year but every minute. We are losing at a tremendous pace." But this was not surprising, "when we look [at] the personnel of the State Department." [27]

On the Senate floor on January 5, 1950—two days before he allegedly "discovered" the Communist issue at the Washington dinner—McCarthy again attacked Service. Why was he "still in charge of personnel and placement in the State Department," he demanded, after he was picked up by the FBI for espionage and was "accused of having had a sizable number of secret documents in his possession which he was handing over to the Communists?" [28] On January 21, he indicted Secretary of State Dean Acheson for supporting Alger Hiss and alleged:

> *There are lots of borers from within—left behind in the State Department, and they are under Acheson's nose every day.* [sic]
> *It is these men who are largely responsible for Acheson's defeatist policy in the Far East.*
> *It is time Acheson either clean the Communists out of the State Department or resign and let President Truman appoint someone who will.* [29]

Four days later he reiterated his remarks on Acheson in a brief statement to the Senate. [30]

Scholars have overlooked the Cedric Parker incident as the origin and stimulant to McCarthy's campaign against Communism. [31] His offensive was a sharp reversal from his previous neglect of the issue. Perhaps the substantial evidence he discovered on Parker convinced him of the real danger of Communists. More likely, the publicity and success he amassed from the incident made him aware of the political potential in the issue. In any case, Communism was the major theme of his speeches for three months before his historic Wheeling address. After his successful attack on Parker and the *Capital Times,* it was no wonder—if Cohn's account is correct—that McCarthy was so receptive to the group with the intelligence report on subversion in the country. And surely he needed no suggestion from Father Walsh to realize the political value of the Communist issue.

By early 1950, then, McCarthy had hitched his career to the rising issue of anti-Communism. The senator could have hardly foreseen the consequences of this commitment, though they were surely foreshadowed by the growing intensity of public concern over spies and subversives. In part this growing concern was the product of the cold war and of the militantly anti-Communist rhetoric that the Truman Administration used to justify its foreign policies. It was also the result of increasingly bitter attacks on the Truman Administration by Republican partisans who believed that they had discovered, in the Communist issue, a means of unseating the Democrats. The explosion of a Soviet nuclear bomb, the fall of China, and the conviction of Alger Hiss all served, therefore, to catalyze popular fears that had already been excited by partisan appeals from both Democrats and Republicans.

McCarthy, fresh from his "triumph" in Wisconsin, intersected this growing national concern on February 9, 1950, in Wheeling, West Virginia. His speech, a logical if extreme outgrowth of his mounting interest in anti-Communist politics, touched a popular nerve with its seeming revelations about Communist infiltration in the State Department. The subsequent reaction made the senator a national figure and marked the beginning of his turbulent five years at the center of American politics.

THE POLITICS OF CULTURE:

Hollywood and

the Cold War

BY
LES K.
ADLER

Between 1947 and 1954, the movie industry in Hollywood engaged in its own miniature cold war. In general, the patterns of anti-Communist activity in the movie capital paralleled those developing throughout American society. Yet because it existed on a highly visible pedestal, with the potential for a powerful impact on the public mind, Hollywood was in a unique position of both vulnerability and power. Financially linked with banking and industrial interests on the production side, the movie colony also had its share of independent-minded artists, writers, and directors whose political and social ideas and activities ranged the full spectrum of American experience. Both external and internal pressures were brought to bear before the industry gave way to the forces of anti-Communism, silenced and exiled its dissenting voices, and lent itself to the creation of unofficial propaganda for the national crusade. Reaching its peak in the years of Senator Joseph McCarthy's ascendancy in Washington, Hollywood's cold war is a fascinating study in both politics and perception.

Behind the banner of a vaguely defined "Americanism," great numbers of political and business leaders, editorial writers, such organized groups as the American Legion and the United States Chamber of Commerce, as well as unorganized individuals, had long rallied against the real and imaginary incursions into the national life of Catholics, Masons, Mormons, immigrants, and most recently Communists.[1] More by accident than design, initially, Senator Joe McCarthy tapped this rich vein of "countersubversive" thought and feeling in America by casting Communism as a negative point of reference for Americans in the postwar world. As Michael Paul Rogin has written, the symbolic weapon he employed was simply that of the charge of "Communism," [2] and if his meteoric rise to prominence is any indication of the issue's effectiveness, it can hardly be doubted that his appeal struck a receptive chord in the American public. Yet the

THE SPECTER

phenomenon of McCarthyism, as Rogin also testifies, existed on other than symbolic levels, levels of politics and power where the actions or inactions of a few greatly influenced the course of events.[3]

It is in this intersection of unconscious symbolism and conscious political activity that Hollywood's cold war occurred. Both in the politics of Hollywood and in the celluloid record of the industry's efforts, it is possible to trace the processes by which an independent industry organized itself to produce unofficial cold-war propaganda, and the nature of the propaganda itself, the graphic images that the American screen made visible for the public. Just as it would be misleading to view McCarthyism outside of the framework of the entire thrust of postwar American anti-Communism, it would be misleading to view American anti-Communism in a historical vacuum. Barraged by more than a half century of anti-radical attacks in politics and in the media, the public's knowledge and perception of Communism and Communists was highly colored, distorted, and selective.[4] Hollywood's particular contribution after 1947 was to capture and interpret in a contemporary setting the negative images created by decades of anti-radical, anti-Communist agitation and feeling.

Like many of his countrymen in early 1947, the relatively unknown, newly elected senator from Wisconsin was aware of the currents of suspicion in the air and was attuned to the apocalyptic image of a world poised between the forces of good and evil. Invited to participate in a radio debate on the popular "Town Meeting of the Air" program in early April of that year, McCarthy argued aggressively and emotionally in favor of outlawing the Communist Party in the United States. Comparing the party to a "huge iceberg in a shipping lane" with the most dangerous part "underwater and invisible," he compressed Communism to the "concept that human life is valueless, that there are no human rights, and that there is no human soul" and concluded that it was therefore "vicious," "dangerous" and "anti-American" and did not deserve the dignity of the ballot.[5]

It is impossible to know how many listeners the young senator convinced, but it is evident that his speech had much less impact than did his unrecorded and distorted statements in Wheeling, West Virginia, scarcely three years later at the outset of his crusade. His words, nevertheless, were reflective of widely shared attitudes, which were prompting new and more stringent federal internal security regulations, state and local laws designed to remove subversives from the public payroll, and test oaths to ferret out those citizens disloyal to the society. Surfacing in labor unions, lodges, church circles, business groups, and very noticeably by 1948 in politics, and given public hearings in all the communications media, the twin fears of subversion from within and aggression from abroad were gradually pervading American life.

Deeply rooted in prewar attitudes, American distrust, dislike, and fear of the Soviet Union and its ideology had never entirely vanished during the wartime alliance with Russia. Even before the war's end, a number of highly placed Americans suggested that Russia would be the successor to Nazi Germany in Europe.[6] To many Americans, the ideological distinctions between Fascism and Communism were less significant than what appeared to be the commitment of both types of regimes to a common "totalitarianism." What this meant to a growing number of Americans was that the "Red Fascists" would follow the path of their Nazi predecessors and seek to take over Europe, Asia, and ultimately the rest of the world by military conquest.[7]

Tied to this conception of a militarily aggressive Soviet state was the recently revived and longer standing American fear of Communism as an internal subversive threat. In the case of domestic Communism, Americans were in the process of es-

tablishing an extensive image that incorporated the usual prewar fears of Communists in unions, in the New Deal, in civil
rights activity with the seemingly documented testimony of ex-
Communists such as Louis Budenz, Elizabeth Bentley, and
Whittaker Chambers that there was a vast underworld of cen-
tralized subversion and espionage that threatened every institution and individual in the Republic. The enemy was already
within the gates and close to the citadel.

It was in this context that Hollywood began to feel external
and internal pressure. Attacks against the industry's size, economic power, and political opinions had been plentiful in previous decades. In the renewed uncertainty of postwar America,
Hollywood again came under attack, particularly by those
already sensitized to the search for a culprit behind the changes
and problems affecting the nation. The movie industry was off-
balance at the time, because of the difficulties of a prolonged
and bitter labor dispute involving the major studios and featur-
ing inter-union charges of Communist influence and infiltration.[8]

The charges were picked up by California State Senator Jack
B. Tenney, chairman from 1941–49 of the Senate's Fact-Find-
ing Committee on Un-American Activities, who charged in a
speech to the State Legislature that the labor disturbances in
Hollywood were Communist-inspired.[9] The industry representative, Eric Johnston, former president of the American Chamber
of Commerce, and then president of the Motion Picture Association, added his voice to the anti-Communist clamor. On
March 5, 1947, Johnston charged that all Communists were
"foreign agents" and asked the U.S. Congress to prevent them
from holding positions of leadership in labor unions.[10] Johnston
repeated his charges before the House Committee on Un-American Activities (HUAC) on March 27, 1947, and then ironically,
in light of the subsequent devastating HUAC investigation of the
industry he represented, he called for the "pitiless spotlight of

The politics of culture

publicity" on Communists.[11] The committee took up his suggestion with a literal fervor, which Johnston clearly had not anticipated.

Scarcely two months later, on May 9, Representative J. Parnell Thomas and his investigators arrived in Hollywood complete with spotlight.[12] Allegations of Communist influence in the industry itself and of Communist-inspired governmental wartime pressure on the industry immediately became national headlines. Film actor Adolphe Menjou, a board member of the militantly anti-Communist Motion Picture Alliance for the Preservation of American Ideals, which had been formed in 1944, informed the committee that Hollywood was one of the main centers of Communist activity in America and that a number of Hollywood films had been influenced by Reds in the industry.[13] Screenwriter Rupert Hughes, who had helped found the Alliance, admitted that no open Communist propaganda was on the screen. But, he told the committee, "where you see a little drop of cyanide in the picture, a small grain of arsenic, something that makes every senator, every businessman, every employer a crook and which destroys our beliefs in American free enterpirse and free institutions, that is Communistic." [14]

Within the film industry there was resistance to the investigation and to the charges that were being made. Ronald Reagan, though a friendly witness before HUAC, cautioned the committee against sacrificing democratic principles in search for Communists and argued from his experience in the Screen Actors Guild that "the best thing to do in opposing these people [Communists] is to make democracy work." Reagan went on to add his hope "that we are never prompted by fear or resentment of Communism into compromising any of our democratic principles in order to fight them." [15] Others went further, often refusing to testify before the committee at all. In testimony originally given before the Tenney committee the previous October but repeated before HUAC, Emmett Lavery, president of the

Screenwriters Guild, presented the often used argument that though some writers may have had Communist sympathies, it hardly mattered since "I have not yet in my ten years' experience in Hollywood found a man who can finance what you would call a Communist picture through Louis B. Mayer or Mr. Sam Katz at Metro. They are anything but Communistic gentlemen." Lavery bluntly told the congressional investigators that the vast majority of writers in his guild were members of the "liberal center" and that he was not afraid of Communist activity in the organization.[16]

Yet this argument failed to satisfy either the Tenney committee or HUAC. The very existence of what Senator Tenney considered "fifth columnists"—the term itself a throwback to the pre-World War II years of Fascist aggression—and of those like Lavery who were prepared to tolerate them in unions and in the studios seemed incomprehensible to the legislators. In assuming that the presence of Communists in various organizations infected the entire membership and that the presence of a Communist screenwriter in a studio meant that the studio's films would somehow carry subversive messages, such legislators and their allies in the film industry were popularizing the widely held stereotype of the Communist as a subtle manipulator capable of running circles around naïve Americans.[17] When Matthew Woll of the rival American Federation of Labor charged members of the Screen Actors Guild with "playing at revolution . . . to justify the possession of a swimming pool" and with being "light-minded . . . window-dressers for the most tyrannical political system in the world," he too was denying the validity of their values and beliefs and validating popular stereotypes by painting them as mindless dupes.[18]

Opposition to the entire investigation was organized in the Committee for the First Amendment, founded by producers William Wyler and John Huston and screenwriter Philip Dunne and embraced by many Hollywood figures including Robert

Ardrey, Larry Adler, Humphrey Bogart, Sterling Hayden, Danny Kaye, Gregory Peck, and Billy Wilder.[19] Most hostile to the investigation, however, were the famous Hollywood Ten, witnesses who refused to testify at all before HUAC. The film industry as a whole, however, despite a brief fling at resisting the investigation, quickly assumed that public opinion would not support such a stand. Though Eric Johnston had reached the point of politely chiding the committee for smearing Hollywood, on November 26, 1947, he announced a new industry-wide hiring policy which pledged:

> *We will forthwith discharge or suspend without compensation those in our employ and we will not re-employ any of the ten until such time as he is acquitted or has purged himself of contempt and declares under oath that he is not a Communist . . .*

> *We will not knowingly employ a Communist or a member of any party or group which advocates the overthrow of the Government by force or by any illegal or unconstitutional methods . . .*[20]

Blacklisting was the industry's answer to the charges aired by HUAC, and despite attacks on the legality and morality of the system, it became and remained a fact of life in Hollywood.[21] The industry's sudden capitulation surprised a great many persons, including, according to one source, J. Parnell Thomas himself.[22]

The national outcry for positive action against both domestic and foreign Communists, however, left no room for an objective analysis of just what influence, if any, Communists had had in Hollywood, and the studios were not slow to catch the hint. In October, 1947, Adolphe Menjou publicly urged the industry to produce anti-Communist films, erroneously predicting that

they would be an enormous public success.[23] Studio owner
Louis B. Mayer told HUAC the following month that M-G-M
was already in the process of preparing such a film,[24] and it
was reported in addition that the studio was hastening a re-
issue of its prewar anti-Communist hit *Ninotchka.*[25]

Though the changing composition of Hollywood films after
1947 cannot be attributed entirely to the impact of HUAC, a
basic change did occur, which oriented the industry further away
from dealing with serious social problems and which seems
clearly related to the investigations. The 1945–47 period had
seen an increase in the film treatment of such themes, and as
calculated in one study, approximately 28 percent of the films
produced in 1947 were of a serious social bent. From 1947–49,
however, the trend was reversed, with only approximately 18
percent of the films in 1949 qualifying. An even sharper break
occurred from 1950–52 with an upsurge in war films, pure
entertainment films, escapist films, and a large number of anti-
Communist films. In 1950 only 11 percent dealt with social
questions, and by 1953 this figure was further reduced to 9 percent.[26] It is possible that the public was tired of controversial
social themes in its motion pictures and that lighter films fit
the popular mood of escape. It is certainly true that audiences
did not flock to most of the anti-Communist productions, and
that as Dorothy B. Jones has pointed out, "studios frankly did
not expect these films to make money, but regarded them as
being necessary for public relations." [27]

It is in the changing film content itself that the most significant side of Hollywood's anti-Communist efforts can be examined. Hollywood's conception of Communists and Communism developed gradually in the prewar period, and it was not
until the late 1930's that a clear perspective emerged. Most
representative, as well as being one of the last prewar films
dealing with the subject, M-G-M's *Ninotchka,* produced in
1939, is notable here chiefly because of its bygone vision of

The politics of culture

Soviet agents, a view touched with humor rather than fear and a view reflecting an American society relatively certain of its own viability.

The story, briefly, is of several Bolshevik agents sent to Paris to sell confiscated royal jewels. The three original agents are portrayed as simple men, unused to the ways of the West, but all sharing artificially repressed desires to enjoy the fruits of the "decadent" society they are visiting. These are bumbling agents, totally harmless, whose ideology is little more than verbal and who are rapidly and easily drawn into enjoyment of material goods forbidden them in their native land. When their superiors learn of their high-living and disregard for orders, a fourth agent, Comrade Ninotchka (Greta Garbo) is sent to take charge of the negotiations. The perfect caricature of Soviet young woman-hood, as perceived in the West, Ninotchka is plain in dress and feature, mannish in behavior, icy cold in temperament, and in-terested only in preserving and furthering the revolution. She is portrayed as a denial of every element of Western femininity, and initially for her, even love is stripped of its romantic sentimentality and made purely functional.

Yet the ways of bourgeois world are not to be denied, and Ninotchka herself begins to lose her revolutionary ardor once she is struck by Cupid's arrow. The genuine emotion of love is the real agent behind her change of heart, and once she has broken with her revolutionary ideals, not only her dress, de-meanor, and outlook change for the better, but her features as well. One basic assumption present in the film is that Soviet life is somehow an "unnatural" denial of man's native instincts; that the desires of the Russian agents for fine wines and clothes in the Western tradition are more natural than the Soviet-made virtues of abstinence and sharing. A second assumption is that given a chance to choose between Communist and Western ways, the Communist will throw over his revolutionary heritage in a moment. Once this occurs, a transformation takes place that for the first time allows the individual to become a full human being, capable of emotions and the enjoyment of life.

Significantly, however, in this prewar film produced prior to the Nazi-Soviet Pact and the Russo-Finnish War, the Soviet state was not portrayed as a malignant force in the world, nor was Communist ideology seen as a sinister threat to the West. Hollywood was free enough for the moment from the anti-Communist dynamic to produce a subtle rather than an overt anti-Soviet film, and Americans could perceive Russia, for a time, with enmity rather than fear. The untested Soviet military projected none of the invincibility that the undefeated Nazi forces did and that the Red Army would project only a few years later. Although scenes portraying life inside Russia employed the familiar images of cramped apartments housing five or six families, each suspicious of the other and careful not to reveal any private thought or feeling for fear of being informed on, there was still room for humor and warmth even in Russia, and life went on.

Between 1948 and 1954, Hollywood film makers produced more than forty anti-Communist films.[28] Roughly divisible into three categories—spy thrillers, films dealing with the infiltration and development of the Communist Party inside the United States, and those dramatizing world-wide events in the cold war—the films were generally quickly made and, as will become evident, produced according to certain formulas. Contrasting sharply with the pro-Russian wartime films designed to strengthen the Allies and with *Ninotchka*'s tolerant and humorous view of the Soviets, the postwar films conveyed a stereotyped view of the enemy that left no room for ambiguous feelings. Evil was clearly external in origin and stemmed from one readily identifiable source. Demanding that the portrayal of non-Communist Americans fit as stereotyped a pattern of purity as Communists in America or Russia fit a pattern of evil, Hollywood's "Reds" tended to become in one critic's phrase "projections

The politics of culture

rather than portraits," while according to another, Americans become "models" rather than people.[29]

Early in 1948, it was rumored in Hollywood that Twentieth-Century Fox Studios was preparing for release an anti-Communist film dealing with the Igor Gouzenko Canadian spy case. The film, *The Iron Curtain,* was to be Hollywood's first major venture into the realm of anti-Communist propaganda, and predictably, the news prompted nationwide interest. In mid-January, the chairman of the National Council of American-Soviet Friendship, the Reverend William Howard Melish, addressed a public letter to Eric Johnston protesting the "war propaganda" contained in the film.[30] Shortly afterward, the New York State chapter of the Progressive Citizens of America also protested the film's release. Clashes between rival picketing groups marred the film's New York opening in early May, and police were required on subsequent nights to guard the actions of both the New York Committee Against War Propaganda, who protested the showing, and the Catholic War Veterans, who were in favor of its showing.[31]

The movie itself, based loosely on the report of the Canadian Royal Commission in 1946, starred as Gouzenko and his wife, crew-cut Dana Andrews and glamorous actress Gene Tierney. This supposedly typical Slavic couple was surrounded by a collection of hard, cold, boorish, secretive, unsentimental marionettes, described by one critic as familiar "granite-faced, super-gangster types who, curiously, speak with heavy accents, while Mr. Andrews does not." [32] "The Russian villains," the critic added in a later review, "are the Nazi villains of years back." Not coincidentally the screenplay was written by Milton Krims who had helped write the prewar thriller *Confessions of a Nazi Spy.*[33] The film reviewer of the liberal Catholic journal *Commonweal* attacked the makers of the film by charging that in portraying the Russians "as so inhuman . . . these characters cease to be people and are merely symbols of a way of life we abhor." [34] This, of course, was the function of the film.

Familiar immoral Communist tricks are employed to test the loyalty of the young Red Army soldier, Gouzenko, when he arrives in Canada to work as a code clerk in the Russian embassy. The secretary of one of the high officials on the embassy staff invites him out and attempts to seduce him, but with firm resolve and righteous anger he rejects the offer. From the beginning of the film, then, a contrast is established between Gouzenko and the other Russians. His morality documented, the film goes on to contrast the sweet innocence of his young wife with the hard-bitten, ideological immorality of such figures as the secretary and various Russians in the embassy. Because her feelings are somehow not deadened by Communist teachings and reasoning, Gouzenko's wife becomes a major influence in drawing him away from doing his duty as a Russian soldier. Like a great many Hollywood portrayals of Communists in Western settings, the free life of the West allows submerged natural feelings to surface and to set up an internal conflict between feeling and logic within the Communist. Inevitably, as in the case of *Ninotchka,* logic, reason, ideology, and the "artificial" structures of twentieth-century thought all yield before the sweep of human emotion. Western "natural"openness and feeling are sharply contrasted with Communist repression and denial of all emotion except devotion to the cause.

Stripped of all the complexities that might emphasize the ambiguities of reality, scientists become naïve dupes, liberals allow themselves to be used, Communists plot endlessly, and in the words of one critic of *The Iron Curtain,* the only good Russian is one who deserts Communism and betrays his country.[35] In thus giving dramatic life to the flat, unreal characters warned against by the FBI, the Chamber of Commerce, HUAC, a host of ex-Communist informers, and politicians anxious to find an issue, films made their particular contribution to the animation of the Red Image. Unlike *Ninotchka,* in which the Soviets are exasperatingly human and often bumbling, *The Iron Curtain*'s treatment of Communists is entirely without humor or satire. "An out-and-out anti-Soviet picture in which 'entertainment' seems a secondary aim," wrote *New York Times* film critic Bosley Crowther, who attacked the film for doing nothing to clarify the issues of the day and only teaching the lesson "hate the Red." [36]

Darryl F. Zanuck of Twentieth-Century Fox bluntly admitted as much in his public answer to Crowther's review of the film. "The picture is calculated to, and does," he argued, "arouse the public to vigilance against a menace." In support of his position, he cited editorials from across the nation, which he claimed praised the film for doing just that.[37] It was an admission of a policy that would govern Hollywood for years to come; not only would the industry produce uncompromising propaganda, but it would actively encourage an oversimplified, stereotyped portrayal of reality without remorse or second thoughts. An unspoken implication, as well, was that films critical of America or Americans would be in disfavor, and that in films dealing with Communism, Americans could not be portrayed critically or honestly.

Reviewing *The Iron Curtain* for the *New Republic,* Robert Hatch considered himself "old-fashioned enough to want my wars declared for me by the President, and not by a motion picture company—not even one blessed by the Thomas committee." [38] *Life*'s reviewer, on the other hand, felt that "the fanaticism, suspicion, and amorality which characterize the Communist mind become more graphic and hideous in this film than in a hundred editorials." [39] Both reviewers, however, recognized that the film was an effective "first shot" in Hollywood's cold war, and that it lived up to its advance billing. If it seemed to liberal critics "excessively sensational and dangerous to the disease of our times to dramatize the myrmidons of Russia as so many sinister fiends," [40] it was *Life*'s appraisal that the public was likely to follow by 1948. The film merely gave visual life to an image already stirring in the imaginations of many.

Perhaps the best example of those films dealing with domestic Communism was Paramount's 1952 production *My Son John*. Unusually well produced and acted, *My Son John* contains the most complete presentation of Hollywood's perception of the nature of Communism, as well as one of its narrowest perceptions and presentations of Americanism. The studio went to great pains on the film, luring Helen Hayes out of retirement to star as the mother, Mrs. Jefferson, and putting together a cast of Dean Jagger, Robert Walker, and Van Heflin as the father, son, and friendly FBI agent, respectively. It was not wholly accidental that *My Son John* appeared at the moment of Senator Joseph McCarthy's greatest power in Washington, for the film industry had developed an extraordinary sensitivity to the currents of congressional anti-Communist feeling after 1947, and was well aware of the national sentiments played upon by the Wisconsin senator. This film, perhaps more than any other, expresses the spirit of McCarthyism and juxtaposes the frozen American perception of both Communism and Americanism while dramatizing in the most explicit manner the conflicts felt by a nation fearful not merely of the future but of itself.

In the film, a small-town, devout Irish-Catholic family, headed by a schoolteacher and rabid American Legionnaire father, is portrayed just at the moment that two big, blond football-playing sons are going off to war in the Pacific. The third son, John, dark rather than blond, an intellectual rather than an athelete, and a Washington government employee with a deferment rather than a soldier, has gone in another direction—to college, atheism, big-city life, and as it is broadly hinted, to Communism. With no proof other than their son's highbrow acquaintances and activities, the parents' "instincts" and suspi-

256

cions are aroused by his behavior. To allay his mother's fears along these lines, John swears on her sacred Bible that he "is not now nor has he ever been a member of the Communist Party." But, of course, as the audience is reminded, nothing is sacred to "Commies" once they become puppets of their mistaken ideals, and John continues lying until he is brutally machine-gunned to death, gangland style, on the steps of the Lincoln Memorial by his unforgiving comrades who have learned of his repentant decision to go to the FBI to confess his sins.[41]

John's skeptical views of religion are sharply contrasted to his family's devout churchgoing, and this incriminating behavior along with his residence in Washington, D.C., clearly defines the symbolic conflict. It is the modern, secular, materialistic, urbanized world versus America's source of strength in the home, church, and small-town Legion post. Unlike the Communists of prewar films such as *Ninotchka,* John and his comrades are not merely garden-variety Westerners momentarily drawn down a false path; they are vicious, alien puppets in the service of foreign masters, men who have truly sold their souls and would as easily sell their country. To make John's motives meaningful to the audience, he is portrayed as having initially been a well-meaning "dupe," manipulated by sinister figures somehow able to play with his good intentions and bend him to their will. Whereas the emotions and feelings of characters in the earlier *Ninotchka* are only repressed, those of the characters in *My Son John* are deadened. Their elementary moral knowledge of right and wrong has been replaced by an inhuman, willful, and blind subservience to the dictates of the human masters who have subverted them.

In essence, John, like the evil Russians in *The Iron Curtain,* appears as an "unnatural" creature who has lost control of his own destiny, and Americans, whose greatest fear seems to be a loss of what they conceive of as their individuality, could not but perceive such a being as an abomination. In John's case, the additional imputation is that his intellectual nature rendered him susceptible to control, and that his choice of professors and books instead of football and faith had led him astray. The turmoil of a nation undergoing profound social change is evident in the film's built-in conflicting images, and it is not surprising that the film powerfully reinforced the definition of morality and Americanism symbolized by John's Legionnaire father and verbalized on the national level by Senator Joseph McCarthy. In their extreme caricature, the film's enemy images were those at which McCarthy and his followers had been directing their forays for years.

Only rarely did Hollywood extend itself on one of its anti-Communist projects as it did for *My Son John*. Producers and studios, for the most part, seemingly aspired only for the Grade B product, and after the initial flurry of controversy over the first films of the genre, public and critical response was minimal. In part this can be explained by the great upsurge in interest in escapist films and by the loss of audience to television, but to a great extent it was the result of the nature and quality of the anti-Communist films themselves. Heavy, pedantic, and generally depressing, despite (or perhaps because of) their inevitable victory of the FBI over Red agents, they lacked the subtlety, spirit, and compelling power of effective propaganda. Humor was almost nonexistent; there was no glamour on either side, no clear-cut decisive action, and, indeed, no real message other than "hate the enemy." In creating such an inhuman caricature of the "enemy," film makers also created a shallow, unreal, and uninteresting caricature of American life.

Unlike wartime films dealing with the Soviet Union and the Russian people, postwar films emphasized the ideology of Communism rather than Russia, concentrating particularly on aspects of worldwide Communist intrigue and subversion. Those actors portraying Russians no longer represented the good Russian

The politics of culture

folk, but the Communist Party elite—the deadliest of secret agents—and the resulting impression left on the screen was that all Communists, whether domestic or foreign, were espionage agents or their dupes. Communist activities were stereotyped as a constant round of intrigue, brutality, and suffocating discipline. American Communists often were portrayed as regretting having entered the Party, but their attempts to escape generally ended either in suicide or murder.[42]

Similarly, Communists were subtly identified with the most negative reference groups available to Americans: the violence-ridden underworld of gangsterism and organized crime, and the Nazis against whom the nation had directed a vast war effort. Film critic Pauline Kael pointed out this later strain in anti-Communist films as she wrote, "The bit players who once had steady employment as S.S. guards are right at home in their new Soviet milieu; the familiar psychopathic faces provide a kind of reassurance that the new world situation is not so different from the old one." [43] Siegfried Kracauer described the 1945–48 turn-about in American films dealing with Russia in like terms. "Gone are the brave Russian women fighters, the happy villagers, and the democratic allures of the rulers," he wrote. "In their places somber bureaucrats, counterparts of the Nazis, spread an atmosphere of oppression." [44]

Ms. Kael has compared such anti-Communist films with medieval morality plays, both in substance and function, and indeed, the melodramatic Hollywood portrayal of a struggle between the forces of good and evil bears a strong resemblance to the earlier drama.[45] Not on the screen alone, however, was such an oversimplified, stereotyped moral struggle portrayed. At all levels of society and government, respected figures brought their own familiar and remarkably similar interpretations to bear on the subject at hand. Speaking at Gonzaga University in 1950, President Truman characterized the Soviet Union as a "modern tyranny led by a small group who have abandoned their faith in God." [46] The leading Republican foreign policy spokesman, John Foster Dulles, referring to Russian imperialism in a 1951 speech, commented that "evil is never irresistible, only truth and righteousness; and these qualities are the peculiar possession of minds and spirits that are free." [47] Asserting that "the Supreme Architect will give us the strength, wisdom, and guidance to triumph against the onrush of Red Fascism and Atheistic Communism," FBI Director J. Edgar Hoover exhorted the public in 1950 against the "force of traitorous Communists, constantly gnawing away like termites at the very foundations of American society. . . ." [48]

By these standards, Senator Joe McCarthy was fully justified when he asserted in the opening speech of his anti-Communist campaign, "The great difference between our Western Christian world and the atheistic Communist world is not political . . . it is moral." [49] The senator's instincts, like those of John's parents in the film, and those of the Americans for whom he spoke, led him to identify the source of all evil with the Communist image projected throughout the culture. It was this image that Hollywood, primarily out of fear, but to some extent also out of shared conviction, captured vividly on the screen. A moderate position on Communism was virtually impossible to maintain in the polarized, highly charged atmosphere of McCarthy's America, and the movie industry, sensing its own vulnerability and responding to organized pressure, moved quickly to rid itself of the onus of radicalism. It then set out to prove its loyalty by turning out a series of crude, propagandistic films that closely adhered to well-defined formulas of ideological purity. Hollywood's main contribution to the new war effort thus was to give dramatic, visual life to the fear-ridden currents and undercurrents of the age, thereby magnifying the fear and strengthening the hands of McCarthy and his followers.

Not coincidentally, the overt propaganda faded from the screen just as the Wisconsin senator faded from the national political stage. Blacklisting lingered on in Hollywood, but it too waned with the cold-war thaw in the late 1950's and early 1960's. Film does not vanish so quickly, however, and late-night television viewers still are able to enjoy a replay of some of Hollywood's cold-war classics in the privacy of their own homes. To those aware of the impact of McCarthyism on American life, it is an experience not easily forgotten.

THE SPECTER

THE POLITICS OF SCHOLARSHIP:

Liberals, Anti-Communism,

and McCarthyism

BY ATHAN THEOHARIS

During the 1950's American liberals, influenced both by their identification with the New Deal presidency and their acceptance of the anti-Communist politics of the cold war years, sought to explain McCarthyism in terms of a mass-based, essentially nonpartisan and nonconservative threat to American institutions. According to such scholars as Daniel Bell, Seymour Martin Lipset, Richard Hofstadter, and the other contributors to *The New American Right,* McCarthyism was an irrational popular response to the rise of the modern secular state. Like Populism, McCarthyism was not only a dangerous popular movement, they argued; it was also rooted in resentments produced by status anxiety. This analysis of the McCarthy phenomenon reinforced the belief of these scholars in the irrationality of mass-based protest and encouraged them to place their confidence in interest-group politics, in public and private bureaucracies, and in the educated elite that governed both. In these institutions, they hoped to find a bulwark against the dangers of popular passion.[1]

Articulating these concerns, Hofstadter lamented the lack in the "populistic culture" of the United States of a "responsible elite with political and moral autonomy." Similarly, Lipset attributed McCarthyism to "the lack of an integrated cultural and political control structure—of a distinct aristocratic elite to play an integrative and leadership function." Peter Viereck, another contributor to *The New American Right,* charged that "The McCarthyites threaten liberty precisely because they are so egalitarian, ruling foreign policy by mass telegrams to the Executive Branch and by radio speeches and Gallup Poll." Finally, Talcott Parsons argued that a political elite composed "of 'politicians' whose specialty consist in the management of public opinion, and of 'administrators' in both civil and military

* The author expresses his appreciation to John Berens, Barton Bernstein, Robert Griffith, Michael Rogin, and Melvin Small for their editorial assistance and to Marquette University, particularly to Eleanor Woodward Sacks for typing assistance.

THE SPECTER

services, must be greatly strengthened. It is here," he concluded, "that the practical consequences of McCarthyism run
most directly counter to the realistic needs of the time." [2]

This interpretation has been subjected to a brilliantly persua-
sive critique by Michael Paul Rogin who argues, in *The Intellectuals and McCarthy: The Radical Specter,* that there was no
continuity between Populism and McCarthyism and that, even
more important, McCarthyism was not a mass movement of the
"radical" right, but rather the product of routine conservative
politics. McCarthyism did not split apart existing coalitions or
create a new mass base; it was created by the actions and inactions of conservative and liberal elites—precisely those groups to
whom the liberal pluralists would turn to in their quest for an
orderly society.[3]

This analysis, however insightful its critique of the deficien-
cies of pluralistic theory, fails to discuss certain basic assumptions of these liberal scholars, especially their identification of
presidential leadership with the national interest and their uncritical acceptance of the containment/loyalty-security policies
of the Truman Administration. This essay intends to extend
Rogin's analysis and specifically to suggest that McCarthyism
can best be understood as the product of the anti-Communist
politics of the early cold-war years.

I

For American liberals, the experiences of the 1950's shaped
their conception of the American past and contributed to the
popularity of consensus historiography. Writing during these
years, liberal scholars came to celebrate the American past and
to extol the beneficence of American political and economic
institutions.[4] Historians and other social scientists were especially supportive of activist presidential leadership. Strongly
influenced by their identification with the New Deal presidency
of Franklin Roosevelt and convinced by the experiences of

The politics of scholarship

World War II and the early cold war that public opinion was a potentially dangerous impediment to the conduct of American diplomacy, many liberal scholars sought to reinterpret democratic principles to justify the need for dynamic, even manipulative, executive leadership. To them, the President was the "central instrument of democracy," the national teacher, the American public's "one authentic trumpet." [5] Because the President alone represented all the people, and because he alone had command of the expertise necessary to make policy, he was therefore "the common reference point for social effort." Reformers were admonished to seek change through a vigorous executive rather than through Congress or through mass public pressure. Foreign policy, these scholars continued, was almost exclusively the preserve of the President. One noted authority, indeed, approvingly quoted Harry Truman's bluntly revealing remark to the Jewish War Veterans: "I make American foreign policy." [6]

This exalted view of the presidency was given wide currency during the 1950's by Clinton Rossiter in *The American Presidency*. Written, as Rossiter himself noted, out of a "feeling of veneration, if not exactly reverence, for the authority and dignity of the presidency," *The American Presidency* extolled the strong-minded executive who bent Congress and the public to his will and who left as his legacy a strengthened executive office. The greatness of presidents, according to this calculus, lay in their success in leading a passive, if not recalcitrant, public into accepting new responsibilities.[7]

Not only did Rossiter and other liberal scholars commend activist presidents; they particularly supported the substantive policy decisions of Presidents Franklin D. Roosevelt and Harry S. Truman. For Rossiter, Roosevelt's greatness lay in the leadership he provided during depression and war, and Truman's in his responses to the international crisis of the cold war. "Not one of [Truman's] grave steps in foreign and military affairs has yet been proven wrong, stupid, or contrary to the best judgment and interests of the American people," Rossiter contended. When Truman left office in January 1953, "we stood before the world a free, liberty-loving people with no more wounds and neuroses than we probably deserved." [8]

Rossiter's judgments, delivered in 1956, reflected the dominant concerns of the "new liberalism" that emerged during the cold-war years. Unlike their predecessors in the thirties, the new liberals did not consider themselves a part of the left but rather what Arthur Schlesinger, Jr., has called the "vital center." [9] As such, they rejected the crusading rhetoric of the thirties with its blunt appeals to class interests and its demands for redistributive social change. Moreover, the new liberals had discovered in the "mixed" economy of the postwar years an alternative both to unregulated capitalism and to socialism. This economy—for them, an interest-group "democracy" presided over by "progressive" businessmen, trade unionists, and pragmatic politicians— had the dual advantage of ensuring prosperity and of providing the means to avoid class conflict. Reform, the new liberals thus argued, could be achieved without conflict through economic growth.[10]

Again unlike the liberals of the thirties, the new liberals were also militantly anti-Communist. An excerpt from the organizational statement of principle and purpose of the Americans for Democratic Action (ADA), the chief vehicle for the new liberalism, captures this concern: "Because the interests of the United States are the interests of free men everywhere, America must furnish political and economic support to democratic and freedom-loving peoples the world over." [11] This language—indistinguishable from the later-announced Truman Doctrine's emphases on freedom and globalism—served to set the ADA apart from the postwar American left. Inevitably, then, with the intensification of the cold war, the ADA emerged as one of the principal and frequently uncritical defenders of the foreign and internal security policies of the Truman Administration.

During the late 1940's specifically, the ADA endorsed the Truman Administration's crusading anti-Communism, its loyalty program, and attacked Henry Wallace and other cold-war critics as naïve and sentimental dupes of the Communists. Their criticisms even of the blatantly partisan and reactionary House Committee on Un-American Activities centered on that Committee's methods not objectives—in the words of Arthur Schlesinger, Jr., the committee's "promiscuous and unprincipled attack on radicalism." Writing in 1949, Schlesinger further extolled the need for a federal loyalty program, objecting only to certain procedural aspects of the recently established presidential program. Even then, Schlesinger muted his criticisms— one might have concluded that Schlesinger's objections were not to specific provisions of Truman's loyalty program (which they were) but to possible future abuses. And, when Schlesinger detailed examples of the precipitous and unfair dismissal of certain federal employees under the program, he lamely maintained that the executive branch only acted thusly because it had been "stampeded" by pressure from "witch-hunters in the Eightieth Congress." [12]

Similarly, in the years after 1947 and as the result of internal decisions, the ADA came to subordinate liberal principles concerning the right to dissent and respect for individual liberties to the attainment of an effective anti-communist program. Dissent, for many ADAers, became a burdensome luxury to be exercised with cautious restraint, if at all. Thus, one ADAer, when recommending a strategy intended to undercut liberal support for Henry Wallace's 1948 presidential bid, lamented

> *Every time a non-Wallace liberal pours forth a volley of criticism of our foreign policy (frequently well deserved) without making clear in the same breath where he stands and what his positive proposals are, he is*

*clasped to the bosom of the Wallace people and drives
another herd of bewildered innocents in that direction.*[13]

A more dramatic index of this shift is contained in the ADA's
disparate responses in 1947 and then in 1950–51 to the loyalty
procedures instituted by Truman and to internal security legislation then under congressional consideration. In 1947 the ADA
publicly condemned what it considered the repressive and unfair
procedures of Truman's loyalty program. At the same time, the
ADA forthrightly opposed congressional enactment of internal
security legislation, arguing that the measures then under consideration by the Congress were unnecessary and unconstitutional. In contrast, by 1950 the ADA would support an internal
security bill drafted by the Administration—a bill that contained
provisions the ADA had condemned in 1947.

Although the ADA opposed the Communist registration bill
urged by Richard Nixon and Pat McCarran, they did not condemn the drastic preventive detention bill which several liberal
Democrats offered as an alternative. Indeed Hubert Humphrey,
an ADA founder, was one of the bill's sponsors, while ADA
executive secretary James Loeb, Jr., defended the measure as
one which was "justified both by realistic justice and by political expediency." Both the registration bill and the preventive
detention plan were included in the McCarran Internal Security
Act, which finally passed Congress in 1950. Following the bill's
passage, the national leadership of the ADA concluded that
effective purpose would be served by continued public opposition to the act on the part of the ADA or a liberal-labor coalition alone. And in 1951 the ADA did not publicly condemn
Truman's executive order amending the dismissal standard of
the loyalty program.* Rather, the ADA leadership sought a

---

* Truman's April 1951 order amended the original standard, "reasonable grounds exist for the belief that the person involved is disloyal,"
to read: "reasonable doubt as to the loyalty of the individual involved."

The politics of scholarship

private meeting with the President to express ADA concern "with many of the injustices of the present program." [14]

The new liberals, moreover, were poorly equipped to resist the conservative reaction that set in during the late forties. Fearful of being labeled radical, they would further mute their demands for social change. Increasingly, they stressed their belligerent anti-Communism, became even more fearful of public debate and an aroused citizenry, and drew closer still to established institutions. These factors, in turn, deeply influenced their perception of the emergent McCarthyism of the early 1950's.

II

Because liberals had come to identify the national interest with executive recommendations, to doubt the rationality of the American public, and to accept uncritically the necessity and sensibility of the anti-Communist politics of the Truman Administration, they were ill-prepared to understand the McCarthy phenomenon. This was true of the "new" liberals in general, and of the contributors to *The New American Right* in particular.

Because they identified with "responsible" conservatives instead of "sentimental" liberals, the contributors to *The New American Right* tended, in the first place, to minimize the continuity between McCarthyism and traditional conservative politics. Instead, they stressed the upper-class background of many of McCarthy's victims. Thus, Richard Hofstadter argued that the McCarthyites were "much happier to have as their objects of hatred the Anglo-Saxon, eastern, Ivy League intellectual gentlemen than they are with such bedraggled souls as, say, the Rosenbergs." Similarly, Seymour Martin Lipset held that "The image of the Communist which emerges time and again in [McCarthy's] speeches is one of an easterner, usually of Anglo-Saxon Episcopalian origins, who has been educated in schools such as Groton and Harvard." In national politics, Lipset continued, "McCarthy's attacks are probably much more important in terms of their appeal to status frustration than to resentful isolationism. In the identification of traditional symbols of status with pro-Communism, the McCarthy followers, of non-Anglo-Saxon extraction, can gain a feeling of superiority over the traditionally privileged groups." [15]

Moreover, Hofstadter denied that McCarthyism was conservative politics; rather it was "pseudo-conservative." ". . . its exponents," Hofstadter contended, "although they believe themselves to be conservative and usually employ the rhetoric of conservatism, show signs of a serious and restless dissatisfaction with American life, traditions, and institutions." [16]

Nowhere, however, do Hofstadter, Lipset, or any of the other contributors to *The New American Right* provide empirical evidence to support these sweeping judgments about the motivations behind popular support for McCarthyism—either by documenting what was "in the minds" of the McCarthy supporters or by establishing that the McCarthyites were "happier" attacking eastern patricians than Jewish scientists. These impressionistic judgments derived substance, and for the time appeared convincing, because they captured the tone and focus of many of Senator McCarthy's speeches.[17]

The denial that McCarthyism was a form of conservative politics, and the disjunction that Hofstadter posited between "real" and "pseudo" conservatism, moreover, constituted an idealization of postwar American conservatism and a serious misreading of McCarthyism. To begin with, such an analysis ignored the fact that the established conservative political leaders, and most notably Senator Robert Taft (Republican-Ohio), did not repudiate McCarthy; in fact, they actively supported him. Conservatives, in addition, did not differ from McCarthy in their conception of the nature of the internal security problem confronting the nation or how to rectify it. In fact, a politics of anti-Communism was central to conservative strategy and deeply influenced the reactions of many conservatives to the Truman Administration's foreign and internal security policies.

Throughout the cold-war years conservatives in Congress sought to Red-bait the Roosevelt and Truman administrations. Even before McCarthy captured the "Communists-in-Government" issue, conservatives had relied upon a politics of anti-Communism in their effort to discredit the New Deal. In this effort, they had utilized the investigative hearing process to expose the "disloyal" beliefs and associations of New Deal personnel. In addition, in their public position on foreign policy questions, as early as 1945, but increasingly after 1948, conservatives had pointedly attributed Soviet expansion to "Communist influence" within the federal government. Following McCarthy's dramatic impact on national politics, these same conservatives rallied to the senator's banner. A serious internal security problem existed, they charged; only an independent, and necessarily Republican, Congress could resolve it.[18]

Hofstadter's distinction between real and pseudo conservatism is further belied by the responses of Herbert Hoover (a "real" conservative if Hofstadter's distinction has any meaning) to an invitation from President Truman. In a letter dated November 25, 1950, Truman asked the former Republican President to accept the chairmanship of a proposed presidential commission on internal security and individual rights.[19]

The idea of establishing such a commission had been seriously discussed within the White House since June 1950. Truman, however, did not act upon this suggestion of his White House staff until after the November 1950 congressional elections, the results of which seemed to demonstrate both McCarthy's appeal and public doubts about the adequacy of the Administration's loyalty program. Having decided to establish the commission, the President and his aides carefully considered whom to appoint. They sought to ensure a blue-ribbon panel balanced to include respected political, religious, and business leaders; more importantly, Truman pressed Hoover to head the study.

Hoover's presence, as chairman of the proposed presidential commission investigating federal loyalty procedures, could have disarmed possible McCarthyite charges of "whitewash" (earlier raised in response to the Tydings committee report*). Insofar as this study might have defused an effective Republican campaign issue, Hoover could not but have been somewhat discomforted. Yet, in 1947 the former Republican President had agreed to accept Truman's offer of the chairmanship of a commission investigating the efficiency of the federal bureaucracy (for Hoover, the New Deal). In this action, Hoover's chairmanship had indirectly served to defuse those Republican criticisms of the New Deal that had emphasized waste and inefficiency.

At the same time, should Hoover have accepted the chairmanship of this proposed internal security commission, he would have commanded considerable leverage vis-à-vis the President in the area of internal security improvements. Given the politics of 1950, it would have been politically inexpedient for Truman to have opposed any recommendations Hoover might make concerning additional internal security legislation or tightened procedures in the federal loyalty program.

Significantly, when declining Truman's offer, Hoover affirmed

* The so-called Tydings committee had been established in March 1950 by special resolution of the Senate to investigate the eighty-one cases of "known" Communists in the State Department enumerated by Senator McCarthy in a February 20, 1950, Senate speech. The majority report of the committee, released in July 1950 and signed only by the Democratic members, had denied the validity of McCarthy's charges.

The politics of scholarship

the current lack of confidence arises from the belief that there are men in Government (not Communists) whose attitudes are such that they have disastrously advised on policies in relation to Communist Russia. The suspicion is abroad that they continue in Government.

. . . Without a wide-spread inquiry into the past and present of such men and the facts, the answer to this problem could not be determined. It would require the authority to examine on oath, . . . and to include access to all files. . . . Such powers could come jointly from yourself and a Congressional Act. The personnel of such a Commission would need be approved by the leaders of both parties in that body. . . .

. . . I suggest that a statement might be issued by you that you would be glad if the Congress would either create such a Commission or would itself make an inquiry on the broadest basis, . . . [20]

In May 1952, moreover, a disparate group of conservatives (including, among others, Fulton Lewis, Jr., Roscoe Pound, Clarence Manion, Felix Morley, Norman Vincent Peale— prominent conservative thinkers who were not directly involved in partisan politics) endorsed a ten-page pamphlet entitled "Senator McCarthy" and published by Freedom Clubs, Inc. The pamphlet conceded that McCarthy's earlier attacks on the State Department had been "rude and crude." It rationalized this crudeness as the natural reaction to the "pugnacious refusal of the Truman Administration to assist Congressional investigations of the loyalty of Federal employees." The recent investigations conducted by the Internal Security Subcommittee of the Senate Judiciary Committee, the pamphlet concluded, had

"already substantiated a large part of the charges of Senator
McCarthy, and well may lead to proof of all of these charges." [21]

III

Because they were enamored with the office of the presidency, and because they feared and distrusted the people, the
new liberals failed to understand how the manipulative and
elitist conduct of the presidency under Roosevelt and Truman
had provided conservative partisans with an important and
popular issue. In their attacks on the Truman Administration's
conduct of foreign and internal security affairs, conservatives
were not responding simply to the personnel in the White House
and State Department, but to the crucial administrative changes
that had been instituted during the preceding decade. Since 1939
President Roosevelt had increasingly relied upon secret diplomacy to effect policy and had often intentionally bypassed the
Congress in resorting to executive agreements and by invoking
his powers as commander-in-chief. Under Truman, executive
authority not only had increased but had become institutionalized and made more immune to congressional surveillance.
The National Security Act of 1947 had created a National Security Council, responsible only to the President, and had thus
strengthened executive control over foreign policy and reduced
congressional influence. Similarly, Truman's 1947 executive
order creating the Federal Employee Loyalty Program had
established exclusive presidential control over federal loyalty
procedures; and Truman's 1948 directive extending classification restrictions to employee loyalty records had denied congressional access to information essential to an independent surveillance function.

In couching their protest in terms of the public's "right to
know," McCarthy and other conservatives during the 1950's
were raising the important issue of accountability, one that was

The politics of scholarship

popular among a people increasingly suspicious of secretive government and among legislators increasingly concerned over executive usurpation of congressional prerogatives. Such a protest, whatever its partisan motivation, cannot be dismissed out of hand as irrational and irresponsible. All the more so since this effort by McCarthy and his conservative supporters was consistent with the major priority of American politicians (administration liberals and congressional conservatives) during the cold-war years: the need to protect the nation from a serious internal security threat. McCarthy and other conservative Republicans were thus raising an issue incapable of compromise: Congress's responsibility to investigate the federal bureaucracy to insure a more effective and adequate internal security program. In this sense, McCarthyism cannot simply be ascribed, as Daniel Bell suggested in his introductory essay to *The New American Right,* as the product of the tendency of interest groups to assume a large identity through sweeping rhetorical appeals and thereby moving the "political debate . . . from specific interest clashes, in which issues can be identified and possibly compromised, to ideologically tinged conflicts which polarize the groups and divide the society.' [22]

IV

More importantly, the new liberals failed to discern the continuity between the anti-Communist politics of Joe McCarthy and anti-Communist politics of the Truman Administration, or to understand how the rhetoric and leadership of the Truman Administration, alarmist in tone and manipulative in form, helped to create the climate that eventually led to McCarthyism.

Instead, the new liberals argued that the anti-Communism of the Truman Administration was realistic and reasonable, while that of the Administration's McCarthyite critics was irrational and dangerous. The McCarthyite, wrote Richard Hofstadter, "sees his own country as being so weak that it is constantly about to fall victim to subversion; and yet he feels that it is so all-powerful that any failure it may experience in getting its way in the world . . . cannot posibly be due to its limitations but must be attributed to its having been betrayed. . . . While he naturally does not like Soviet Communism, what distinguishes him from the rest of us who also dislike it is that he shows little interest in, is often bitterly hostile to such realistic measures as might actually strengthen the United States vis-à-vis Russia." The "self-styled conservatives," agreed David Riesman and Nathan Glazer, were "isolationists with overtones of manifest-destiny jingoism" who were ill-prepared to consider complex foreign policy issues. "Asians and Europeans ought never to confuse genuine American anti-Communism, a necessary shield for peace and freedom against aggression, with pseudo-anti-Communism of the demagogues, which is not anti-Communism at all but a racket," concluded Peter Viereck.

When the Truman Administration acted unwisely, these scholars attributed these actions to McCarthyite pressures. Thus, Riesman and Glazer contended that "In the last years of Truman's term, . . . many demagogic anti-Communist steps were taken by a reluctant Administration." Similarly, Seymour Martin Lipset argued that the restrictions on civil liberties instituted during the cold-war years "were initiated in response to radical right activity." [23]

But this disjunction between the anti-Communism of the right and that of the center, together with the depiction of the Truman Administration as the hapless victim of McCarthyism, obscures the complex reality of cold-war politics. Since 1947 the Truman Administration had increasingly resorted to a rhetoric of crusading anti-Communism in order to arouse public support for its policy of containment. In speech after speech, the President and other Administration spokesmen stressed American omnipotence and innocence, Soviet depravity, and the subversive nature of the Soviet threat. Thus, in a March 17,

The politics of scholarship

1948, nationwide radio broadcast, Truman described the international situation as a morally dichotomous struggle between good and evil. "We must not be confused about the issue which confronts the world today," he declared. ". . . It is tyranny against freedom." ". . . even worse," he continued, "Communism denies the very existence of God." Or again, as in a May 11, 1950, address at Gonzaga University, Truman charged that "The greatest obstacle to peace is a modern tyranny led by a small group who have abandoned their faith in God." Stressing American righteousness and omnipotence, he concluded that "Our effort to resist and overcome this tyranny is essentially a moral effort. . . . In everything we do, at home and abroad, we must demonstrate our clear purpose, and our firm will, to build a world order in which men everywhere can walk upright and unafraid, and do the work of God." [24]

At the same time, the Truman Administration sought to brand critics of its policies, both those on the left and the right, as irrational or even disloyal. In September 1946 Truman privately denounced Henry Wallace as a dreamer who "wants us to disband our armed forces, give Russia our atomic secrets, and trust a bunch of adventurers in the Kremlin Politburo. . . . The Reds, phonies, and the 'parlor pinks' seem to be banded together and are becoming a national danger." During the 1948 campaign, the Administration sought, in the words of Clark Clifford, "to identify [Wallace] and isolate him in the public mind with the Communists." As then Democratic National Chairman J. Howard McGrath bluntly put it, "a vote for Wallace . . . is a vote for the things for which Stalin, Molotov, and Vishinsky stand." Truman would later publicly attack McCarthy as "the greatest asset that the Kremlin has" and denounce Republican "isolationism" as an attempt to "sabotage the foreign policy of the United States [which] is just as bad in the cold war as it would be to shoot our soldiers in the back in a hot war." [25]

THE SPECTER

At home, Administration spokesmen stressed the gravity of
the threat of Communist subversion and called for measures that
would insure absolute security. When speaking around the country in 1949 and 1950, Truman's Attorney General, J. Howard
McGrath, sought to arouse the public to recognize the all-perva-
sive menace of Communism. He urged those who believed "in
God's law and the dignity of human personality" to take up the
"modern struggle against pagan Communist philosophies that
seek to enslave mankind." Warning against the subtle subversion of students' minds by their teachers, he emphasized the
need to invite anti-Communist speakers onto the college cam-
puses and to ensure that anti-Communist books were promoted
in local bookstores. Communists, the Attorney General warned,
were "everywhere—in factories, offices, butcher shops, on street
corners, in private businesses—and each carries in himself the
germs of death for society." They were "busy at work," he
pointed out, "undermining your government, plotting to destroy
the liberties of every citizen, and feverishly trying, in whatever
they can, to aid the Soviet Union." [26]

In a similar fashion in 1947 the Truman Administration had
legitimized Red-baiting at home through its loyalty program
(which applied sweeping standards to all federal employees, not
just those in sensitive positions), its compilation and public release of the so-called Attorney General's list (which, based on
the concept of guilt by association, became the most widely used
litmus for confirming "subversive tendencies"), and through its
public quest for total internal security (which raised an impossible standard by which the Administration itself would subsequently be judged and found wanting).[27]

V

With spokesmen for the Truman Administration calling for a
holy war against Communism, it is hardly surprising that Mc-
Carthyism flourished during the early 1950's, or that McCar-

The politics of scholarship

thyite congressmen effectively attacked the Administraton for failing to act in accordance with its own alarmist and conspiratorial rhetoric. Given the rhetoric of the Truman Administration, the McCarthyite attack was neither irrational nor abberrational so much as the logical extension of Administration policies and assumptions. On February 9, 1950, at Wheeling, West Virginia, the crows simply began coming home to roost.

By 1950 the rhetoric and policies of the Truman Administration had created a political climate conducive to McCarthy-style politics. Ironically, perhaps, given the solid anti-Communist credentials of the President, Joe McCarthy and the conservative Republicans who supported him were in many ways more faithful to the assumptions and logic of the Administration's public pronouncements than the specific policy actions of Truman himself.

The liberal scholars who contributed to *The New American Right* were unable, however, to discern the continuities between Trumanism and McCarthyism, or to understand how competing conservative and liberal elites contributed to the politics of anti-Communist hysteria. Their identification with presidential leadership and with the anti-Communist politics of the cold war instead led them to represent McCarthyism only in terms of status anxieties, mass hysteria, and social irresponsibility.

If *The New American Right,* and the scholarship that gave rise to and sustained this interpretation, offer any lessons to historians of McCarthyism, however, it is the need for analyses centering on American politics not American culture, and on partisan tactics and strategy not status anxieties. Further, it requires that future students of the cold-war political debate appreciate that those who made anti-executive and subversion charges were raising political issues as rational and non-status-in-motivation as those who commended the foreign and internal security policy decisions of the Truman Administration.

THE SPECTER

NOTES

AMERICAN POLITICS AND
THE ORIGINS OF "McCARTHYISM"

1. For a summary of this view, see Daniel Bell, ed., *The New American Right* (New York, 1955), and its revised edition, *The Radical Right* (New York, 1963). Contributors to the original collection included Bell, Richard Hofstadter, David Riesman, Nathan Glazer, Peter Viereck, Talcott Parsons, and Seymour Martin Lipset. Disillusioned by what they believed to be the consequences of mass democracy, these "pluralist" scholars distrusted popular rule and hoped that America's conservative, elite-managed institutions would serve as a bulwark against the dangers of popular passion. This represented a dramatic shift from the New Deal era during which intellectuals had allied themselves with the dispossessed. By the mid-fifties, as Riesman and Glazer somewhat uncomfortably note, intellectuals were seeking "allies among the rich and well-born, rather than among the workingmen and farmers they had earlier courted and cared about. . . ." The interested reader should also consult the individual works of the various contributors, especially Hofstadter, *The Paranoid Style in American Politics* (New York, 1965), Daniel Bell, *The End of Ideology* (New York, 1962), and Peter Viereck, *Shame and Glory of the Intellectuals* (New York, 1953). For somewhat similar appraisals see Will Herberg, "McCarthy and Hitler: A Delusive Parallel," *New Republic,* Vol. 131 (August 23, 1954), and Leslie Fiedler, *An End to Innocence* (Boston, 1955). For a recent restatement of the pluralist position, see Seymour Martin Lipset and Earl Raab, *The Politics of Unreason* (New York, 1970).

For an early and provocative critique of the "radical right" thesis, see Nelson Polsby, "Toward an Explanation of McCarthyism," *Political Studies,* Vol. 8 (October 1960). The best and most sustained criticism of the pluralist position, however, is Michael Paul Rogin, *The Intellectuals and McCarthy: The Radical Specter* (Cambridge, Mass., 1967). For further discussion of this important study, see Robert Griffith, "The Politics of Anti-Communism: A Review Article," *Wisconsin Magazine of History,* Vol. 54 (Summer 1971).

For the argument that McCarthy was a charismatic and unusually talented demagogue, see Richard Rovere, *Senator Joe McCarthy* (New York, 1959) and, more recently, Fred Cook, *The Nightmare Decade: The Life and Times of Senator Joe McCarthy* (New York, 1971).

2. For public opinion on McCarthy, see John Fenton, *In Your Opinion* (Boston, 1960); Louis Harris, *Is There a Republican Majority* (New York, 1954); and Angus Campbell and Homer C. Cooper, *Group Differences in Attitudes and Votes* (Ann Arbor, Mich., 1956). On attitudes toward Communists in the thirties, see Hadley Cantril, *Public Opinion,*

1935–46 (Princeton, 1946). The best examination of public opinion toward Communism and civil liberties is Samuel A. Stouffer, *Communism, Conformity, and Civil Liberties* (Garden City, N.Y., 1955).

3. Seymour Martin Lipset, "Three Decades of the Radical Right," in Bell, ed., *The Radical Right,* p. 421.

4. Polsby, *op. cit.,* pp. 250–271.

5. Rogin, *op. cit.,* Also see David A. Shannon, "Was McCarthy a Political Heir of La Follette," *Wisconsin Magazine of History,* Vol. 45 (Autumn 1961).

6. Stouffer, *op. cit.,* pp. 58–88.

7. See especially, Alan Harper, *The Politics of Loyalty: The White House and the Communist Issue, 1946–1952* (Westport, Conn., 1969); Robert Griffith, *The Politics of Fear: Joseph R. McCarthy and the Senate* (Lexington, Ky., 1970); and Athan Theoharis, *Seeds of Repression: Harry S. Truman and the Origins of McCarthyism* (Chicago, 1971).

8. Rogin, *op. cit.,* pp. 216–260.

9. Griffith, *Politics of Fear,* pp. 30–32.

10. The standard history of America's first anti-Communist scare is Robert K. Murray, *Red Scare: A Study in National Hysteria* (Minneapolis, 1955). On Attorney General Palmer, see Stanley Coben, *A Mitchell Palmer* (New York, 1963). William Preston, *Aliens and Dissenters: Federal Suppression of Radicals, 1903–1933,* is especially good on the antecedents of the Red Scare. John Higham touches on the popular linkage of radicalism and nativism in *Strangers in the Land: Patterns of American Nativism, 1960–1925* (New Brunswick, N.J., 1955). Murray B. Levin, *Political Hysteria in America: The Democratic Capacity for Repression* (New York, 1971), is provocative but superficial. Julian F. Jaffe, *Crusade Against Radicalism: New York During the Red Scare, 1914–1924,* is an unsuccessful attempt to study the Red Scare in a local context. Jean Jensen, *The Price of Vigilance* (Chicago, 1969), provides a valuable account of the American Protective League and the Wilson Administration's violation, of civil liberties.

11. Taft is quoted in James T. Patterson, *Mr. Republican: A Biography of Robert A. Taft* (Boston, 1972), p. 157. The Republican National Committee is quoted in Arthur Schlesinger, Jr., *The Politics of Upheaval* (Boston, 1960), p. 625.

12. On the House Committee on Un-American Activities, see August R. Ogden, *The Dies Committee* (Washington, D.C., 1945); Robert K.

NOTES

Carr, *The House Committee on Un-American Activities, 1945–50* (Ithaca, N.Y., 1952); Frank Donner, *The Un-Americans* (New York, 1961); and Walter Goodman, *The Committee* (New York, 1968). For a defense of the committee, see William F. Buckley, *The Committee and Its Critics* (New York, 1962). Also see Lewis H. Carlson, "J. Parnell Thomas and the House Committee on Un-American Activities, 1938–1948" (unpublished Ph.D. dissertation, Michigan State University, 1967).

13. The best account of the Smith Act remains Zechariah Chafee, Jr., *Free Speech in the United States* (Cambridge, Mass., 1941). As originally drafted, the Smith bill would have included provisions for deporting any alien who "advises a change in the form of government of the United States" or who "engages in any way in domestic political agitation." The sedition section of the Smith bill was drawn, in part, from the Palmer-sponsored Sedition bill of 1920, which had failed of passage.

14. Franklin Roosevelt to Oswald Garrison Villard, July 19, 1940, in Roosevelt Papers, O.F. 133, Box 1, cited in David Sullivan, "A Legislative History of the Alien Registration Act of 1940" (unpublished paper in author's possession).

15. Lawrence H. Chamberlain, *Loyalty and Legislative Action: A Survey of Activity by the New York State Legislature, 1919–1949* (Ithaca, N.Y., 1951), 53–67. Edward L. Barrett, Jr., *The Tenney Committee: Legislative Investigation of Subversive Activities in California* (Ithaca, N.Y., 1951), pp. 1–10. E. Houston Harsha, "Illinois: The Broyles Commission," Robert J. Mowitz, "Michigan: State and Local Attack on Subversion," and Walter Gellhorn, "A General View," all in Walter Gellhorn, ed., *The States and Subversion* (Ithaca, N.Y., 1952). All three of the above are part of a series of books on the impact of government on civil liberties sponsored by Cornell University and funded by the Rockefeller Foundation. Also see Chafee, *op. cit.*, pp. 490–493, 577. For an informative local study see George K. Gardner and Charles D. Post, "The Constitutional Questions Raised by the Flag Salute and Teachers' Oath Acts in Massachusetts," *Boston University Law Review*, Vol. 16 (November 1936), pp. 803–844.

16. For standard acounts of these years, see Eric Goldman, *The Crucial Decade: America, 1945–1955* (New York, 1956), and Herbert Agar, *The Price of Power: America Since 1945* (Chicago, 1957).

17. For this thesis, see Theoharis, *op. cit.*, and Richard M. Freeland, *The Truman Doctrine and the Origins of McCarthyism: Foreign Policy, Domestic Politics, and Internal Security, 1946–1948* (New York, 1972).

18. On Taft, see Patterson, *op. cit.*, especially Chapters 20, 24, 25, 28, 29, 31.

Notes

19. On the role of the Chamber of Commerce, see Leslie K. Adler, "The Red Image: American Attitudes Toward Communism in the Cold War Era" (unpublished Ph.D. dissertation, University of California, Berkeley, 1970), pp. 94–114; and Peter H. Irons, "America's Cold War Crusade: Domestic Politics and Foreign Policy, 1942–1948" (unpublished Ph.D. dissertation, Boston University, 1972), pp. 46–116. To the right of the Chamber of Commerce, of course, stood many smaller and more extreme organizations, such as the Committee for Constitutional Government and the National Economic Council.

20. The role of the American Legion is touched on briefly in Adler, *op. cit.,* and in Rodney G. Minott, "The Organized Veteran and the Spirit of Americanism, 1898–1959" (unpublished Ph.D. dissertation, Stanford, 1960). Raymond Moley, Jr., *The American Legion Story* (New York, 1966), contains some useful information on the Legion's role in the creation of the Special House Committee on Un-American Activities. For the Legion's role in the states, see Barrett, *The Tenney Committee,* pp. 11–12, and Gellhorn, *op. cit.,* pp. 55, 67, 86, 158, 193, 371. For the role of the Legion in the Hollywood controversy, see John Cogley, *A Report on Blacklisting* (New York, 1956), I, 118–143.

21. *Life,* July 30, 1945, p. 20, quoted in Adler, *op. cit.,* pp. 71–72. On the roll of Catholics, see Donald F. Crosby, "The Angry Catholics: Catholic Opinion of Senator Joseph R. McCarthy, 1950–1957" (unpublished dissertation, Brandeis University, 1973). On the Polish-American Congress, see Irons, *op. cit.,* pp. 245–332.

22. On the Communists, see Joseph R. Starobin, *American Communism in Crisis, 1943–1957* (Cambridge, 1972). Two sympathetic accounts of the emergence of cold-war liberalism are Alonzo Hamby, "Harry S. Truman and American Liberalism" (unpublished Ph.D. dissertation, University of Missouri, 1965), and Clifton Brock, *Americans for Democratic Action* (Washington, 1962). For more critical treatments see Norman Markowitz, *The Rise and Fall of the People's Century: Henry Agard Wallace and American Liberalism, 1941–1948* (New York, 1973), and Allen Yarnell, "The Impact of the Progressive Party on the Democratic Party in the 1948 Presidential Election" (unpublished Ph.D. dissertation, University of Washington, 1969). The best study of cold-war liberalism, however, is Mary Sperling McAuliffe, "The Red Scare and the Crisis in American Liberalism, 1947–1954" (unpublished Ph.D. dissertation, University of Maryland, 1972).

23. For further elaboration of this theme, see Griffith, *Politics of Fear,* pp. 30–51, and Harper, *op. cit.,* pp. 5–124.

NOTES

24. For a summary of congressional investigations into Communism, see U.S. Senate, 84th Congress, *Internal Security Manual* (Washington, 1955), pp. 309–326.

25. On the 1946 elections, see Samuel Lubell, *The Future of American Politics,* 3rd ed. (New York, 1965), p. 100; Lubell, *Revolt of the Moderates* (New York, 1956), p. 213; Irons, *op. cit.,* pp. 336–358; Adler, *op. cit.,* pp. 338–339. On the response of the Truman Administration, see Theoharis, *op. cit.,* and Freeland, *op. cit.* On the 1948 campaign, see especially Robert A. Divine, "The Cold War and the Election of 1948," *Journal of American History,* Vol. 59 (June 1972), pp. 90–110. On the conservative attack following 1949, see Griffith, *Politics of Fear,* and Harper, *op. cit.*

26. See footnotes 19 and 20.

27. William B. Prendergast, "Maryland: The Ober Anti-Communist Law," in Gellhorn, *op. cit.,* pp. 148–149. For the text of the Ober Law and its progeny, see Fund for the Republic, *Digest of the Public Record of Communism in the United States* (New York, 1955), pp. 347–382 *passim.*

28. Fund for the Republic, *ibid.,* pp. 77–78, 347–402, 459–472, *passim.* For an early survey of state legislation, see William B. Prendergast, "State Legislatures and Communism: The Current Scene," *American Political Science Review,* Vol. 44 (September 1950), pp. 556–574.

The only notable exception to the trend of state action following federal action involved laws seeking to outlaw the Communist Party. In 1951 four states—Indiana, Massachusetts, Pennsylvania, and Texas—enacted such laws. Not until 1954 did Congress, led by liberal Democrat Hubert Humphrey, seek to outlaw the Communist Party. The *desirability* of outlawing the party, however, had been frequently argued at the national level. Harold Stassen had made it a major issue in his 1948 campaign for the Republican presidential nomination; while the Truman Administration, though publicly opposing efforts to outlaw the party, nevertheless prosecuted Communist Party leaders under the 1940 Smith Act. In 1950 Congress settled for the registration procedure embodied in the McCarran Act, though many congressmen continued to call for sterner measures.

29. "Either senators are for recognizing the Communist Party for what it is," declared Hubert Humphrey in a 1954 speech supporting a bill that imposed criminal penalties for membership in the Communist Party, "or they will continue to trip over the niceties of legal technicalities and details." The bill was co-sponsored by Humphrey and Senators Wayne

Morse, John F. Kennedy, Herbert Lehman, and John Pastore. Its under-lying purpose was to show, as Wayne Morse declared, that in the Senate there is no division of opinion among liberals, conservatives, and those in between when it comes to our utter detestation of the Communist conspiracy." For a further discussion of this measure, see Griffith, "The Political Context of McCarthyism," *The Review of Politics,* Vol. 33 (January 1971), pp. 24–35; and Mary Sperling McAuliffe, "Outlawing the Communist Party: A Crisis in American Liberalism" (unpublished paper in author's possession).

THE POLITICS OF RELIGION
American Catholics and the Anti-Communist Impulse

1. Especially see Daniel Bell, "Interpretations of American Politics," pp. 47–73; Peter Viereck, "The Revolt Against the Elite," pp. 161–183; Tal-cott Parsons, "Social Strains in America," pp. 209–229; and Seymour Martin Lipset, "The Sources of the 'Radical Right,'" pp. 307–371, all of which were originally published in Daniel Bell, ed., *The New American Right* (New York, 1955), and then republished with additional, updated essays in *The Radical Right* (New York, 1963). All page citations are to the second, expanded edition. Similar viewpoints are expressed by Leslie Fiedler in *An End to Innocence* (Boston, 1955) and by Will Herberg in "McCarthy and Hitler: A Delusive Parallel," *New Republic,* Vol. 131 (August 23, 1954), pp. 13–15. For a trenchant critique of this line of thought, see Michael Paul Rogin, *The Intellectuals and McCarthy: The Radical Specter* (Cambridge, Mass., 1967).

2. Roy Deferrari, trans., Denziger, *The Sources of Catholic Dogma* (St. Louis, 1957), pp. 429–437, 451–454. See also, W. F. Hogan, "Syllabus of Errors," *New Catholic Encyclopedia,* Vol. 13 (New York, 1967), p. 854; John Tracy Ellis, *American Catholicism* (Chicago, 1964), p. 146; Richard L. Camp, *The Papal Ideology of Social Reform* (Leiden, Netherlands, 1969), pp. 50–51.

3. George N. Shuster, *Religion Behind the Iron Curtain* (New York, 1954), pp. 16–17; Albert Galter, *The Red Book of the Persecuted Church* (Westminster, Md., 1957), pp. 44–46; *New Catholic Encyclo-pedia,* Vol. 14 (New York, 1967), p. 410. The Russian Revolution had initially led to a relaxation of Czarist and Russian Orthodox discrimina-tion against Roman Catholics in Russia, and many Roman Catholics re-mained optimistic about the Church's future throughout the early twen-ties. Such optimism vanished by the mid-twenties, however, in a series of disputes over religious freedom and the confiscation of Church proper-ties. Ralph Lord Roy, *Communism and the Churches* (New York, 1960), pp. 125–126.

NOTES

4. On Ryan, see Francis Broderick, *Right Reverend New Dealer* (New York, 1963); David O'Brien, *American Catholics and Social Reform* (New York, 1968), *passim.* On Day, see Dorothy Day, *The Long Loneliness* (New York, 1952), and O'Brien, *ibid.*

5. *Ibid.*, pp. 81–83.

6. *Ibid.*, pp. 79–80.

7. For a reliable study of the war, see Gabriel Jackson, *The Spanish Republic and the Civil War* (Princeton, 1965). On Catholic reaction to the Spanish Civil War, see Hugh Jones Parry, "The Spanish Civil War: A Study in American Public Opinion" (unpublished Ph.D. dissertation, University of Southern California, 1939), p. 373, cited in Foster J. Taylor, *The United States and the Spanish Civil War* (New York, 1956), p. 161. Also see Allen Guttmann, *The Wound in the Heart* (New York, 1962), p. 65. For a study of Catholic reaction to the war in a single community, see Donald F. Crosby, "Boston's Catholics and the Spanish Civil War," *New England Quarterly,* Vol. 44 (March 1971), pp. 82–100.

8. O'Brien, *op. cit.*, p. 96.

9. *National Catholic Almanac, 1942* (Paterson, N.J., 1942), p. 762.

10. *Ibid., 1944,* p. 723.

11. *New York Times,* February 18, 1945, p. 24; *National Catholic Almanac, 1946,* pp. 689, 704–705. Gillis is quoted in Peter H. Irons, "America's Cold War Crusade: Domestic Politics and Foreign Policy, 1942–1948" (unpublished Ph.D. dissertation, Boston University, 1972), p. 170.

12. *New York Times,* April 18, 1945, p. 25; *National Catholic Almanac, 1946,* pp. 703, 714.

13. *New York Times,* May 27, 1945, p. 11; *National Catholic Almanac, 1946,* pp. 722, 735, 772.

14. Quoted in Irons, *op. cit.*, p. 318.

15. *New York Times,* October 19, 1946, p. 6.

16. *Ibid.*, December 2, 1946, p. 14.

17. *Boston Pilot,* March 8, 1947, and August 8, 1947.

18. Robert Gannon, *Cardinal Spellman Story* (Garden City, N.Y., 1962), p. 338.

19. *National Catholic Almanac, 1948,* pp. 727, 800; *New York Times,*

February 10, 1947, p. 19; October 5, 1947, p. 3; October 7, 1947, pp. 5, 7; October 12, 1947, p. 7.

20. *National Catholic Almanac, 1949,* p. 793.

21. Gannon, *op. cit.,* pp. 340–346.

22. *New York Times,* January 6, 1949, p. 18; February 7, 1949, pp. 1, 3; February 10, 1949, p. 4.

23. *Ibid.,* May 16, 1949, p. 13.

24. Confidential sources.

25. For a fuller discussion of Cronin's activities, see Irons, *op. cit.,* pp. 177–183.

26. Gannon, *op. cit.,* pp. 276–282. Also see "Speeches" file, Spellman Mss., St. Joseph's Seminary, Dunwoodie (Yonkers), N.Y.

27. *New York Times,* October 7, 1946, p. 5; October 25, 1946, p. 48; September 25, 1948, p. 32; February 10, 1949, p. 1; Eric Goldman, *The Crucial Decade* (New York, 1959), pp. 130–131; Gannon, *op. cit.,* pp. 336–337.

28. See especially, Fulton J. Sheen, *Communism and the Conscience of the West* (Indianapolis, 1948), and Sheen, *Philosophy of Religion* (New York, 1948).

29. Sheen is quoted in Irons, *op. cit.,* p. 185.

30. Thus, Sheen presided over the return to the Church of Louis F. Budenz, the onetime editor of the *Daily Worker* who subsequently became a zealous informant in government trials and investigations and a warm supporter of Joe McCarthy. See especially, Louis F. Budenz, *This Is My Story* (New York, 1947), and *Bolshevik Invasion of the West* (Linden, N.J., 1966); *New York Times,* January 23, 1947, p. 20; *National Catholic Almanac, 1948,* p. 729.

31. *New York Times,* March 25, 1946, p. 6.

32. *Ibid.,* June 26, 1946, p. 6; *Boston Pilot,* February 8, 1947; *National Catholic Almanac, 1950,* p. 784.

33. *New York Times,* March 22, 1948, p. 41; March 23, 1948, p. 27; March 24, 1948, p. 5; March 31, 1948, p. 1; April 1, 1948, p. 5.

34. *Ibid.,* March 24, 1949, pp. 1, 2; March 27, 1949, p. 47.

35. *Ibid.,* March 20, 1946, p. 8; March 24, 1947, p. 23; March 27, 1947, p. 2; October 14, 1947, p. 29.

NOTES

36. *Ibid.*, June 12, 1946, p. 3; August 23, 1946, p. 38; March 11, 1948, p. 9.

37. *Ibid.*, July 17, 1948, p. 28.

38. *Ibid.*, November 8, 1949, p. 13.

39. *Boston Pilot,* March 15, 1947.

40. *National Catholic Almanac, 1949,* p. 788.

41. *New York Times,* September 9, 1947, p. 19.

42. Goldman, *op. cit.,* p. 131.

43. On social programs as the answer to Communism, see the following citations from *Commonweal:* Vol. 44 (July 5, 1946), p. 276; Vol. 45 (November 8, 1946), pp. 84–85; Vol. 45 (January 17, 1947), p. 341. For support of the Marshall Plan, see Vol. 46 (June 27, 1947), pp. 251, 252; Vol. 46 (July 18, 1947), pp. 323–324; Vol. 46 (July 25, 1947), pp. 347–348; Vol. 47 (November 21, 1947), p. 131; Vol. 47 (March 26, 1948), p. 582. For guarded criticism of HUAC, see Vol. 48 (August 13, 1948), p. 417; Vol. 48 (August 27, 1948), p. 464. For their belief that fellow travelers ought to be lured from Communism by (1) friendship and understanding and (2) the presentation of responsible social programs, see Vol. 49 (April 8, 1949), p. 628; Vol. 48 (August 27, 1948), p. 465. For criticism of anti-Communist legislation, see Vol. 45 (April 4, 1947), p. 604; Vol. 50 (July 8, 1949), pp. 312–315. For belief that the repression of civil liberties to eliminate Communists from government would wreck democracy, see Vol. 45 (April 11, 1947), p. 631. For criticism of the Mundt-Nixon bill, see John Cort, "The Mundt-Nixon Bill," Vol. 48 (July 2, 1948), pp. 285–286. But for a *Commonweal* contributor who dissented, see Christopher Emmet, "Mundt-Nixon Bill," Vol. 48 (June 25, 1948), pp. 253–256.

44. Aaron I. Abell, *American Catholicism and Social Action* (Notre Dame, Ind., 1963), pp. 275–278. On the ACTU also see Philip Taft, "The Association of Catholic Trade Unionists," *Industrial and Labor Relations Review,* Vol. 2 (January 1949), pp. 210–218; Roger J. Ward, "The Role of the Association of Catholic Trade Unionists in the Labor Movement," *Review of Social Economy,* Vol. 14 (September 1956), pp. 79–100.

45. Seymour Martin Lipset, "The Sources of the 'Radical Right,' " in Bell, *The Radical Right,* p. 351; Samuel A. Stouffer, *Communism, Conformity, and Civil Liberties* (New York, 1955), pp. 144–145. For a detailed study of the polls, see Donald F. Crosby, "The Angry Catholics:

Catholic Opinion of Senator Joseph R. McCarthy, 1950–1957" (unpublished Ph.D. dissertation, Brandeis University, 1973).

46. On Spellman, see Washington *Evening Star,* October 24, 1953, and *New York Times,* April 5, 1954, p. 12.

47. For a survey of Catholic press attitudes on McCarthy, see Vincent P. deSantis, "American Catholics and McCarthyism," *Catholic Historical Review,* Vol. 51 (April 1965), pp. 1–30. On Sheil, see *New York Times,* April 10, 1954, p. 8. On Cronin, see Milwaukee *Journal,* April 2, 1950. On Mitchell, see *New York Times,* February 27, 1954, p. 6. On Eugene McCarthy, my interview with him, February 3, 1972, and Eugene McCarthy, *Year of the People* (Garden City, N.Y., 1969), pp. 6–7.

48. On Catholic voting patterns, see Lou Harris, *Is There a Republican Majority* (New York, 1954), pp. 90–103 and Samuel Lubell, *The Future of American Politics,* 3rd ed., rev. (New York, 1965), pp. 14, 200–203, 213–214. For Clifford's comment, see Clark Clifford, Memorandum for the President, November 1947, Clifford Papers, Harry S. Truman Library, Independence, Mo. On Tydings' defeat, see Louis Bean, *Influences in the 1954 Mid-Term Elections* (Washington, 1954), pp. 28–30.

A VIEW FROM THE RIGHT:
Conservative Intellectuals, the Cold War, and McCarthy

1. Barton Bernstein, ed., *Politics and Policies of the Truman Administration* (Chicago, 1970); Richard M. Freeland, *The Truman Doctrine and the Origins of McCarthyism: Foreign Policy, Domestic Politics, and Internal Security, 1946–1948* (New York, 1972); Robert Griffith, *The Politics of Fear: Joseph R. McCarthy and the Senate* (Lexington, Ky., 1970); Alan D. Harper, *The Politics of Loyalty: The White House and the Communist Issue, 1946–1952* (Westport, Conn., 1968); and Athan Theoharis, *Seeds of Repression: Harry S. Truman and the Origins of McCarthyism* (Chicago, 1971).

2. Daniel Bell, ed., *The Radical Right* (Garden City, N.Y., 1963), an expanded and updated version of *The New American Right* (New York, 1955).

3. A recent study that focuses on the conservative political roots of McCarthyism is Michael P. Rogin, *The Intellectuals and McCarthy* (Cambridge, Mass., 1967). Rogin demonstrates that most of those who encouraged Senator McCarthy, particularly at the national level, were "conservative politicians and publicists, businessmen, and retired military leaders discontented with the New Deal, with bureaucracy, and with military policy" (p. 250). I would emphasize, however, that the doctrinal

beliefs of conservative intellectuals also figured importantly in first creating the climate in which McCarthy could command a hearing.

In his book on political conservatives, *The Yalta Myths: An Issue in U.S. Politics, 1945–1955* (Columbia, Mo., 1970), Athan Theoharis has shown how conservative and partisan Republicans, responding to cold-war pressures, were able to increase their political support by exploiting the Yalta issue, thereby helping to create a political climate serviceable to Senator McCarthy.

4. Ronald Lora, *Conservative Minds in America* (Chicago, 1971), pp. 16–17 *passim*.

5. The conservative intellectuals who supported McCarthy diverged sharply from many varieties of European conservatism, particularly in failing to respect constitutional procedures and in failing to cultivate a sense of limits in politics. But in the main, the doctrinal distinctions outlined in the text hold true. The cold-war conservatives discussed herein were an extreme variant of traditional conservative ideology that arose in response to the international tensions existent in the early cold-war era and to the continued popularity of New Deal and Fair Deal domestic policies. They were no more "pseudo-conservatives" (Richard Hofstadter's term) than postwar liberals were pseudo-liberals, i.e., fallen disciples of John Dewey, Rexford Tugwell, or David Lilienthal. To argue thusly, credits "pathology" too much and thought too little. For Hofstadter's position, see his "The Pseudo-Conservative Revolt" and "Pseudo-Conservatism Revisited: A Postscript" in Bell, ed., *The Radical Right*, pp. 75–103. For dissenting views on the "pathological" and "pseudo-conservative" explanations, see Earl Latham, *The Communist Controversy in Washington: From the New Deal to McCarthy* (Cambridge, Mass., 1966), pp. 410–413; and Lora, *op. cit.*, pp. 212–215.

6. Herbert Hoover, *40 Key Questions About Our Foreign Policy* (Scarsdale, N.Y., 1952), pp. 3, 5. Senator Robert A. Taft in June 1941 counseled a similar course, saying that "The victory of Communism in the world would be far more dangerous to the United States than the victory of Fascism"; quoted in James T. Patterson, *Mr. Republican: A Biography of Robert A. Taft* (Boston, 1972), pp. 245–246. So did Harry S. Truman, who declared that "If we see that Germany is winning the war, we ought to help Russia, and if Russia is winning, we ought to help Germany and in that way kill as many as possible" (*New York Times*, July 24, 1941).

7. Herbert Hoover, *Addresses Upon the American Road, World War II, 1941–1945* (New York, 1946), pp. 257–261; Hoover, *Addresses Upon the American Road, 1948–1950* (Stanford, Calif., 1951), p. 66.

Notes

294

8. Clare Boothe Luce, "The Twilight of God," Human Affairs Pamphlets No. 44–45 (Chicago, 1949), pp. 11, 16.

9. George Sokolsky, "The Peace of Truth," *Vital Speeches,* Vol. 17 (November 1, 1950), p. 46.

10. William F. Buckley, *God and Man at Yale* (Chicago, 1951), p. xii.

11. Whittaker Chambers, *Witness* (New York, 1952), p. 8. Also see Chambers, *Odyssey of a Friend: Whittaker Chambers' Letters to William F. Buckley, Jr., 1954–1961,* William F. Buckley, Jr., ed. (New York, 1969).

12. Peter Viereck, *Shame and Glory of the Intellectuals* (Boston, 1952), pp. 141–142.

13. William S. Schlamm, "Across McCarthy's Grave," *National Review,* Vol. 3 (May 18, 1957), pp. 469, 470.

14. Chambers, *Witness,* p. 798; Buckley, *God and Man at Yale,* p. 194. James Burnham, *The Coming Defeat of Communism* (New York, 1949), pp. 145–148.

15. The habitual use of the technique of moral dichotomization differentiated conservative intellectuals from other opponents of Communism. Their deeply internalized anti-Communism flowed naturally from their particular ideology of absolutes. The defense of truth demanded emotion. James Burnham expressed this in one of his many analyses of the containment doctrine: "In estimating basic attitudes, psychology suggests as the most accurate rule: By their emotions shall you know them. Whom does a man hate, whom does he love, at what is he bitter, toward whom tolerant? Although George Kennan is unquestionably anti-Soviet and from a rational standpoint anti-Communist, nowhere in his published writings does one ever find expressed in the texture of his style a powerful emotion concerning Communism, a hatred of Communism. The analysis and rejection, which are there, are always pale and abstract"; *Containment or Liberation?* (New York, 1953), p. 208. In his analysis of Lenin, Trotsky, and Stalin, Burnham contended that it was naïve to differentiate between Stalinism and Communism: "Stalinism *is* Communism." See "Lenin's Heir," *Partisan Review,* Vol. 12 (Winter 1945), pp. 61–72.

16. Hoover, *Addresses, 1941–1945,* pp. 86, 257.

17. Felix Morley, "Black Umbrella and Black Cigar," *Human Events,* Vol. 1 (January 14, 1944), p. 8; "The Trend Since Teheran," *Human Events,* Vol. 1 (February 9, 1944), pp. 13, 15.

NOTES

18. Frank C. Hanighen, "Europe's Lost Equilibrium," *Human Events,* Vol. 1 (February 16, 1944), p. 19.

19. William Henry Chamberlain, in the following articles from *Human Events,* Vol. 1: "Stalin, *Pravda* and Churchill" (February 2, 1944), pp. 10–12; "The True Soviet Challenge" (April 12, 1944), pp. 44–46; "Soviet Aims in Asia" (October 4, 1944), pp. 122–124; and "Russia Moves West" (October 25, 1944), pp. 131–133. See also the following Chamberlain articles from *American Mercury,* Vol. 58: "Can Stalin's Russia Go Democratic?" (February 1944), pp. 142–148; "Will Stalin Dictate an Eastern Munich?" (March 1944), p. 271; and "The Tragic Case of Finland" (July 1944), pp. 7–15.

20. Quoted in William Henry Chamberlain, "The Status of the Atlantic Charter," *Human Events,* Vol. 1 (March 22, 1944), p. 36.

21. Felix Morley, "For Yalta, Read Munich," *Human Events,* Vol. 2 (February 21, 1945), pp. 29–32. See also William Henry Chamberlain, "Some Truths About Poland," *American Mercury,* Vol. 60 (February 1945), pp. 204–212.

22. Eugene Lyons, "Appeasement in Yalta," *American Mercury,* Vol. 60 (April 1945), pp. 461–468.

23. David Dallin, *The Real Soviet Russia* (New Haven, 1944); *The Big Three* (New Haven, 1945).

24. David Dallin, "What Russia Wants in the Far East," *American Mercury,* Vol. 61 (July 1945), p. 27; Dallin, *The Real Soviet Russia,* rev. ed. (New Haven, 1947), p. v.

25. Freda Utley, "Why Pick on China," *American Mercury,* Vol. 59 (September 1944), pp. 345–351; the following from *Human Events,* Vol. 1: Frank C. Hanighen, "Our Dilemma in China" (August 2, 1944), pp. 95–97; William Henry Chamberlain, "Soviet Aims in Asia" (October 4, 1944), pp. 122–124; Chamberlain, "How Strong Is China?" (June 28, 1944), pp. 80–82; and from Vol. 2: Hanighen, "The Far Eastern Dilemma" (August 15, 1945), pp. 136–139, and Chamberlain, "Stalin Stakes Out an Asiatic Claim" (April 11, 1945), pp. 59–62. See also Lin Yutang, "The Civil War in China," *American Mercury,* Vol. 60 (January 1945), pp. 7–14.

26. Freda Utley, *Last Chance in China* (Indianapolis, 1947), pp. 17–21, 355–393.

27. James Burnham, *The Struggle for the World* (New York, 1947), p. 135.

28. *Ibid.*, pp. 59, 62–71, 210.

29. *Ibid.*, pp. 53, 170. China was a case in point. With an adequate comprehension of world politics, Burnham wrote, "it would have been *easy* for the United States to deduce a workable application in China" (emphasis added). The United States should have given all material aid necessary to Chiang Kai-shek and aided him "in extending the sovereignty of the Central Government over all of China, which could be done only by destroying the sovereignty of the rebel government and liquidating its attributes of independent power—armies, police, political administration, finance system." In all probability this would have "settled the basic issue within a very short time and at a minimum cost" (p. 171).

30. In Burnham's view, "the total internal influence of its [Communism's] combined forces, supplemented by the pressures from without of its world apparatus, is already so powerful as to be a major challenge to the sovereignty of the [U.S.] government" (*The Struggle for the World,* p. 208).

31. For a similar proposal by a member of the Republican National Committee, see Bonner Fellers, " 'Thought War' Against the Kremlin," Human Affairs Pamphlet No. 46 (Chicago: Henry Regnery, 1949). During World War II Fellers worked as a psychological warfare officer against Japan, and in the Philippine campaign served as General Mac-Arthur's personal combat observer at the front.

32. *American Mercury,* Vol. 64 (April 1947), pp. 389–406; *Life,* Vol. 22 (March 31, 1947), pp. 59–64ff; *Time,* Vol. 49 (March 24, 1947), pp. 26–27; and three editorials in *Christian Century,* Vol. 64: May 21, 1947, pp. 646–648; May 28, 1947, pp. 678–679; and June 4, 1947, pp. 702–703.

33. Eric Johnston, "The New Deal Appraised," *American Mercury,* Vol. 58 (April 1944), pp. 396–403, and *American Unlimited* (New York: American Mercury-Doubleday, Doran Book, 1945). Johnston in 1944 was president of the U.S. Chamber of Commerce. Also see James T. Patterson, *Congressional Conservatism and the New Deal* (Lexington, Ky., 1967).

34. See especially co-editor Frank C. Hanighen's weekly column "Not Merely Gossip." Representative articles appearing in *Human Events,* Vol. 5, are: Howard H. Buffett, "Our Irredeemable Paper Money" (July 28, 1948), n.p.; Edna Lonigan, "The Republicans and the Republic" (August 4, 1948); and two articles by Frank Chodorov, "Christianity

and the Planned Economy" (July 7, 1948) and "The Political Viscosity of Oil" (November 3, 1948).

35. Felix Morley, "Politics and Principles," *Human Events*, Vol. 5 (October 27, 1948); and in the same volume, Morley's "The South Secedes?" (March 3, 1948), "What the Democrats Are Doing" (July 21, 1948), and "America Turns Toward Socialism" (November 17, 1948).

36. William Henry Chamberlain, "Civil Liberties and Communist Conspiracy," *Human Events*, Vol. 5 (July 11, 1948). Also see Burnham, *The Coming Defeat of Communism*, Chapters 6 and 7, and Chambers, *Witness*, p. 617.

37. John T. Flynn, *The Roosevelt Myth* (New York, 1948), p. 309.

38. Edna Lonigan, "More Than Espionage," *Human Events*, Vol. 5 (September 8, 1948); Oliver Carlson, "The Communist Record in Hollywood," *American Mercury*, Vol. 66 (February 1948), pp. 135–143; Roscoe Drummond, "Are Communists Traitors to America?" *American Mercury*, Vol. 67 (October 1948), pp. 389–396.

39. The outlines of this school of thought are expressed in Robert Strausz-Hupé, et al., *Protracted Conflict* (New York, 1959); and William R. Kintner and Joseph Z. Kornfeder, *The New Frontier of War: Political Warfare, Present and Future* (Chicago, 1962).

40. Burnham, *The Coming Defeat of Communism*, p. 138. Eisenhower's arrangement of the Korean truce in 1953 left a disappointed Burnham still hoping that "liberation" would supercede containment: "At most, containment can be a temporary expedient, a transition. As the transition is completed, containment must move toward one or the other of the two major poles, toward appeasement or liberation" (*Containment or Liberation?* p. 218). Other conservatives, although differing among themselves, agreed with Burnham that the containment policies of the Truman Administration were grossly inadequate. Edna Lonigan wrote that the Marshall Plan, instead of providing a better way of containing Communism, meant the abandonment of the Truman Doctrine; "Re-examination of the Marshall Plan," *Human Events*, Vol. 7 (August 30, 1950). See also Lonigan, "Wanted: A Military Policy for Survival," *Human Events*, Vol. 8 (January 17, 1951), and Senator Styles Bridges, "Blueprint for Victory," *Vital Speeches*, Vol. 17 (February 15, 1951), pp. 265–267. For Peter Viereck, peaceful coexistence with Communism was "too risky an aim." "Heartless are those who prefer 'containment' to liberation" (*Shame and Glory of the Intellectuals*, pp. 157, 163).

While Viereck thought Burnham's prescriptions somewhat heavy-handed, he was nevertheless busily engaged in resurrecting a new hero for postwar conservatives in the person of Clemens von Metternich, the "last European." Long before President Nixon's chief foreign affairs adviser, Henry Kissinger, attempted to reenact Metternichian policy, Viereck had reinterpreted the Hapsburg foreign minister as the successful creator of the first League of Nations, "the last hope" of internationalism and human survival; "Warning for a Western Union," *Current History*, Vol. 17 (July and August 1949), pp. 7–10, 75–78, later published in *Conservatism Revisited* (New York, 1949).

41. Burnham, *The Coming Defeat of Communism*, pp. 159–160.

42. *Ibid.*, pp. 147, 155, 161–162. James Gilbert has traced Burnham's intellectual pilgrimage from radicalism through Trotskyism and Musteism to the conservative right in "James Burnham: Exemplary Radical of the 1930's," in Ronald Radosh and Murray N. Rothbard, eds., *A New History of Leviathan* (New York, 1972).

43. *Congressional Record*, 81st Congress, 2nd Session (July 28, 1950, 96: 5475–6 (Appendix).

44. Representative articles appearing in *American Mercury* are: David J. Dallin, "Communism Means War," Vol. 71 (October 1950), pp. 400–409; Max Eastman, "Can Truman Be Educated?" Vol. 71 (December 1950), pp. 726–732; William Bradford Huie, "Untold Facts in the Korean Disaster," Vol. 72 (February 1951), pp. 131–139; Alice Widener, "The Korean Failure," Vol. 74 (May 1952), pp. 12–24; Boris Shub, "Why America Is Losing World War III," Vol. 74 (July 1952), pp. 11–24; and in *Human Events:* William Henry Chamberlain, "Repudiate Yalta and Potsdam," Vol. 8 (April 25, 1951); and in *Vital Speeches:* Representative Walter Judd, "How Can We Be So Stupid?" Vol. 17 (March 1, 1951), pp. 293–300; and Senator Styles Bridges, *op. cit.*

45. *New York Times*, July 13, 1950, p. 6; December 2, 1950, p. 3; October 6, 1951, p. 3; October 12, 1951, p. 17; November 10, 1951, p. 5; November 13, 1951, p. 3; *Vital Speeches*, Vol. 17 (February 15, 1951), pp. 265–267; *American Mercury*, Vol. 75 (November 1952), pp. 11–19.

46. *New York Times*, July 21, 1950, p. 4; January 13, 1952, p. 5; December 6, 1952, p. 6; December 2, 1950, p. 14; March 9, 1953, p. 8; and November 3, 1952, p. 13. It is instructive to note in this connection that a regional survey by the *New York Times* in December 1950 found little public sentiment either for war with Communist China or for the use of the atom bomb (*New York Times*, December 17, 1950, p. 3).

47. Libertarian, or perhaps more accurately, the "quasi-libertarian" right, because conservatives of the fundamentalist persuasion, con-

trary to a principled libertarianism, had all too seldom opposed state-granted privileges to business enterprise achieved through taxing and fiscal policies, protective tariffs, and the like.

48. For a personal account of this transformation, see Murray N. Roth-bard, "Confessions of a Right-Wing Liberal," *Ramparts,* Vol. 6 (June 15, 1968), pp. 47–52.

49. William F. Buckley, Jr., "The Party and the Deep Blue Sea," *Commonweal,* Vol. 55 (January 25, 1952), p. 391.

50. *Ibid.,* pp. 392–393.

51. James T. Patterson's *Mr. Republican* is an excellent biography and the only one based on the voluminous Taft papers deposited in the Library of Congress. I have drawn freely from it. Three helpful articles are Henry W. Berger, "A Conservative Critique of Containment: Senator Taft on the Early Cold War Program," in *Containment and Revolution,* David Horowitz, ed. (Boston, 1967), pp. 125–139; Berger, "Senator Robert A. Taft Dissents from Military Escalation," in *Cold War Critics,* Thomas G. Paterson, ed. (Chicago, 1971), pp. 167–204; and John P. Armstrong, "The Enigma of Senator Taft and American Foreign Policy," *Review of Politics,* Vol. 17 (April 1955), pp. 206–231.

52. Robert A. Taft, "Let Us Stay Out of War," *Vital Speeches,* Vol. 5 (February 1, 1939), pp. 254–256; Taft, "Let's Mind Our Own Business," *Current History,* Vol. 50 (June 1939), pp. 32–33; Patterson, *Mr. Republican,* pp. 291, 292–298.

53. Berger, "Senator Robert A. Taft Dissents," p. 176; Berger, "A Conservative Critique," p. 129; *New York Times,* March 13, 1947, p. 3 and March 16, 1947, p. 1.

54. Patterson, *Mr. Republican,* pp. 437–438.

55. Robert A. Taft, "The Republican Party," *Fortune,* Vol. 39 (April 1949), p. 118.

56. Quoted in Patterson, *Mr. Republican,* p. 449.

57. Berger, "Senator Robert A. Taft Dissents," pp. 178–182, 190–192; Patterson, *Mr. Republican,* pp. 476–492.

58. Robert A. Taft, *A Foreign Policy for Americans* (Garden City, N.Y. 1951), pp. 6–7, 48–49, 50–54, 74, 86, 89, 91, 117–121.

59. For an extensive discussion of the issue of liberation in the 1952 presidential campaign, see Theoharis, *The Yalta Myths,* Chapter 8, especially pp. 135–146.

Notes

60. In this connection, William F. Buckley once defined conservatism as "the tacit acknowledgment that the truly important in human experience is behind us; that the truly crucial battles have been fought, and that it is given to man to know what are the great truths that emerged from them." Quoted in "The Isms in 1957," *Saturday Review of Literature,* Vol. 40 (June 8, 1957), p. 37.

61. Willmoore Kendall, *The Conservative Affirmation* (Chicago, 1963), p. 77. In his enthusiastic review of the book, William F. Buckley declared that Kendall "makes sense . . . and for the very first time in America, of the whole McCarthy business (tempers got as heated as they got precisely because the fight involving McCarthy *was* a fight over heresy)"; "Hang On to Your Hats," *National Review,* Vol. 14 (April 23, 1963), p. 324.

62. Kendall, *Conservative Affirmation,* pp. 74, 76.

63. Herbert McClosky, "Conservatism and Personality," *American Political Science Review,* Vol. 52 (March 1958), p. 41.

64. William F. Buckley, Jr., and L. Brent Bozell, *McCarthy and His Enemies* (Chicago, 1954), p. 327. A highly favorable review of Buckley and Bozell's argument from a conservative perspective is Max Eastman, "Facts and Logic re McCarthy," *Freeman,* Vol. 4 (April 19, 1954), pp. 532–534.

65. Buckley and Bozell, *ibid.,* pp. 317–318, 334.

66. *Ibid.,* p. 334. During an October 1952 television and radio campaign broadcast, Senator McCarthy delivered an invective-laden attack on Adlai Stevenson and his advisers Archibald MacLeish, Bernard De Voto, and Arthur Schlesinger, Jr. In commenting on this, Buckley and Bozell warned that someday "the patience of America may at last be exhausted, and we will strike out against Liberals," not because they are Communists but because, in James Burnham's words, "They are mistaken in their predictions, false in their analyses, wrong in their advice, and through the results of their actions injurious to the interests of the nation. That is reason enough to strive to free the conduct of the country's affairs from the influence of them and their works" (*McCarthy and His Enemies,* p. 333; *Freeman,* June 15, 1953, pp. 661–662). In point of fact, Buckley and Bozell were less interested in warning of future conservative attacks on "mistaken" individuals than in providing a rationale for the way in which McCarthyites in Congress used the Communist issue to exclude men from public office.

67. Buckley and Bozell, *ibid.,* pp. 247, 248, 249. Freda Utley had used the same argument three years earlier in *China Story* (Chicago, 1951),

pp. 171–173. And the Truman Administration offered a similar rationale in defending the loyalty program and in extending the scope of that program.

68. Buckley and Bozell, *ibid.*, pp. 247, 249.

69. *Ibid.*, pp. 3, 4. It had been acknowledged by other conservatives as well that innocent persons would suffer. Testifying before the Tydings committee in 1950, Freda Utley stated that "the Communist cancer must be cut out if we are to survive as a free nation. Perhaps in this operation some healthy tissues on the fringe will be destroyed" (quoted in Griffith, *Politics of Fear*, p. 86).

70. Buckley and Bozell, *ibid.*, p. 122. Interestingly, the Loyalty Review Board adopted the same standard when denying loyalty clearance to John Stewart Service in 1951 and John Paton Davies in 1952. The others were Dorothy Kenyon, Esther Brunauer, Harlow Shapley, and Gustavo Duran.

71. Hoover, *Addresses, 1950–1955*, pp. 111–118. Eugene Lyons, "Is Freedom of Expression Really Threatened?" *American Mercury*, Vol. 76 (January 1953), pp. 22, 23, 33.

72. "The Necessity of 'Red-Baiting,' " *Freeman*, Vol. 3 (June 1, 1953), pp. 619–620. Also see C. Dickerman Williams, "The Duty to Investigate," *Freeman*, Vol. 3 (September 21, 1953), pp. 917–920.

73. Russell Kirk, *Beyond the Dreams of Avarice* (Chicago: Henry Regnery, 1956), pp. 114, 121, 162.

74. The *American Mercury* was especially embittered at the Republican retreat from the liberationist rhetoric of the 1952 presidential campaign. Representative selections are John T. Flynn, "Our Phony War on Communism," Vol. 78 (February 1954), pp. 17–21; Flynn, "What Is Joe McCarthy Really Trying to Do," Vol. 78 (March 1954), pp. 69–72; Frank S. Meyer, "Where Is Eisenhower Going?" Vol. 78 (March 1954), pp. 123–126; Meyer, "The Booby-Trap of Internationalism," Vol. 78 (April 1954), pp. 85–88; and two editorials by Russell Maguire, "It's Hard to Keep the Dog Out of the House," Vol. 78 (April 1954), pp. 45–46, and "In the Mercury's Opinion," Vol. 79 (August 1954), pp. 87–89.

AMERICAN BUSINESS AND THE ORIGINS OF McCARTHYISM:
The Cold War Crusade of the United States Chamber of Commerce

1. William F. Buckley, Jr., and L. Brent Bozell, *McCarthy and His Enemies* (Chicago, 1954), p. 58.

2. Two comprehensive accounts of this anti-Communist campaign are in Peter Irons, "America's Cold War Crusade: Domestic Politics and Foreign Policy, 1942–1948" (unpublished Ph.D. dissertation, Boston University, 1973), and Leslie K. Adler, "The Red Image: American Attitudes Toward Communism in the Cold War Era" (unpublished Ph.D. dissertation, University of California, Berkeley, 1970).

3. On the Liberty League, see George Wolfskill, *The Revolt of the Conservatives: A History of the American Liberty League, 1934–1940* (Boston, 1962).

4. The role of both the BAC and the CED is discussed in David W. Eakins, "The Development of Corporate Liberal Policy Research in the United States, 1885–1965" (unpublished Ph.D. dissertation, University of Wisconsin, 1966). Also see Eakins, "Business Planners and America's Postwar Expansion," in David Horowitz, ed., *Corporations and the Cold War* (New York, 1969), pp. 143–171. For a semiofficial account of the founding and early years of the CED, see Karl Schriftgeisser, *Business Comes of Age* (New York, 1960).

5. The best source on the role of business in the making of foreign economic policy is Thomas G. Paterson, "The Economic Cold War: American Business and Economic Foreign Policy, 1945–1950" (unpublished Ph.D. dissertation, University of California, Berkeley, 1968). See also Gabriel Kolko, *The Politics of War: The World and United States Foreign Policy, 1943–1945* (New York, 1968), pp. 333–336.

6. "America and the Future," *Fortune,* 31 January 1945, p. 147.

7. "What Business With Russia?" *Fortune,* 31 January 1945, p. 202. The American-Russian Chamber of Commerce's membership derived from the elite of the corporate world. Its president was Reeve Schley of Chase National Bank and it included members from International General Electric, RCA, IBM, Socony-Vacuum, and other corporate giants. Paterson, *op. cit.,* p. 220.

8. "U.S. Opinion on Russia," 32 *Fortune,* September 1945, p. 238.

9. Junius B. Wood, "How Russia Trades With Us," *Nation's Business,* 33 March 1945, p. 46.

10. Charles Prince, "The Things Russia Wants," *Nation's Business,* 33 September 1945, pp. 28–29.

11. Quoted in Carl Marzani, *We Can Be Friends* (New York, 1952), pp. 80–81.

NOTES

12. John Jay Daly, "Red Blight in Union Gardens," *Nation's Business,* 34 September 1946, pp. 57, 58, 100.

13. Interview with Emerson Schmidt, Washington, D.C., August 4, 1971.

14. Ralph Bradford to Francis Matthews, December 11, 1945, Francis P. Matthews Papers, Box 10, Harry S. Truman Library, Independence, Mo. (henceforth HSTL).

15. John J. Sullivan to Francis Matthews, January 21, 1946, Matthews Papers, Box 10, HSTL.

16. L. Ward Bannister to Francis Matthews, January 29, 1946, Matthews Papers, Box 10, HSTL. Also see John Roy Carlson, *The Plotters* (New York, 1946) for data on the organizations listed above.

17. At the time, Matthews was Secretary of the Navy, having been appointed to the post in May 1949. Because of this speech, President Truman fired Matthews, demoting him to U.S. Ambassador to Ireland. *Congressional Record,* Vol. 96, Part 17, 81st Congress, 2nd Session, pp. A6230–6231.

18. Emerson Schmidt to Francis Matthews, August 27, 1946, Matthews Papers, Box 10, HSTL.

19. Father Cronin's anti-Communist activities within the Catholic Church are discussed in Irons, *op. cit.,* pp. 158–197. See also Gary Wills, *Nixon Agonistes* (New York, 1971), pp. 35–39.

20. Father John F. Cronin, *Communism: A World Menace* (Washington: National Catholic Welfare Conference, 1947), p. 12.

21. John Cronin to Francis Matthews, March 18, 1946, Matthews Papers, Box 10, HSTL.

22. Francis Matthews to John Cronin, September 23, 1946, Matthews Papers, Box 10, HSTL.

23. *New York Times,* October 8, 1946, p. 1.

24. U.S. Chamber of Commerce, *Communist Infiltration in the United States* (Washington, 1946), pp. 27–29.

25. *Ibid.,* p. 37.

26. The role of the commission is discussed in Irons, *op. cit.,* pp. 224–233. See also Alan D. Harper, *The Politics of Loyalty: The White House and the Communist Issue, 1946–1952* (Westport, Conn., 1969), Chapter 3.

Notes

27. Memo of January 17, 1947, Stephen Spingarn Papers, Box 7, HSTL.

28. *Ibid.*

29. On Mandel's early years, see Theodore Draper, *American Communism and Soviet Russia* (New York, 1960), p. 412.

30. Interview with Emerson Schmidt, August 4, 1971.

31. *Ibid.*

32. *Ibid.*

33. U.S. Chamber of Commerce, *Communists Within the Government* (Washington, 1947), p. 14.

34. *Ibid.*

35. *Ibid.*

36. The Chamber of Commerce proposals are in *Communists Within the Government,* pp. 27–37. The text of Executive Order 9835 is reprinted in Harper, *op. cit.,* pp. 255–263.

37. Interview with Emerson Schmidt, August 4, 1971.

38. U.S. Chamber of Commerce, *Communists Within the Labor Movement* (Washington, 1947), p. 6.

39. *Ibid.,* p. 27.

40. Francis Matthews to Theodore Aubert, March 26, 1947, Matthews Papers, Box 10, HSTL.

41. U.S. House of Representatives, Committee on Un-American Activities, *Investigation of Un-American Propaganda Activities in the United States,* 80th Congress, 1st Session, p. 226.

42. *Ibid.,* p. 233.

43. *Ibid.,* pp. 222, 227.

44. Harper, *op. cit.,* p. 149.

45. Robert K. Carr, *The House Committee on Un-American Activities* (Ithaca, N.Y., 1952), pp. 193–194.

46. *Nation's Business,* 34 October 1946, p. 25.

47. *Steel,* 80 November 4, 1946, p. 72.

NOTES

48. Adler, *op. cit.* Adler discusses the Chamber of Commerce's anti-Communist program on pp. 94–114.

49. Charles J. V. Murphy, "McCarthy and the Businessman," *Fortune,* 42 April 1954, p. 180.

50. Michael P. Rogin, *The Intellectuals and McCarthy: The Radical Specter* (Cambridge, Mass., 1967), pp. 222–223. On the role of Benton, Flanders, and Hoffman, see Robert Griffith, *The Politics of Fear: Joseph R. McCarthy and the Senate* (Lexington, Ky., 1970).

A VIEW FROM THE LEFT:
From the Popular Front to Cold War Liberalism

1. For a sophisticated look at public responses to the Communist question in the early 1950's, see Samuel Stouffer, *Communism, Conformity, and Civil Liberties* (New York, 1955).

2. Arthur Schlesinger, Jr., *The Vital Center* (Boston, 1962, Sentry edition), p. 130. For the history of the Congress for Cultural Freedom, see Christopher Lasch, *The Agony of the American Left* (New York, 1966), pp. 63–114.

3. Schlesinger, *ibid.,* pp. 129–130. During World War II, Sidney Hook had decried the "new failure of nerve" on the left. See Sidney Hook, "The New Failure of Nerve," *Partisan Review,* January–February 1943, pp. 2–23.

4. For a fuller treatment of social liberalism, including the interrelationship between European and American social liberalism, see Norman Markowitz, *The Rise and Fall of the People's Century: Henry Agard Wallace and American Liberalism, 1941–1948* (New York, 1973), Chapter 1. On the doctrine of the positive state, see Sidney Fine, *Laissez-Faire and the General Welfare State* (Ann Arbor, Mich., 1956). On the differences between corporate and humanitarian reform, see Robert Wiebe, *The Search for Order* (New York, 1967). On corporate liberalism, see especially William A. Williams, *Contours of American History* (Chicago, 1966), pp. 343–488; James Weinstein, *The Corporate Ideal in the Liberal State* (Boston, 1968); and Martin J. Sklar, "Woodrow Wilson and the Political Economy of Modern United States Liberalism," in Ronald Radosh and Murray Rothbard, eds., *The New Leviathan* (Chicago, 1972).

5. For a critical treatment of liberal identification with the state, see Arthur Ekirch, *The Decline of American Liberalism* (New York, 1955).

Notes

For a penetrating critique of contemporary liberalism's interest-group approach, see Theodore Lowi, *The End of Liberalism* (New York, 1969).

6. For the first popular front, see Frank Warren III, *Liberals and Communism* (Bloomington, Ind., 1966). For the second popular front, see Markowitz, *op. cit.,* Chapter 6.

7. Eugene Lyons, *Red Decade* (New York, 1941); Schlesinger, *op. cit.,* pp. 40–46. Lewis Coser and Irving Howe also depict "totalitarian liberals" as blind worshippers of Soviet power and efficiency. See Coser and Howe, *The American Communist Party* (Boston, 1957), p. 435. More recently, historians Frank Warren and R. Alan Lawson have sought to rebut these charges, either by minimizing the degree of interaction between liberals and Communists or by arguing that where such interaction took place the Communists were largely at the mercy of the liberals. Warren, *ibid., passim,* Lawson, *The Failure of Independent Liberalism* (New York, 1971), p. 158.

8. Coser and Howe, *ibid.,* pp. 332–333.

9. See Woody Guthrie, *Bound for Glory* (New York, 1943); Robert Shelton, ed., *Born to Win* (New York, 1965); and John Steinbeck, *The Grapes of Wrath* (New York, 1939). For a colorful history of folk music and the left, see R. Serge Denisoff, *Great Day Coming* (Urbana, Ill., 1971).

10. For an account of the popular-front left and the Spanish Civil War, see Allen Guttman, *The Wound in the Heart* (New York, 1962).

11. See Ernest Hemingway, *For Whom the Bell Tolls* (New York, 1940).

12. For a fuller presentation of these themes, see Markowitz, *op. cit.,* Chapters 2 and 5.

13. *Ibid.*

14. Max Lerner, Bruce Bliven, and George Soule, "America and the Postwar World," *New Republic,* Vol. 109 (November 29, 1943), pp. 763, 780–782.

15. Markowitz, *op. cit.,* Chapter 2.

16. George P. West, "Communists and Liberals," *New Republic,* Vol. 110 (May 10, 1944), pp. 631–633.

17. Earl Browder, *The People's Front* (New York, 1936); Coser and Howe, *op. cit.,* p. 340; Campaign Circular, n.d., Fred Basset Blair Pa-

pers, Box 1, Wisconsin State Historical Society (henceforth WSHS), Madison, Wis.

18. Coser and Howe, *op. cit.,* pp. 395–396.

19. *Ibid.,* pp. 425–427. For a revealing look at the pro- and anti-Communist disputes that rent the CIO even during the war, see the Adolph Germer Papers, WSHS.

20. For the most important statement of Browder's position, see Earl Browder, *Teheran* (New York, 1943). Also see Joseph Starobin, *American Communism in Crisis* (Cambridge, 1972).

21. The popular-front left was a New Deal left, acting within the American system for specific social reforms and an anti-Fascist foreign policy. Its achievements are not separable from the overall achievements of the New Deal.

22. For a prophetic article on the failures of popular-front politics while the popular front was at its peak, see Will Herberg's critique of New York's American Labor Party, "The Stillborn Party," in *Common Sense,* Vol. 13 (May 1944), pp. 161–164.

23. John Dewey, "Why I Am Not a Communist," *The Modern Monthly,* Vol. 8 (April 1934), pp. 125–137.

24. For liberal critics of the popular front, see Warren, *op. cit., passim.* The Norman Thomas Papers, New York Public Library (NYPL), contain extensive correspondence with opponents of the popular-front left.

25. *New York Times,* April 24, May 15, 17, 1939.

26. *Partisan Review*'s "Trotskyism" was diluted enough by the war so that it mixed condemnation of both sides with a militant defense of art and artistic freedom against the demands of politics. For a brilliant critique of the *Partisan Review,* see James Gilbert, *Writers and Partisans* (New York, 1968).

27. Almost any number of the *New Leader* for the 1940's exhibits strong anti-Soviet and anti-Communist tendencies.

28. Norman Thomas to Ray F. Carter, April 18, 1944, Thomas Papers, Box 46, NYPL. Norman Thomas to Mr. and Mrs. Carl Whitehead, December 2, 1947, Thomas Papers, Box 52, NYPL.

29. UDA, for example, militantly attacked isolationist congressmen and was in turn attacked as a Communist-front group by the Dies committee. Jerry Voorhis, the one liberal on the Dies committee, issued a statement criticizing both the committee's attack on UDA and the UDA's at-

tack on "anti-Communists in Congress." *New Republic,* Vol. 106 (May 18, 1942), pp. 683–711, and Jerry Voorhis in Washington *Times-Herald,* June 26, 1942.

30. For UDA's and Loeb's attempt to use George Norris as a rallying point for the creation of a national liberal organization during the war, see Adam Clymer, "George Norris and Progressive Unity, 1942–1943," undated MS, FDR Library, Hyde Park, N.Y.

31. For Loeb's enthusiasm over the Political Action Committee, see James Loeb, Jr., "The Rising Tide of Progressivism," *New Republic,* Vol. 109 (August 9, 1944), pp. 185–187.

32. For material relating to UDA's joint sponsorship of a testimonial dinner for Henry Wallace (with the *New Republic*), see ADA Papers, Series I, Box 33, WSHS.

33. Jacque Duclos, "On the Dissolution of the Communist Party of the United States," *Political Affairs,* Vol. 24 (August 1945), p. 656. William Z. Foster, "Leninism and Some Practical Problems of the Postwar Period," *Political Affairs,* Vol. 25 (April 1946), p. 106.

34. Adam Lapin, "Truman and the Republicans," *Political Affairs,* Vol. 24 (October 1945), p. 881; Eugene Dennis, *America at the Crossroads* (New York, 1945), p. 28.

35. Although the Communists were largely destroyed from the top by the government and by the trade union bureaucracies, they may have contributed to their own destruction by consistently retreating in their mass organizations. For an example of the conservatism that would continue to plague the Communists even during the Foster period, see Rob F. Hall, "Labor in the 1946 Primaries," *Political Affairs,* Vol. 25 (August 1946), pp. 704–712.

36. Although perhaps exaggerating the Communist strength up to the disastrous Progressive Party campaign, Joseph Starobin provides the best account of the Party's decline (Starobin, *op. cit.*).

37. *New Republic,* Vol. 112 (June 4, 1945), p. 774.

38. For a fuller presentation of this thesis, see Markowitz, *op. cit.,* Chapter 6.

39. For a criticism of popular-front thinking on the Communist and Soviet questions, see Granville Hicks, "The *P.M.* Mind," *New Republic,* Vol. 112 (April 16, 1945), pp. 514–516.

40. Markowitz, *op. cit.,* Chapters 7–9.

41. James Loeb, Radio Address, September 26, 1946, ADA Papers, Series 7, Box 105, WSHS.

42. James Loeb, Jr., Letter to the *New Republic,* Vol. 114 (May 13, 1946), p. 699. Memorandum, Proposed Conference of Democratic Progressives, undated, Reinhold Niebuhr Papers, Box 10, Library of Congress; Alonzo Hamby, "Harry S. Truman and American Liberalism, 1945–1948" (unpublished Ph.D. thesis, University of Missouri, 1965), p. 150.

43. Popular fronters Frank Kingdon and Clark Foreman were among those questioned, along with Loeb and Niebuhr. "Liberals and Labor," *New Republic,* Vol. 114 (June 12, 1946), pp. 830–831. Philip Murray to Norman Cousins, September 13, 1946, Murray Papers, Box A-32, Catholic University of America, Washington, D.C.

44. Report of the Conference of Progressives, September 28–29, 1946, Box A-33; Baldwin to Murray, February 3, 1947, Box A-33, both in the Murray Papers. Ickes to Norman Thomas, November 25, 1946, Box 50, New York Public Library, Thomas Papers.

45. "Picking Up the Pieces," *Nation,* Vol. 163 (November 16, 1946), p. 543. For press and radio comment on the elections, see Harry S. Truman Papers, Editorial Comment, Box 3, HSTL.

46. Jerry Voorhis, *Confessions of a Congressman* (Garden City, N.Y., 1947), p. 230; Robert La Follette, Jr., "Look Out, Liberals," *Progressive,* Vol. 10 (November 25, 1946), p. 2; "The CIO Meets," *New Republic,* Vol. 115 (December 2, 1946), p. 716.

47. Niebuhr to Oscar Chapman, November 30, 1946, Oscar Chapman Papers, Box 89, ADA Folder, HSTL.

48. Right after the war, for example, Niebuhr criticized liberals for being "corrupted by the immense self-righteousness and sense of power of a victorious nation." Reinhold Niebuhr. "A Lecture to Liberals," *Nation,* Vol. 161 (November 10, 1945), p. 491.

49. Paul Carter, *The Decline and Revival of the Social Gospel* (Ithaca, N.Y., 1956), p. 156; Reinhold Niebuhr, "The Confusion of Good and Evil," Sermon Outline, Niebuhr Papers, Box 14, Library of Congress.

50. For the most succinct statement of Niebuhr's view of power, see Reinhold Niebuhr, *The Children of Light and the Children of Darkness* (New York, 1944).

51. Reinhold Niebuhr, "New Allies, Old Issues," *Nation,* Vol. 153 (July 19, 1941), pp. 50–52; Reinhold Niebuhr, Letter to the Editor of the

Nation, Nation, Vol. 162 (March 30, 1946), p. 383; Reinhold Niebuhr, "Europe, Russia, and America," *Nation,* Vol. 163 (September 14, 1946), pp. 691–692.

52. Niebuhr to Oscar Chapman, November 30, 1946, Chapman Papers, Box 89, HSTL.

53. Program for Political Action, PCA Founding Conference, December 29, 1946, Progressive Party Papers, Box 11, Folder 35, University of Iowa, Iowa City, Iowa.

54. Freda Kirchway, "Mugwumps in Action," *Nation,* Vol. 164 (January 18, 1947), p. 62. Hamby, *op. cit.,* pp. 159–161.

55. *Ibid.;* Minutes of UDA Expansion Meeting, January 4, 1947, ADA Papers, Series I, Box 53, WSHS.

56. The text of the ADA declaration is reprinted in full in Curtis D. MacDougall, *Gideon's Army* (New York, 1965), Vol. I, pp. 121–122.

57. Robert Bendiner, "Revolt of the Middle," *Nation,* Vol. 164 (January 18, 1947), pp. 65–66; James Loeb, Jr., to Hubert Humphrey, July 30, 1947, ADA Papers, Series I, Box 53, WSHS.

58. ADA Press Release, December 9, 1947, in Records of the Dean of the Maxwell School of Journalism, RG 4, Syracuse University, Syracuse, N.Y.

59. *New York Times,* December 30, 1947.

60. For a fuller presentation, see Markowitz, *op. cit.,* Chapter 8.

61. *Ibid.* For the ADA's major attacks on Wallace, see ADA, "Henry A. Wallace: The First Three Months" (Washington, 1948) and ADA, "Henry A. Wallace: The Last Seven Months" (Washington, 1948).

62. Clark Clifford, Confidential Memorandum to the President, November 19, 1947, Clark Clifford Papers, Political File, Box 21, HSTL; Markowitz, *op. cit.,* Chapter 8.

63. *New York Times,* July 23, 1948.

64. Schlesinger, *op. cit.; ADA World* rather prematurely announced "Truman Triumph Heralds New Era: Liberal Labor Forces in Key Role," *ADA World,* November 10, 1948.

LABOR'S COLD WAR:
The CIO and the Communists

1. The most influential accounts are, Max Kampelman, *The Communist Party vs. The CIO,* (New York, 1957); David Saposs, *Communism in*

American Unions, (New York, 1959); Philip Taft, *Organized Labor in American History,* (New York, 1964).

2. Kampelman, *The Communist Party vs. The CIO,* p. 249.

3. See, for example, Frank Emspak, "The Break-Up of the Congress of Industrial Organizations, 1945–1950," unpublished doctoral dissertation, University of Wisconsin, 1972; James Prickett, "Some Aspects of the Communist Controversy in the CIO," *Science and Society,* vol. XXXIII, (Summer-Fall, 1968); F.S. O'Brien, "The Communist-Dominated Unions in the United States Since 1950," *Labor History,* vol. LX (Fall, 1968); For the accounts of left-wing participants, see, Art Preis, *Labor's Giant Step: Twenty Years of the CIO,* (New York, 1964); Len DeCaux, *Labor Radical,* (Boston, 1970). Mr. Preis is a Trotskyist, while Mr. DeCaux was a Communist Party member.

4. *Report of the Proceedings of the Fifty-Fifth Annual Convention of the American Federation of Labor,* 1935, pp. 778–779.

5. See, Saul Alinsky, *John L. Lewis: An Unauthorized Biography,* (New York, 1949), pp. 370–376; James Green, "Working Class Militancy in the Depression," *Radical America,* vol. 6, no. 6 (November–December, 1972), pp. 1–30.

6. See, Bernard Karsh and Phillips Garman, "The Impact of the Political Left," in Milton Derber and Edwin Young, *Labor and the New Deal,* (Madison, 1957), p. 87.

7. DeCaux, *Labor Radical,* p. 162.

8. Karsh and Garman, "The Impact of the Political Left," pp. 105–107.

9. Kampelman, *The Communist Party vs. The CIO,* pp. 14–23.

10. *Ibid.,* pp. 25–27.

11. See, Preis, *Labor's Giant Step,* p. 46.

12. James Prickett, "Communism and Factionalism in the United Automobile Workers, 1939–1947," *Science and Society,* vol. XXXII (Summer-Fall, 1968) p. 260.

13. Quoted in *Steel Labor,* July 28, 1939.

14. *Proceedings of the Fifth Annual Convention of the United Automobile Workers,* 1940, pp. 101–104; *Proceedings of the Sixth Annual Convention of the United Automobile Workers,* 1941, pp. 77–83, 328–332.

15. See, DeCaux, *Labor Radical,* pp. 330–331.

Notes

16. *Ibid.*, p. 379.

17. *Proceedings of the Third Constitutional Convention of the CIO,* 1941, p. 192.

18. See, Irving Howe and Lewis Coser, *The American Communist Party,* (Boston, 1957), pp. 411–412; Preis, *Labor's Giant Step,* p. 222.

19. See, National Association of Manufacturers, *Freedom From Victory: A Program Adopted by the War and Reconversion Committee of American Industry,* (New York, 1944); Eric Goldman, *The Crucial Decade,* (New York, 1956), pp. 16–46; Taft, *Organized Labor in American History,* pp. 563–578.

20. "Work Stoppages Caused by Labor-Management Disputes in 1945," *Monthly Labor Review,* vol. 62, no. 5 (April, 1946), pp. 718–735.

21. See, R. Alton Lee, *Truman and Taft-Hartley,* (Lexington, Kentucky, 1966), p. 52.

22. John Fitch, "The New Congress and the Unions," *Survey-Graphic,* vol. XXXVI (April, 1947), p. 231.

23. An excellent analysis of the Duclos letter can be found in Joseph Starobin, *American Communism in Crisis, 1943–1957,* (Cambridge, Mass., 1972), pp. 71–106.

24. The *San Antonio Light* editorial is quoted, Les Adler, "The Red Image: American Attitudes Towards Communism in the Cold War Era," unpublished doctoral dissertation, University of California, Berkeley, 1970, p. 74. On the Chamber, see Chamber of Commerce of the United States, *Communist Infiltration in the United States,* (Washington, 1946), pp. 21–22.

25. Quoted, *Newsweek,* vol. XXVIII (July 22, 1946), p. 28.

26. *Proceedings of the 75th Annual Convention of the American Federation of Labor,* 1946, p. 553.

27. Nine affiliates—the Mine, Mill and Smelter Union, the Food and Tobacco Union, the United Office and Professional Workers, the United Public Workers, the International Longshoremans' and Warehousemans' Union, the Marine Cooks and Stewards, the International Fur and Leather Workers, and the International Fisherman and Allied Workers—were expelled, while two others—the United Electrical Workers and the Farm Equipment Workers—departed before they could be removed.

NOTES

28. Murray's quotes are in Kampelman, *The Communist Party vs. The CIO*, p. 129; and DeCaux, *Labor Radical*, p. 239.

29. *Proceedings of the Eighth Constitutional Convention of the CIO,* 1946, pp. 111–113.

30. *Sixteenth Biennial Convention of the Fur and Leather Workers Union,* 1946, p. 253.

31. *Proceedings of the Fifteenth Biennial Convention of the Amalgamated Clothing Workers,* 1946, p. 96.

32. Irwin Ross, *The Loneliest Campaign,* (New York, 1968), p. 146.

33. Murray's quote is in Preis, *Labor's Giant Step,* p. 337. See also, Kampelman, *The Communist Party vs. The CIO,* pp. 107–109.

34. *Proceedings of the Ninth Constitutional Convention of the CIO,* 1947, pp. 258–262.

35. *Ibid.,* p. 277.

36. *Ibid.,* p. 283.

37. *Ibid.,* p. 292.

38. *Ibid.*

39. Quoted in Walter Galenson, *The CIO Challenge to the AFL,* (Cambridge, Mass., 1960), p. 255.

40. *UE News,* March 22, 1941.

41. *Ibid.,* July 12, 1941.

42. Quoted, *Proceedings of the Seventh Annual Convention of the United Electrical Workers,* 1941, p. 172.

43. See, Galenson, *The CIO Challenge to the AFL,* pp. 254–265.

44. Quoted, *Proceedings of the Seventh Annual Convention of the United Electrical Workers,* 1941, pp. 111, 137.

45. Quoted in Kampelman, *The Communist Party vs. the CIO,* p. 130.

46. Quoted, *Proceedings of the Eleventh Annual Convention of the United Electrical Workers,* 1946, p. 80.

47. Quoted, *Proceedings of the Fifth Constitutional Proceedings of the United Rubber Workers,* 1940, p. 5.

48. See, Michael Harrington, "Catholics in the Labor Movement," *Labor History,* vol. I (Fall, 1960), pp. 253–261.

49. James Matles, "The Members Run This Union," UE Publication #94, pp. 33–34.

50. Although employer responses to Communist-dominated unions varied greatly during this period, a movement was begun by several business periodicals to encourage management to favor anti-Communist union groups over pro-Communist ones. *The Management Review,* for example, wrote that "If a Communist group is attempting to secure control of a union with which you deal, tough management policy toward non-Communist leaders may drive employees into the Communist camp. Therefore, carefully examine all details of your collective bargaining policies to insure that you are not providing the Communist elements with ammunition . . . And under no circumstances accept cooperation from a dissident Communist group within the union in opposing demands of a non-Communist element." (*Management Review,* April, 1946, p. 36). Similarly, the Research Institute of America advised businessmen, "Employers should carefully examine their collective bargaining policies to determine whether they help arm the Communist drive for power in the union . . . You may run up against an offer of apparent cooperation from a Communist wing of a union in your plant. From any long range point of view, acceptance of such an offer is dangerous." (See, *Industrial Relations,* vol. 6, no. 6 October, 1948, p. 33.)

51. See, Kampelman, *The Communist Party vs. The CIO,* p. 134.

52. Quoted in Saposs, *Communism in American Unions,* pp. 234–235.

53. *Communist Domination of Unions and National Security, Hearings Before a Subcommittee of the Senate Committee on Labor and Public Welfare,* U.S. Senate, 82nd cong., 2nd sess., p. 459.

54. See, Harrington, "Catholics in the Labor Movement," pp. 262–263; James Prickett, "The NMU and the Ambiguities of Anti-Communism," *New Politics,* vol. VII (Winter, 1968) pp. 54–59.

55. Harrington, "Catholics in the Labor Movement," pp. 262–263.

56. Prickett, "Communism and Factionalism in the UAW," p. 260.

57. *Proceedings of the Sixth Annual Convention of the United Automobile Workers,* 1941, pp. 690–702.

58. Galenson, *The CIO Challenge to the AFL,* p. 178.

59. *The Wage Earner,* March 29, 1946.

NOTES

60. *Ibid.,* April 4, 1947.

61. *UAW Press Release,* March 28, 1947.

62. See, Robert Ozanne, "The Effects of Communist Leadership on American Trade Unions," unpublished doctoral dissertation, University of Wisconsin, 1954, pp. 273–300; Thomas Gavett, *The Development of the Labor Movement in Milwaukee,* (Madison, 1965), pp. 190–196.

63. Quoted in Irving Howe and B. J. Widick, *The UAW and Walter Reuther,* (New York, 1947), p. 166.

64. *Proceedings of the Eleventh Convention of the United Automobile Workers,* 1947, pp. 75–83.

65. Emspak, "The Break-Up of the CIO," pp. 174–179.

66. See, Howe and Widick, *The UAW and Walter Reuther,* pp. 149–171; Frank Cormier and William Eaton, *Reuther,* (Englewood Cliffs, New Jersey, 1970), pp. 231–254.

67. Prickett, "Communism and Factionalism in the UAW," pp. 257–277.

68. Kampelman, *The Communist Party vs. The CIO,* p. 143; Preis, *Labor's Giant Step,* pp. 345–346; 369–370.

69. "CIO-PAC Speakers Book of Facts," 1948.

70. Quoted in Kampelman, *The Communist Party vs. The CIO,* p. 141.

71. *Official Reports on the Expulsion of Communist-Dominated Organizations From the CIO,* 1954, pp. 14–15, 26–27, 106–118.

72. F. S. O'Brien, "The Communist Dominated Unions in the United States Since 1950," p. 43.

73. *CIO News,* March 6, 1950.

74. See, Harrington, "Catholics in the Labor Movement," pp. 262–263; Prickett, "Some Aspects of the Communist Controversy in the CIO," pp. 319–321.

75. *CIO News,* November 20, 1950.

76. Paul Jacobs, *The State of The Unions,* (New York, 1956), p. 263.

THE POLITICS OF CIVIL LIBERTIES:
The American Civil Liberties Union During the McCarthy Years

1. The National Civil Liberties Bureau, the predecessor of the American Civil Liberties Union, was founded in 1917. The ACLU itself was estab-

lished in 1920. For the history of the ACLU's founding and early years, see Donald Johnson, *The Challenge to American Freedoms: World War I and the Rise of the American Civil Liberties Union* (Lexington, Ky., 1963, pp. 145–203.

2. The ACLU's problems during the McCarthy years were not reflected in its membership rolls, however. The American Civil Liberties Union, *Security and Freedom: The Great Challenge* (New York, 1951), p. 87, showed on January 1, 1950, a national membership (excluding membership of local affiliates) of 9,355, a net gain of almost 15 percent for the fiscal year. By January 31, 1955, net total membership was almost 30,000, a figure only partially acounted for by the inclusion of local affiliates with the national membership figure (The American Civil Liberties Union, *Clearing the Main Channels* [New York, 1955], p. 136).

3. In 1939, Congressman Martin Dies labeled the ACLU a Communist front and planned to call the Union for a hearing before the House Committee on Un-American Activities. The hearing did not take place, however; quite unexpectedly, Dies announced that the ACLU was not a Communist organization and therefore need not be investigated. In a letter to Corliss Lamont, a longtime ACLU board member, Dies later said that in consultation with the ACLU's two general counsels, Morris Ernst and Arthur Garfield Hays, he had proposed "that if we worked together, we could destroy the Communist apparatus and influence within a few months, and that the liberals would share in the credit." Unfortunately, Dies continued to Lamont, the ACLU attorneys had not agreed to his plan. Lamont continued to suspect, however, that some sort of understanding was reached between Dies and the two ACLU attorneys at this time; the ACLU dropped its original plan to challenge the constitutionality of the committee's procedure on the basis of the First Amendment (Corliss Lamont, *Freedom Is as Freedom Does: Civil Liberties Today* [New York, 1956], pp. 268–270).

4. The American Civil Liberties Union, *In the Shadow of War: The Story of Civil Liberty, 1939–1940* (New York, 1940), pp. 6, 48–50; The American Civil Liberties Union, *Crisis in the Civil Liberties Union: A Statement, Including the Basic Documents Concerned, Giving the Minority Position in the Current Controversy in the A.C.L.U.* (New York, 1940), p. 5; Osmond K. Fraenkel, "Extracts from Diaries of Osmond K. Fraenkel Relating to American Civil Liberties Union," 3 vols. (1933–1968), Manuscript Division, Princeton University Library, Princeton, N.J., pp. 2–3; Corliss Lamont, ed., *The Trial of Elizabeth Gurley Flynn by the American Civil Liberties Union* (New York, 1968), pp. 13–14; Lucille Milner, *Education of an American Liberal* (New York, 1954), pp. 262–268.

NOTES

Roger Baldwin, executive director of the ACLU from its founding until 1950, concluded that the 1940 anti-Communist resolution, which he drafted, was the means of settling the controversy that threatened to split the ACLU board. He acted for what he believed was the majority view, "which so turned out." Baldwin later stated that he was "satisfied with the resolution's results and the effect of Miss Flynn's expulsion, which cleared up the troublesome question of how a civil liberties organization could tolerate in its councils an apologist for dictatorship" (Roger Baldwin to author, March 6, 1972).

5. The American Civil Liberties Union, *In the Shadow of Fear: American Liberties, 1948–1949* (New York, 1949), p. 71.

6. "Proposed Revisions of Constitution and By-Laws of American Civil Liberties Union, Inc.," June 13, 1951; Board of Directors agenda for September 17, 1951, both in Vol. 1, 1951, American Civil Liberties Union Archives, Princeton University Library, Princeton, N.J. (hereafter cited as ACLU Papers).

7. The statement was as follows: "The American Civil Liberties Union is an organization devoted to the protection and expansion of the guarantees contained in the Bill of Rights. Because this proceeding is alleged to involve a member of the Communist Party, we believe that it is pertinent to state our views. The American Civil Liberties Union as a champion of civil liberties is opposed to any governmental or economic system which denies fundamental civil liberties and human rights. It is therefore opposed to any form of the police state or to any single party state and any movement in support of them, whether fascist, Communist, or known by any other name. In opposing these dictatorial or totalitarian systems, the Union takes no position on their economic, social or political practices or politics not affecting civil liberties" (Herbert M. Levy [staff counsel] to Emil Oxfeld, October 6, 1949, Vol. 34, 1950, ACLU Papers). Also see minutes, Board of Directors, June 26, 1950, Vol. 7, 1950, ACLU Papers.

8. The ACLU had only recently emerged from an attack from the right following its attempt to uncover and halt blacklisting in the broadcasting industry. The Union's sponsorship of *The Judges and the Judged* (Garden City, N.Y., 1952), an investigatory book on blacklisting by a board member, Merle Miller, had created a storm of controversy within the Union itself when another of the board's members, Merlyn Pitzele, challenged the book's accuracy. A special committee of the ACLU board studied Pitzele's charges and upheld the book's overall accuracy; the board, by a large majority, then approved the special committee's report and voted to continue ACLU sponsorship. The core of Pitzele's criticism,

however, was not that the book was factually inaccurate but that it had failed to recognize that Communism, rather than McCarthyism, was the real danger in America. Consequently, Pitzele's quarrel was with the book's basic purpose, which was to fight a form of McCarthyism. Unfortunately, Miller's self-defense, that he was as good an anti-Communist as Pitzele or anybody else, reflected a fear of attack from the right which became increasingly evident among many members of the ACLU's board, particularly following the controversy over *The Judges and the Judged*. See Merlyn S. Pitzele, "Is There a Blacklist?" *New Leader,* May 12, 1952, pp. 21–23; Pitzele, " 'This Book Is a Bad Mistake. . . .,' " *New Leader,* June 16, 1952, pp. 15, 18; Merle Miller, "Is 'The Judges and the Judged' an Honest Book?" *New Leader,* June 16, 1952, pp. 12–14; "Report of Special Committee to Investigate the Charges Against Merle Miller's 'The Judges and the Judged,' " July 14, 1952, p. 7, Vol. 1, 1952; minutes, Board of Directors, July 21, 1952, pp. 1–2, Vol. 1, 1952, both in ACLU Papers; Fraenkel, *op. cit.,* p. 43.

9. "Now," wrote ACLU director Patrick Murphy Malin in a 1954 reformulation of the ACLU's anti-Communist statement, "when American civil liberties are threatened from the outside by the aggressions of Soviet Communism, and on the inside by excrescences of our people's natural and indispensable determination to guard against acts of treasonable or revolutionary subversion, a new statement [of the ACLU's post-1940 policy on Communism] is necessary. . . ." (Patrick Murphy Malin to [ACLU Corporation], "Reformulation of the Form of Statements 1, 2, 3," January 28, 1954, Vol. 1, 1954, ACLU Papers).

Malin, formerly professor of economics at Swarthmore College and vice-director of the Intergovernmental Committee on Refugees from 1943 to 1947, replaced Roger Baldwin as the ACLU's director in 1950.

10. "In view of the continuing though irresponsible charges and insinuations that the American Civil Liberties Union is equivocal in its attitude toward Communism, or unaware of the nature of the Communist Party in the U.S.," wrote the Reverend John Paul Jones, "the Board of Directors desires once and for all to set the record straight" ("Statement to be submitted to Board of ACLU," March 15, 1954, Vol. 1, 1954, ACLU Papers). Varian Fry, one of the more conservative members of the board, argued that "many feel that we have failed badly in our major duty today: to show how a secret, deadly and worldwide conspiracy against our basic freedoms can be successfully combated without sacrifice of our immediate civil liberties" (Varian Fry to Patrick Murphy Malin, January 20, 1954, Vol. 1, 1954, ACLU Papers).

11. Lamont, *Freedom Is as Freedom Does,* p. 280.

By 1951, a small group of men had concluded that a new organiza-

NOTES

tion was needed "to augment the American Civil Liberties Union, but with guts enough to fight the evils of McCarthyism without fear of being sullied by the label of 'pro-Communist.' " They founded the Emergency Civil Liberties Committee, a non-Communist organization, in which Corliss Lamont became active ("Emergency Civil Liberties Committee, First Fifteen Years: 1951–1966," *Rights,* December 1966, pp. 4–6).

12. The special committee consisted of Norman Thomas, Morris Ernst, the Reverend John Paul Jones, and James Wechsler, the editor of the New York *Post.*

13. The second section of the statement, on academic freedom and educational and United Nations employment, advocated a United Nations security program and stated that "commitments of any kind which interfere with [the free and unbiased pursuit of truth and understanding] are incompatible with the objectives of academic freedom." The third section, on the proper uses of the Fifth Amendment privileges, stated that "the ACLU recognizes that there are certain situations in which a person's exercise of the [Fifth Amendment] privilege may be inconsistent witih his duty of full disclosure toward an employer," particularly in the fields of government service, the United Nations, and education. The statement held that employers in these fields did not violate employees' civil liberties by considering their use of the Fifth Amendment and by giving "such weight to the refusal [to answer] as may be appropriate in the particular circumstances" ("Proposal #1, As Adopted by the Board on April 20, 1953," Vol. 1, 1953, ACLU Papers).

14. ACLU, *In the Shadow of War,* p. 48. This section of the 1940 resolution read: "The American Civil Liberties Union does not make any test of opinion on political or economic issues a condition of membership. . . ."

15. Fraenkel, *op. cit.,* p. 45; The American Civil Liberties Union, *America's Need: A New Birth of Freedom* (New York, 1954), p. 128.

16. W. [William] L. White to [ACLU], March 15, 1954, American Civil Liberties Union Papers, American Civil Liberties Union, New York (hereafter cited as ACLU Papers, New York). Contemplating the possibility of Communists controlling ACLU policy, White, editor of the Emporia (Kansas) *Gazette* and an ACLU board member, commented, "As maybe they already have."

17. Minutes, Board of Directors, April 15, 1953, pp. 1–3; May 4, 1953, pp. 1–2; Board to Corporation members, May 8, 1953, all in Vol. 1, 1953, ACLU Papers.

Notes

18. "Affirmative Arguments, Negative Arguments," September 1, 1953, Vol. 1, 1953, ACLU Papers; Fraenkel, *op. cit.,* p. 47.

19. Minutes, Board of Directors, August 31, 1953; Ernest Angell to Corporation members, September 1, 1953, both in Vol. 1, 1953, ACLU Papers; Fraenkel, *op. cit.,* p. 47.

Corliss Lamont objected to the impropriety of Angell's action and sent telegrams to each affiliate stating his objections and, further, indicating that the board had only approved the policy statement because its members had become tired of arguing (Corliss Lamont to George E. Rundquist, September 11, 1953, Vol. 1, 1953, ACLU Papers). One board member, Herbert R. Northrup, a labor economist and member of the National Industrial Conference Board, was so angered by Lamont's action that he proposed censuring him for it, but was prevented by a quick adjournment of the meeting (Fraenkel, *op. cit.,* p. 47). Edward J. Ennis, an attorney and board member, later proposed a motion to censure Lamont, which the board tabled after Lamont apologized for his remarks to the affiliates about the board (Minutes, Board of Directors, October 5, 1953, p. 2, ACLU Papers, New York).

20. The ACLU's "general" members, as differentiated from the corporate members, had little formal power in the organization. See Barton Bean, "Pressure for Freedom: The American Civil Liberties Union" (Ph.D. dissertation, Cornell University, 1955), p. 123.

21. Bean, *ibid.,* pp. 208–215, 227–231, 239; "Proposed Revisions of Constitution and By-Laws of American Civil Liberties Union, Inc.," June 13, 1951, p. 7; Board of Directors agenda for September 17, 1951, both in Vol. 1, 1951, ACLU Papers; Lamont, *Freedom Is as Freedom Does,* pp. 279–280.

22. Lamont, *Freedom Is as Freedom Does,* pp. 279, 281; "The ACLU's Directors Prepare to Jettison Its Principles," *I. F. Stone's Weekly,* October 31, 1953, p. 2; Corliss Lamont, "Corliss Lamont's Inside Story After 21 Years," *I. F. Stone's Weekly,* March 1, 1954, p. 5.

The corporate vote was taken by a weighted voting procedure, a complex arrangement that gave the national committee and the national board of directors proportionately a far greater voice than the affiliates in the total vote.

I. F. Stone, who analyzed the vote on the referendum, observed that the national committee and national board of directors were three to one in favor of the new policy statement, whereas the affiliates cast all but 600 of their 16,000 votes against the statement ("Convulsions at the ACLU," *I. F. Stone's Weekly,* December 14, 1953, p. 3).

NOTES

23. Minutes, Board of Directors, October 19, 1953, p. 2; November 16, 30, 1953, all in Vol. 1, 1953, ACLU Papers; "ACLU's Directors Prepare to Jettison Its Principles," p. 2; Fraenkel, *op. cit.,* pp. 48–49.

Following the referendum, Patrick Murphy Malin had conducted an investigation of the affiliates' votes; during this procedure, Chicago, the largest of the affiliates, decided to change its original vote to one of concurrence with the board's policy statement, and thus reversed the outcome of the entire referendum. Lamont contested Chicago's vote switch on the grounds that the October 16 deadline for the referendum had passed, that it would be illegal "to alter the ballot totals after the referendum had been officially concluded," and that the procedure involved in the vote switch was "based chiefly on a hasty and incomplete telephone poll." Following a telephone call from Lamont, the Chicago group restored its original vote at its next meeting, thus again reversing the outcome of the entire referendum to the original vote for rejection (Lamont, *Freedom Is as Freedom Does,* p. 281). Malin complained to the board of Lamont's action and in particular objected to Lamont's implication that Malin was acting illegally by telephoning the affiliates. Malin stated that he was not trying to conduct a telephone ballot but to produce more ballots, as in the case of the Chicago affiliate, where only 29 percent of the Chicago board was represented in the first vote (Patrick Murphy Malin to Board, November 13, 1953, Vol. 1, 1953, ACLU Papers).

Fraenkel noted that at the October 19 meeting, those in favor of rejecting the referendum included: James Fly, Norman Thomas, Morris Ernst, Ernest Angell, Merlyn Pitzele, Herbert Northrup, Varian Fry, Whitney North Seymour (an attorney), William Fitelson (managing director of the "Theatre Guild on the Air"), Katrina McCormick Barnes (former publisher of *Common Sense*), James Kerney (editor of the *Trenton Times*), and Norman Cousins (editor of the *Saturday Review*). Those opposed were: Osmond Fraenkel, Arthur Garfield Hays, Walter Gellhorn, Corliss Lamont, the Reverend John Paul Jones, Edward Ennis, the Reverend John Haynes Holmes (former chairman of the ACLU board), General Telford Taylor, Elmer Rice (the playwright), Judge Dorothy Kenyon (one of the first persons McCarthy accused of being part of the Communist conspiracy), Dorothy Dunbar Bromley (Scripps-Howard columnist), Richard Childs (chairman of the Council of the National Municipal League), Walter Frank (an attorney), and Judge J. Waties Waring (retired judge of the Federal District Court in South Carolina) (Fraenkel, *op. cit.,* p. 48).

Shortly after the October 19 meeting, several board members who had voted to accept the referendum as final began to change their minds. Five of them (Dorothy Bromley, Edward Ennis, Walter Frank, John Paul Jones, and Judge Waring) circulated a memorandum to the other board members seeking to reject the referendum's results (Patrick

Murphy Malin to Board members, October 23, 1953, Vol. I, 1953, ACLU Papers).

24. Minutes, Board of Directors, November 30, 1953, pp. 2–3, Vol. I, 1953, ACLU Papers.

25. "Statement by Special Graham Committee Unanimously Adopted at Biennial Conference, February 14, 1954," ACLU Papers, New York; Fraenkel, *op. cit.,* p. 56.

26. Minutes, Board of Directors, February 15, 1954, pp. 1–2, Vol. I, 1954, ACLU Papers; Lamont, *Freedom Is as Freedom Does,* p. 283.

27. Norman Thomas to Board members, March 5, 1954; W. [William] L. White to [ACLU], March 15, 1954, both in ACLU Papers, New York; Lamont, *Freedom Is as Freedom Does,* p. 283.

28. John Finerty to [Patrick Murphy] Malin, March 15, 1954, Vol. I, 1954, ACLU Papers.

29. Minutes, Board of Directors, March 15, 1954, pp. 1–2, Vol. I, 1954, ACLU Papers; Fraenkel, *op. cit.,* p. 59.

30. New York *World-Telegram,* March 17, 1954.

31. Patrick Murphy Malin to Board members, March 18, 1954, p. 1, Vol. I, 1954, ACLU Papers.

32. The committee, announced on March 29, 1954, consisted of Judge Waring as chairman and Walter Gellhorn, Dorothy Kenyon, and Norman Thomas from the board. Fraenkel later took Gellhorn's place. The national committee of the ACLU and the affiliates were each represented by two other committee members (Fraenkel, *op. cit.,* pp. 60, 63).

33. The statement also condemned the loss of any job, public or private, solely because of an employee's availing himself of the privilege of the Fifth Amendment: "The use of the privilege against self-incrimination does not justify any inference as to the character of the answer which might have been given to the question." In addition, the statement opposed security probes into the beliefs and associations of United Nations employees other than for connection with possible subversion (Fraenkel, *op. cit.,* pp. 61, 63; Special Committee on Statements 1, 2 and 3, to Board members, July 9, 1954; Patrick Murphy Malin to Board members, July 21, 1954, both in Vol. I, 1954, ACLU Papers).

34. Patrick Murphy Malin to Board members, July 21, 1954, pp. 1–2; minutes, Board of Directors, August 2, 1954, p. 1; November 22, 1954, all in Vol. I, 1954, ACLU Papers; Fraenkel, *op. cit.,* p. 64.

NOTES

35. Corliss Lamont to the Senate Permanent Subcommittee on Investigations of the Senate Committee on Government Operations, September 23, 1953, ACLU Papers, New York; Lamont, *Freedom Is as Freedom Does,* pp. 33–47.

36. Minutes, Board of Directors, October 5, 1953, p. 1; Special Committee on Mr. Lamont's Appearance before Senator McCarthy's Subcommittee to Board members, October 29, 1953, pp. 1–2; Philip Wittenberg to American Civil Liberties Union, November 25, 1953; minutes, Board of Directors, November 30, 1953, all in Vol. 1, 1953, ACLU Papers.

37. Those supporting Fraenkel's proposal were Edward Ennis and Arthur Garfield Hays. Those opposed were Ernest Angell, Morris Ernst, James Fly, and Judge Waring (Fraenkel, *op. cit.,* p. 51).

38. Minutes, Board of Directors, December 14, 1953, Vol. 1, 1953; ACLU news release, January 7, 1954, Vol. 1, 1954, both in ACLU Papers; Fraenkel, *op. cit.,* p. 52.

In March 1954, the ACLU protested to the Senate Committee on Government Operations when that committee voted to cite Lamont for contempt. In August 1954, the United States Senate voted seventy-one to three to cite Lamont for contempt of Congress. The ACLU office, attempting to prevent the citation, had contacted the Senate's majority and minority leaders and had distributed its memorandum on the case to all members of McCarthy's committee. In addition, it filed a friend-of-the-court brief supporting Lamont's motion to dismiss the indictment against him (Patrick Murphy Malin to Board members, March 18, 1954, p. 1; minutes, Board of Directors, September 13, 1954, both in Vol. 1, 1954, ACLU Papers; ACLU Feature Press Service, November 29, 1954, pp. 1–2, ACLU Papers, New York).

In October 1954, a federal grand jury in New York City indicted Lamont for contempt of the United States Senate. In November, Lamont filed motion for dismissal of the indictment, citing a new point: that neither the Senate nor the Senate Committee on Government Operations "had ever passed any resolution or minute formally and legally establishing the McCarthy Subcommittee." In July 1955, Judge Edward Weinfeld of the United States District Court, Southern District of New York, granted the motion for dismissal based upon his findings that the McCarthy subcommittee had acted beyond the scope of its authority and was not duly empowered by the Senate to conduct the particular inquiry. The government gave notice that it would carry this decision to a federal court of appeals, but it made no move to reindict Lamont, who had won a considerable victory (Lamont, *Freedom Is as Freedom Does,* pp. 46–47).

Notes

39. Minutes, Board of Directors, November 16, 1953, p. 1; November 30, 1953, p. 2; Lamont, *Freedom Is as Freedom Does,* pp. 281–282; "Corliss Lamont's Inside Story After 21 Years," pp. 5–6; New York *World-Telegram,* December 11, 1953; Fraenkel, *op. cit.,* p. 50.

Fraenkel also recorded that he, Roger Baldwin, John Finerty, Edward Ennis, and John Paul Jones "all agreed" that Lamont was "a useful member of the Board" (Fraenkel, *op. cit.,* p. 50). Somewhat later, at a January 1954 ACLU board meeting, Fraenkel insisted that while on the board, Lamont "had always stood for the civil liberties of all" (Fraenkel, *op. cit.,* p. 53).

40. Minutes, Board of Directors, November 30, 1953, p. 2; Corliss Lamont to the National Committee and Affiliates of the A.C.L.U., January 22, 1954, p. 1, Vol. 1, 1954, ACLU Papers.

41. Patrick Murphy Malin to Board, January 14, 1954, p. 1; minutes, Board of Directors, January 4, 1954, p. 1; January 18, 1954, p. 2; Herbert M. Levy [staff counsel] to Judge Thurman Arnold, October 28, 1954; Arnold to Levy, October 29, 1954; minutes, Board of Directors, November 8, 1954, all in Vol. 1, 1954, ACLU Papers; Fraenkel, *op. cit.,* pp. 52, 65.

42. Minutes, Due Process Committee, April 29, 1952; Herbert M. Levy to "whom it may concern," May 2, 1952, pp. 1, 3; minutes, Due Process Committee, June 12, 1952; September 15, 1952; Herbert M. Levy to Due Process Committee, September 10, 1952, pp. 1–2; minutes, Due Process Committee, November 10, 1952; minutes, Board of Directors, November 17, 1952; "Statement of the National Board of Directors Regarding Commutation of Death Sentences in Rosenberg Atomic Espionage Case," December 1, 1952; HML [Herbert M. Levy] to PMM [Patrick Murphy Malin], March 3, 1953, all in Vol. 51, 1953, ACLU Papers; Fraenkel, *op. cit.,* pp. 41, 44.

43. Minutes, Board of Directors, June 12, 1950, p. 2; August 28, 1950, p. 2, both in Vol. 7, 1950; minutes, Board of Directors, December 1, 1952, p. 1, Vol. 1, 1952; minutes, Board of Directors, April 20, 1953, p. 2, Vol. 1, 1953, all in ACLU Papers.

44. On the grounds that the Smith Act abridged free speech and, "even if constitutional, the statute as applied to the eleven is invalid because it was applied in the absence of a 'jury finding of a clear and present danger to carry out the ideas advocated' " ("Justice Department Denies Mass Prosecution of Communists," ACLU Feature Press Service, July 3, 1950, Vol. 33, 1950, ACLU Papers).

45. Minutes, Policy Committee, March 29, 1950, p. 1; minutes, Board of Directors, May 1, 1950, p. 1; August 28, 1950, p. 1; minutes, Policy

Committee, May 9, 1950, p. 2; November 1, 1950, all in Vol. 7, 1950;
Executive Director to Board, June 20, 1951, pp. 12, 14, 16–17; minutes,
Board of Directors, July 25, 1951, both in Vol. 1, 1951; ACLU news
release, June 28, 1951; [Roger Baldwin] to Palmer Weber, June 23,
1951; [Roger Baldwin] to Patrick Murphy Malin, June 27, 1951, all three
in Vol. 49, part II, 1951, all above in ACLU Papers.

46. Minutes, Board of Directors, December 4, 1950, p. 2, Vol. 7, 1950,
ACLU Papers; Fraenkel, *op. cit.,* p. 32; American Civil Liberties Union,
Freedom, Justice, Equality (New York, 1953), p. 103.

47. George Soll [associate staff counsel] to Board, July 31, 1950; minutes,
Alien Civil Rights Committee, November 29, 1950, both in Vol. 7,
1950; "Positions on the Provisions of the Internal Security Act Section
22: Exclusion of Certain Types of Aliens," January 15, 1951, pp. 1–3,
Vol. 1, 1951, all in ACLU Papers; Fraenkel, *op. cit.,* p. 33.

48. ACLU, *Freedom, Justice, Equality,* pp. 75–76; Fraenkel, *op. cit.,*
p. 31.

49. Alan Reitman [associate director, ACLU] to author, March 8, 1972,
p. 2. See also: ACLU, *Freedom, Justice, Equality,* pp. 9–10.

It should be noted that the ACLU returned to active involvement at
the trial stage during the 1960's, "when it became apparent that the
winning of Supreme Court decisions was not enough to achieve realistic
civil liberties gains" (Reitman to author, March 8, 1972, p. 2).

50. Fraenkel, *op. cit.,* p. 56; [Roger Baldwin] to Palmer Weber, June 23,
1951, Vol. 49, part II, 1951, ACLU Papers.

LEGISLATIVE POLITICS AND "McCARTHYISM":
The Internal Security Act of 1950

1. 64 *Stat.* pp. 987–1031. For a legislative history of this act see William R. Tanner, "The Passage of the Internal Security Act of 1950,"
Ph.D. dissertation, University of Kansas, 1971.

2. The Espionage and Sedition Acts of 1917–18 not only punished disloyal actions, but also speech and writings considered detrimental to
American security. The Hatch, McCormack, Voorhis and Smith Acts of
1938–40 were aimed more directly at domestic Nazi and Communist
organizations and propaganda. James M. Smith, *Freedom's Fetters*
(Ithaca N. Y., 1956); Robert K. Murray, *Red Scare* (Minneapolis,
1955); John Higham, *Strangers in the Land* (New York, 1955); Zechariah Chafee, Jr., *Free Speech in the United States* (Cambridge, 1941,
1946); William Preston, *Aliens and Dissenters* (Cambridge, 1963);

Roger Daniels, *Concentration Camps, USA: Japanese Americans and World War II* (New York, 1971).

3. For a survey of the Roosevelt-Truman years, consult Earl Latham, *The Communist Controversy in Washington* (Cambridge, 1966). See also Robert K. Carr, *The House Committee on Un-American Activities. 1945–1950* (Ithaca N. Y., 1952); Walter Goodman, *The Committee* (New York, 1968); Robert Griffith, *The Politics of Fear* (Lexington, Ky., 1970), and Athan Theoharis, *Seeds of Repression* (Chicago, 1971).

4. *New York Times,* January 31, 1946; February 3, 1946; March 17, 1946; April 3, 1946; May 18, 1946; *Congressional Record* (February 26, 1946), pp. A967–968; (March 1, 1946), pp. A1056–1058; (April 1, 1946), pp. A1831–1832; (May 2, 1946), pp. A2441–2443; (June 3, 1946), pp. A3153; (July 8, 1946), pp. A3922–3925; (August 1, 1946), pp. A4726–4727. *Congressional Record* (August 7, 1948), pp. A5114–5115; *New York Times,* October 22, 1948.

5. U.S. House of Representatives, Committee on Un-American Activities, *Protecting the United States Against Un-American and Subversive Activities,* 80th Congress, 2nd Session, House Report No. 1844 (Washington: Government Printing Office, 1948). Copy of H.R. 5852, Harry S. Truman Library, Independence, Mo.

6. Memorandum, American Civil Liberties Union, May 1948, Papers of Emanuel Celler, Internal Security File, 1947–1948, Library of Congress; *Baltimore Sun,* June 1, 1948; *New York Times,* June 1, 2, 3, 1948; U.S. Senate Committee on the Judiciary, *An Act to Protect the United States Against Un-American and Subversive Activities,* 80th Congress, 2nd Session, Hearings (Washington: GPO, 1948), pp. 420–425; *Congressional Record* (June 19, 1948), pp. 9028–9032; Letter, Attorney General Tom C. Clark to Alexander Wiley, June 16, 1948, Papers of Stephen J. Spingarn, Internal Security File, HSTL; *Congressional Record* (May 14, 1948), pp. 5838–5845, 5848–5861, 5869, 5873, 5889; (May 18, 1948), pp. 5851–5853, 5867–5874; (May 19, 1948), pp. 6122–6124.

7. Stephen J. Spingarn to Clark M. Clifford, April 19, 1949, National Defense-S2311, Papers of Stephen J. Spingarn, HSTL; *New York Times,* June 23, 1948; *Congressional Record* (August 5, 1948), pp. 4867–4868. May 2, 1948, p. 1; May 5, 1948, p. 4; May 18, 1948, pp. 1, 16. Taft is quoted in James T. Patterson, *Mr. Republican: A Biography of Robert A. Taft* (Boston, 1972), p. 447.

8. Alan D. Harper, *The Politics of Loyalty* (Westport, Conn., 1969), Chapter 7; Memorandum, Stephen J. Spingarn to Harry S. Truman,

July 14, 1950, Papers of Stephen J. Spingarn, Internal Security File, HSTL; *New York Times*, July 2, 1950; *Congressional Record* (July 14, 1950), pp. 10146–10147.

9. Reprint of speech, *Congressional Record* (January 7, 1947), pp. A27–28; Copy of Address by Tom Clark, September 18, 1948, Papers of Stephen J. Spingarn, White House Assignment File, HSTL: Copy of Remarks by J. Howard McGrath, April 19, 1950, Papers of Emanuel Celler, Internal Security-HUAC, Library of Congress.

10. Stephen J. Spingarn, Memorandum for the Files, July 22, 1950, Papers of Stephen J. Spingarn, HSTL; U.S. House of Representatives, *Hearings on Proposed Legislation to Curb or Control the Communist Party of the United States,* 80th Congress, 2nd Session (Washington: GPO, 1948), pp. 15–27; Reprint of President's Message to Congress, *Congressional Record* (September 22, 1950), pp. 15629–15632.

11. These included H.R. 10, which authorized the Attorney General to detain indefinitely deportable aliens who could not secure permission to enter another country, and S. 595, which sought, among other things, to tighten laws against unauthorized disclosure of information relating to the national security. The original version of the latter had authorized wire-tapping until objections from the Treasury Department and Senator Harley W. Kilgore (Democrat-West Virginia) forced their deletion. See Harper, *op. cit.,* pp. 147–152 and Theoharis, *op. cit.,* Chapter 6. For specific recommendations by the Justice Department: Memorandum, Robert Ginnane to Peyton Ford, September 11, 1950, Papers of Stephen J. Spingarn, Internal Security File, HSTL; Memorandum, Office of the Solicitor General to Patrick A. McCarran, September 14, 15, 1950, Senate Judiciary Committee Legislative Records, National Archives and Records Service, Washington, D.C.

12. *Hearings on Proposed Legislation* (1948), pp. 70–71, 77, 105–130, 256–257.

13. *Congressional Record* (September 22, 1950), pp. 15820, 15835.

14. *Congressional Record* (September 7, 1950), pp. 14319–14321. Also, Memorandum, American Civil Liberties Union, May 1948, Papers of Emanuel Celler, Internal Security File, 1947–1948, Library of Congress. Labor leaders were especially concerned that the registration bill might be used against unions. "I was deeply impressed with the dangers it carries for liberal and labor organizations," wrote CIO leader Phillip Murray. Murray to Senator Herbert Lehman, September 14, 1950, in Senate Legislative File, Drawer 3, Papers of Herbert H. Lehman,

Columbia University. Also see William Green to Lehman, September 5, 1950, and Jacob S. Potovsky to Lehman, August 8, 1950, Senate Files, Drawer 2, Lehman Papers.

15. Stephen J. Spingarn to Charles S. Murphy, et al., August 1, 1950, National Defense—Internal Security and Individual Rights, Papers of Stephen J. Spingarn, HSTL; Joseph L. Rauh to Zechariah Chafee, Jr., June 13, 1949, Legislative File, Box 44, Americans for Democratic Action Papers, State Historical Society of Wisconsin; *New York Times,* August 7, 1950; Statement by Harley W. Kilgore, Herbert H. Lehman, et al., on their opposition to the McCarran Act, in Frank W. McCulloch to Estes Kefauver, September 28, 1950, Legislation, 81st Congress, Papers of Estes Kefauver, University of Tennessee. Communist Party leaders encouraged this association. Simon W. Gerson of the CPUSA, in testimony, before HUAC in May 1950 thus stated: "The Communist Party wishes to associate itself in general with the nationwide opposition already registered against the bill [Mundt-Nixon bill]—that of the whole labor movement, AFL, CIO, Railway Brotherhoods, and independent unions; the National Association for the Advancement of Colored People, the American Jewish Congress, the American Civil Liberties Union, Americans for Democratic Action, . . .". U.S. House of Representatives, Committee on Un-American Activities, *Hearings on Legislation to Outlaw Certain Un-American and Subversive Activities,* 81st Congress, 2nd Session, (Washington, GPO, 1950), pp. 2267–2276. Lehman wrote to a constituent in late September: "In my opposition to the McCarran bill I was furthering my strong and unremitting dislike and antagonism toward Communist activities." Letter, Lehman to John Rizzo, September 20, 1950, Papers of Lehman, Research Drawer #2, Internal Security, Columbia University.

16. Lucas did not, however, follow through with this plan. Harper, *op. cit.,* pp. 154–155. White House aide Spingarn records the President as stating that the situation "was the worst it had been since the Alien and Sedition laws of 1798, that a lot of people on the Hill should know better but had been stampeded into running with their tails between their legs." Memorandum for the File, Spingarn, July 22, 1950, Papers of George M. Elsey, Internal Security File, McCarthy charges, HSTL.

17. Memorandum, Stephen J. Spingarn to Charles S. Murphy, Donald Dawson, and George M. Elsey, July 20, 1950; Memorandum for the Record, Spingarn, July 21, 1950, Internal Security File, National Defense-S2311, Papers of Stephen J. Spingarn, HSTL. *Congressional Record* (August 17, 1950), p. 12693.

18. S. 2311, the Mundt-Nixon (or Ferguson) bill; S. 1832, to allow the Justice Department to bar or deport "subversive" aliens, including em-

ployees of the United Nations organization in New York City; H.R. 10, which authorized the Justice Department to detain indefinitely deportable aliens; S. 595, an Administration-supported bill for stiffening espionage and sedition laws; S. 3069, to create an independent Bureau of Passports and Visas within the State Department, and portions of a McCarran-sponsored bill to overhaul the entire immigration and nationality laws, S. 3455. (S. 3069 was later omitted from the omnibus bill) *Congressional Record* (August 17, 1950), p. 12693.

19. *Congressional Record* (August 29, 1950), p. 13909.

20. *Congressional Record* (September 6, 1950), p. 14229; Memorandum for the Files, Stephen J. Spingarn, July 12, 1950, National Defense— Internal Security and Individual Rights, Papers of Stephen J. Spingarn, HSTL; Herbert H. Lehman to Ralph Barton Perry, November 1, 1952, Senate Legislative File, Drawer 24, Papers of Herbert H. Lehman, Columbia University.

21. Stephen J. Spingarn, Memorandum for the Files, July 12, 1950, Internal Security File, National Defense-S2311, Papers of Stephen J. Spingarn, HSTL; Memorandum, Julius C. C. Edelstein to Herbert Lehman, September 4, 1950, Senate Files, Research Drawer #1, Herbert H. Lehman Papers, Columbia University; Harley M. Kilgore to Truman, September 15, 1950, OF 2750C, Papers of Harry S. Truman, HSTL; Memorandum for the Files, September 6, 1950, Stephen J. Spingarn, Internal Security File, National Defense, Papers of Stephen J. Spingarn, HSTL.

22. *Congressional Record* (September 8, 1950), pp. 14401–14420. In a prepared speech, Douglas noted that the detention provision had precedents in the Japanese-American relocation program during WWII, enemy sedition laws, and the British Emergency Power Act of 1939. These were, he added, not "uniformly satisfactory" but the Emergency Detention Act of 1950 was designed to eliminate their "shortcomings." The Kilgore Bill (S. 4130), he concluded, "offers a greater measure of real security for the nation against Communism and greater safeguards for individual freedom, while the McCarran bill imperils basic freedom and provides only illusionary protection for the safety and peace of the country." Copy of Speech, Senator Paul H. Douglas, September 8, 1950, Papers of Herbert H. Lehman, Research Drawer #2, Internal Security, Columbia University.

23. *Congressional Record* (September 11, 1950), pp. 14457–14490.

24. *Ibid.*, pp. 14547–14549.

Notes

25. Memorandum, Stephen J. Spingarn to George M. Elsey, September 7, 1950, Papers of Stephen J. Spingarn, Internal Security File, National Defense—Internal Security and Individual Rights, HSTL; *Chicago Tribune,* September 10, 1950.

26. Voting against the bill were Senators Graham, Kefauver, Lehman, Theodore Green (Democrat-Rhode Island), Edward L. Leahy (Democrat-Rhode Island), James E. Murray (Democrat-Montana), and Glen H. Taylor (Democrat-Idaho). Senator Langer was opposed to the bill but voted yea in order to be able to move for reconsideration. *Congressional Record* (September 12, 1950), pp. 14580–14628; William Benton to Francis Biddle, November 7, 1950, Legislative File, Box 34, Americans for Democratic Action Papers, SHSW; Herbert H. Lehman to Ralph Barton Perry, November 1, 1952, Senate Legislative File, Drawer 24, Papers of Herbert H. Lehman, Columbia University; William Langer to Harry S. Truman, September 18, 1950, PPF 5491, Papers of Harry S. Truman, HSTL.

27. John Steele to Senator Arthur Vandenberg, September 27, 1950, Papers of Arthur Vandenberg, W. L. Clements Library, Ann Arbor, Michigan; J(ohn) D. E(rwin) to Estes Kefauver, September 24, 1950 and Hubert H. Humphrey to Estes Kefauver, September 19, 1950, Papers of Estes Kefauver, Legislative File, 81st Congress; William Benton to Francis Biddle, November 7, 1950, Americans for Democratic Action Papers, Legislative Files, Box 34.

28. Tom Connally to Mrs. W. A. Nauwald, April 11, 1951, Papers of Tom Connally, Library of Congress; William Benton to Francis Biddle, November 7, 1950, Americans for Democratic Action Papers, Legislative File, Box 34; Charles Neese to R. E. Grubb, September 14, 1950, Papers of Estes Kefauver, Legislative Files, 81st Congress. However, Kefauver did not want a "permanent" detention program, but one designed for the Korean "wartime" situation. "I take no pride of authorship in the bill . . . ." For Kefauver bill (S. 4163), *Congressional Record* (September 14, 1950), p. 14993. *Congressional Record* (September 22, 1950), pp. 15780–15781.

29. Harley W. Kilgore to Harry S. Truman, September 15, 1950; Herbert Lehman, James Murray, and Estes Kefauver to Harry S. Truman, September 20, 1950, Papers of Harry S. Truman, OF 2750C, HSTL; Memorandum for the Files, Stephen J. Spingarn, September 19, 1950, Papers of Stephen J. Spingarn, National Defense—Internal Security and Individual Rights, HSTL.

30. President's Message to Congress, *Congressional Record* (September 22, 1950), pp. 15629–15632.

NOTES

31. *Congressional Record* (September 22, 1950), p. 14632; *Washington Post,* September 24, 1950; *Congressional Record* (September 22, 23, 1950), pp. 15520–15872. Senator Douglas, who took the floor following Langer's collapse, later wrote: "I had to step over Bill's prostrate body in order to get to the front of the crowded chamber. I could not hear him breathe, and he seemed to be dead. A surge of sympathy and admiration went through me." Paul H. Douglas, *In the Fullness of Time* (New York: Harcourt Brace Jovanovich, 1971), p. 308; *Congressional Record* (September 23, 1950), pp. 15793–15816, 15872; *New York Times,* September 24, 1950; Memorandum for the Files, Stephen J. Spingarn, September 25, 1950, Papers of Stephen J. Spingarn, National Defense—Internal Security and Individual Rights, HSTL.

ELECTORAL POLITICS AND McCARTHYISM:
The 1950 Campaign

1. William A. Glaser in Glaser and William N. McPhee, eds., *Public Opinion and Congressional Elections* (Glencoe, 1962), p. 275; Washington *Post,* November 10, 1950, p. 22; November 28, 1950, p. 17B.

2. *Congressional Record,* 82nd Congress, 1st Session, Vol. 97 (August 9, 1951), pp. 9703–9704.

3. *Ibid.,* (February 12, 1951), p. 1224; (February 28, 1951), pp. 1657, 1659; *New York Times,* November 9, 1950, p. 36.

4. Arthur M. Schlesinger, Jr., *The Age of Roosevelt: The Politics of Upheaval* (Boston, 1960), p. 606; *New York Times,* September 21, 1944, p. 15; October 8, 1944, p. 36; October 26, 1944, p. 15; November 2, 1944, p. 14; May 29, 1946, p. 2; June 2, 1946, p. 12.

5. State of New York, *Public Papers of Governor Thomas E. Dewey, 1948* (Albany, 1949), pp. 620–632; Irwin Ross, *The Loneliest Campaign: The Truman Victory of 1948* (New York, 1968), pp. 51–53.

6. *New York Times,* September 22, 1948, p. 19; September 26, 1948, p. 60; September 28, 1948, p. 19; October 2, 1948, pp. 1, 9.

7. Earl Latham, *The Communist Controversy in Washington From the New Deal to McCarthy* (Cambridge, 1966), pp. 394–399; H. Bradford Westerfield, *Foreign Policy and Party Politics: Pearl Harbor to Korea* (New Haven, 1955), pp. 325–326; *New York Times,* September 20, 1949, p. 21; October 4, 1949, p. 23; October 15, 1949, p. 13; February 7, 1950, pp. 1, 20.

8. Athan Theoharis, *Seeds of Repression: Harry S. Truman and the Origins of McCarthyism* (Chicago, 1971); Richard M. Freeland, *The*

Truman Doctrine and the Origins of McCarthyism: Foreign Policy, Domestic Politics, and Internal Security, 1946–1948 (New York, 1972).

9. *Public Papers of the Presidents of the United States, Harry S. Truman, 1948* (Washington, 1964), pp. 189, 860 (and cf. *ibid.*, pp. 559, 609–614, 802, 845, 882–896, 926–929); *Public Papers of . . . Harry S. Truman, 1950* (Washington, 1965), p. 234.

10. *Time,* Vol. 55 (May 15, 1950), p. 25; Anthony F. Malafronte, "Claude Pepper: Florida Maverick, the 1950 Florida Senatorial Primary," unpublished master's essay (University of Miami, 1964), pp. 11–12, 39, and *passim.* A valuable biography is Alexander Rudolph Stoesen, "The Senatorial Career of Claude D. Pepper," unpublished Ph.D. dissertation (University of North Carolina, 1964). On Pepper's foreign policy views: Thomas G. Paterson, "The Dissent of Senator Claude Pepper," in Paterson, ed., *Cold War Critics: Alternatives to American Foreign Policy in the Truman Years* (Chicago, 1971), pp. 114–139.

11. Smathers quotations in Stoesen, *op. cit.,* pp. 329, 332; *Time,* Vol. 55 (April 3, 1950), p. 23; *New York Times,* April 7, 1950, p. 8; Malafronte, *op. cit.,* p. 33; Ralph McGill, "Can He Purge Senator Pepper?" *Saturday Evening Post,* Vol. 222 (April 22, 1950), p. 33; *Newsweek,* Vol. 35 (April 10, 1950), p. 23.

12. H. D. Price, *The Negro and Southern Politics: A Chapter of Florida History* (New York, 1957), pp. 56, 60–61; Stoesen, *op. cit.,* pp. 339–343, 351; *Time,* Vol. 55 (April 3, 1950), p. 23, (April 17, 1950), p. 28.

13. *New Republic,* Vol. 122 (May 15, 1950), p. 5; Malafronte, *op. cit.,* p. 107; *New York Times,* April 9, 1950, p. 52; Stoesen, *op. cit.,* pp. 341–343; *Newsweek,* Vol. 35 (April 10, 1950), p. 23.

14. Price, *op. cit.,* pp. 63, 86; Stoesen, *op. cit.,* pp. 360–362.

15. Malafronte, *op. cit.,* p. 115 and, quoting Pepper, p. 52.

16. Pepper to Herbert H. Davidson, August 28, 1950, Box 86, Pepper MSS., Federal Records Storage, Alexandria, Va.: Price, *op. cit.,* p. 63; Price, "The Negro and Florida Politics, 1944–1954," *Journal of Politics,* Vol. 17 (May 1955), pp. 216–217; Herbert L. Doherty, "Liberal and Conservative Voting Patterns in Florida," *ibid.,* Vol. 14 (August 1952), pp. 413–414.

17. *U.S. News & World Report,* Vol. 28 (April 28, 1950), p. 17; *Newsweek,* Vol. 35 (April 10, 1950), p. 24; *New Republic,* Vol. 122 (May 15, 1950), p. 5; Pepper to W. G. Ward, June 8, 1950, Box 85, Pepper MSS.

18. Malafronte, *op. cit.*, pp. 25–26, 86–87, 108; Stoesen, *op. cit.*, pp. 338–339; interview with Congressman Claude D. Pepper, June 19, 1967. The 1950 elections marked the entry of the medical profession, alarmed by Truman's health insurance proposals, into a number of campaigns against liberals, Frank P. Graham and Elbert D. Thomas among them. Stanley Kelley, Jr., *Professional Public Relations and Political Power* (Baltimore, 1956), Chapter 3; Joseph G. LaPalombara, "Pressure, Propaganda, and Political Action in the Elections of 1950," *Journal of Politics,* Vol. 14 (May 1952), pp. 308–309.

19. Raleigh *News and Observer,* May 5, 1950, p. 4 (Marquis Childs); *Time,* Vol. 55 (May 15, 1950), p. 25.

20. Raleigh *News and Observer,* May 2, 1950, p. 6; May 3, 1950, pp. 1, 4, 14; May 4, 1950, pp. 4, 8; May 7, 1950, IV, p. 4; Jefferson D. Johnson, Jr., (Graham's campaign manager) to William J. Smith, April 14, 1950, Johnson MSS., Duke University; Jonathan Daniels to Isador Lubin, May 5, 1950, Box 49, Daniels MSS., University of North Carolina.

21. Raleigh *News and Observer,* May 4, 1950, p. 8; May 5, 1950, p. 16; May 20, 1950, p. 18; May 21, 1950, p. 5. For Graham and the Civil Rights Committee, see letters of other committee members, with related correspondence, in Johnson MSS. and in Personal Files, 1949, 1950, Frank P. Graham MSS., University of North Carolina.

22. Raleigh *News and Observer,* May 21, 1950, p. 5; May 24, 1950, p. 4; May 25, 1950, p. 1; Greensboro *Daily News,* May 24, 1950, p. 1. Copies of this and other handbills are in Political Campaign Literature, 1841–1964, Box 3, Misc. Collections, North Carolina State Department of Archives and History.

23. Raleigh *News and Observer,* May 11, 1950, p. 16; May 13, 1950, p. 2; May 16, 1950, p. 7; May 18, 1950, p. 21; May 19, 1950, p. 15; May 21, 1950, p. 9.

24. *Ibid.,* May 20, 1950, p. 18; May 21, 1950, IV, p. 1; May 4, 1950, p. 4; Greensboro *Daily News,* May 28, 1950, p. 1.

25. Graham received 303,605 votes (49.1 percent of the total vote) to Smith's 250,842 votes. Raleigh *News and Observer,* June 3, 1950, p. 1; Greensboro *Daily News,* June 26, 1950, p. 1; Jonathan Daniels to Will Alexander, June 27, 1950, Box 50, Daniels MSS.

26. Raleigh *News and Observer,* June 14, 1950, pp. 1, 2; June 17, 1950, p. 1; June 20, 1950, p. 1; Greensboro *Daily News,* June 21, 1950, p. 1; pamphlet in Political Campaign Literature, Box 3, North Carolina State

Department of Archives and History; cf. Samuel Lubell, *The Future of American Politics* (New York: Harper Colophon edition, 1965), p. 109.

27. Lubell, *op. cit.*, pp. 110–111; Daniels to Maurice Rosenblatt, June 27, 1950, Box 50, Daniels MSS.; Jefferson D. Johnson, Jr., to D. Hiden Ramsey, July 3, 1950, Johnson MSS.; Charlotte *Observer,* June 26, 1950, p. 1; Greensboro *Daily News,* June 25, 1950, p. 1; June 26, 1950, p. 1.

28. Lubell, *op. cit.*, p. 111. Another analysis of the election confirmed the salience of the race issue with the finding that there was a high (0.71) correlation between a county's black population and its tendency to switch to Smith in June. Taylor McMillan, "Who Beat Frank Graham?" unpublished ms., University of North Carolina Political Studies Program, Research Report #1 (May 20, 1959), pp. 3–6.

29. *New York Times,* June 4, 1950, IV, p. 9; Los Angeles *Times,* May 11, 1950, p. 14; May 16, 1950, p. 14; May 20, 1950, p. 6; May 24, 1950, p. 17; October 1, 1950, p. 16; October 6, 1950, p. 7; October 29, 1950, p. 27; press release, California Democrats for Nixon, September 28, [1950], Box 7, George Creel MSS., Library of Congress; Earl Mazo and Stephen Hess, *Nixon: A Political Portrait* (New York, 1968), pp. 67–68.

30. On Taylor, see Frank Ross Peterson, "Liberal from Idaho: The Public Career of Senator Glen H. Taylor," unpublished Ph.D. dissertation (Washington State University, 1968). On Communist charges: *ibid.,* pp. 206–214; William C. Pratt, "Senator Glen Taylor: Questioning American Unilateralism," in Paterson, *op. cit.*, pp. 160–161; Boyd A. Martin, "The 1950 Elections in Idaho," *Western Political Quarterly,* Vol. 4 (March 1951), pp. 76–79; *New York Times,* July 16, 1950, p. 50; August 6, 1950, p. 49.

31. *Congressional Record,* Vol. 96 (June 28, 1950), p. 9322; *New York Times,* August 13, 1950, pp. 13 & IV, 3; August 14, 1950, p. 1; August 17, 1950, p. 1; August 20, 1950, p. 69.

32. Charles S. Murphy, George M. Elsey, and Stephen J. Spingarn, Memorandum to the President, July 11, 1950; Spingarn, "Memorandum for the Record," July 21, 1950, both National Defense and Individual Rights, Vol. I, Spingarn Papers, Harry S. Truman Library; Washington *Post,* July 9, 1950, p. 5B (Drew Pearson); *New York Times,* June 28, 1950, p. 22; *Christian Science Monitor,* July 3, 1950, p. 1.

33. *New York Times,* September 13, 1950, p. 25.

34. *Ibid.,* July 19, 1950, p. 8; August 1, 1950, p. 18; August 4, 1950, p. 1; August 6, 1950, p. 1; August 14, 1950, p. 1; September 23, 1950, p. 6; Detroit *Free Press,* July 19, 1950, p. 1.

NOTES

35. *New York Times,* September 24, 1950, p. 1; September 25, 1950, p. 10; Washington *Post,* October 23, 1950, p. 9; Herbert H. Lehman to Harry S. Truman, January 7, 1959, Special File, Lehman MSS., Columbia University. On the McCarran Act and attendant maneuvering: Douglass Cater, "A Senate Afternoon: The Red Hunt," *Reporter,* Vol. 3 (October 10, 1950), pp. 27–30; Cornelius P. Cotter and J. Malcolm Smith, "An American Paradox: The Emergency Detention Act of 1950," *Journal of Politics,* Vol. 19 (February 1957), pp. 20–33; Robert Griffith, "The Political Context of McCarthyism," *Review of Politics,* Vol. 33 (January 1971), pp. 26–31. `

36. Kenneth W. Hechler to John Gunther, October 18, 20, 1950, Series 5, Box 17, ADA MSS., State Historical Society of Wisconsin; copy, Michel Cieplinski to William M. Boyle, Jr., November 29, 1950, Box 584, Theodore F. Green MSS., Library of Congress; Anderson article, *The Democratic Digest* (August, 1950), pp. 13–14; Radio Address by J. Howard McGrath, November 1, 1950, Campaign Files, Drawer 4, Lehman MSS.

37. "Address in Kiel Auditorium, St. Louis," November 4, 1950, *Truman Papers, 1950,* pp. 697–703; Philadelphia *Inquirer,* October 25, 1950, p. 10; Seattle *Post-Intelligencer,* November 3, 1950, p. 9B. On the "isolationist" theme: *New York Times,* September 17, 1950, pp. IV, 12; September 22, 1950, p. 25; October 15, 1950, p. 32; October 27, 1950, p. 21; November 4, 1950, p. 10.

38. Philadelphia *Inquirer,* October 26, 1950, p. 12; November 6, 1950, p. 7; *New York Times,* November 5, 1950, p. 38; *Public Opinion Quarterly,* Vol. 15 (Summer 1951), pp. 386–387. On the electoral impact of the Korean fighting: *New York Times,* October 29, 1950, IV, p. 7; Detroit *Free Press,* October 5, 1950, p. 16; November 5, 1950, p. 10; Cleveland *Plain Dealer,* October 22, 1950, p. 3; Chicago *Tribune,* November 7, 1950, p. 4; November 8, 1950, p. 1; San Francisco *Chronicle,* November 6, 1950, p. 8.

39. Los Angeles *Times,* October 1, 1950, p. 16; October 3, 1950, p. 17; October 5, 1950, p. 8; October 6, 1950, p. 9; October 7, 1950, p. 5; October 29, 1950, p. 27; November 2, 1950, II, p. 2; San Francisco *Chronicle,* November 5, 1950, p. 9; Mazo and Hess, *op. cit.,* pp. 71–72.

40. Douglas speech to International Oil Workers of America, August 18, 1950, Box 206, Douglas MSS., University of Oklahoma; *New York Times,* October 15, 1950, p. 80; November 1, 1950, p. 32; San Francisco *Chronicle,* November 3, 1950, p. 5; November 5, 1950, p. 9; Washington *Post,* October 22, 1950, p. 13; March 3, 1951, p. 1; Los Angeles *Times,* October 17, 1950, p. 14; October 24, 1950, p. 14; *U.S. News & World*

Report, Vol. 29 (November 17, 1950), p. 30; Mazo and Hess, *op. cit.,* pp. 72–74.

41. *New York Times,* October 22, 1950, IV, p. 7; *New Republic,* Vol. 123 (November 20, 1950), p. 8; Burton R. Brazil, "The 1950 Elections in California," *Western Political Quarterly,* Vol. 4 (March 1951), p. 67.

42. McCarthy quoted in William Costello, *The Facts About Nixon* (New York, 1960), p. 70; Milwaukee *Journal,* November 8, 1950, p. 4.

43. Frank H. Jonas, "The 1950 Elections in Utah," *Western Political Quarterly,* Vol. 4 (March 1951), pp. 83, 88–90; Jonas, "The Art of Political Dynamiting," *ibid.,* Vol. 10 (June 1957), pp. 374–378; Denver *Post,* October 18, 1950, p. 16; *Deseret News* [Salt Lake City], October 3, 1950, p. 8; October 4, 1950, p. 1B; October 10, 1950, p. 1B; October 12, 1950, p. 1B; October 19, 1950, p. 12. Minions of Gerald L. K. Smith also were active against Thomas. Benjamin R. Epstein and Arnold Forster, *The Trouble-Makers* (Garden City, N.Y., 1952), p. 248.

44. Thomas also suffered because the Mormon Church hierarchy gave the appearance of opposing his candidacy. Elbert D. Thomas to Theodore Cannon, February 24, 1950, Box 291, Thomas MSS., Franklin D. Roosevelt Library; Jonas, "The 1950 Elections in Utah," *loc. cit.,* pp. 86–88; Jonas, "Setting the Stage for the Political Dynamiter," in Jonas, ed., *Political Dynamiting* (Salt Lake City, 1970), pp. 70–71; *New Republic,* Vol. 123 (November 20, 1950), p. 10; *Deseret News,* October 14, 1950, p. 1; October 15, 1950, p. 1; October 24, 1950, p. 6.

45. Seattle *Post-Intelligencer,* October 26, 1950, p. 1; October 27, 1950, p. 1; *New York Times,* October 23, 1950, p. 19; Hugh D. Bone, "The 1950 Elections in Washington," *Western Political Quarterly,* Vol. 4 (March 1951), p. 94.

46. Boyd A. Martin, "The 1950 Elections in Idaho," *Western Political Quarterly,* Vol. 4 (March 1951), pp. 76–79; Richard Neuberger, "Standoff in the Northwest," *Nation,* Vol. 171 (October 30, 1950), p. 334; Seattle *Post-Intelligencer,* November 8, 1950, p. 5.

47. Curtis Martin, "The 1950 Elections in Colorado," *Western Political Quarterly,* Vol. 4 (March 1951), pp. 73–74; Denver *Post,* October 3, 1950, p. 3; October 17, 1950, p. 17; November 2, 1950, pp. 1, 32; November 5, 1950, p. 19C; Epstein and Forster, *op. cit.,* p. 248. The Denver *Post* and Millikin's speech files reveal only occasional and vague references to Hiss and Communist infiltration. E.g., speech of October 2, 1950, Book III; speech of November 3, 1950, Book IV, Millikin MSS., University of Colorado.

NOTES

48. Des Moines *Register,* June 4, 1950, p. 1; October 11, 1950, p. 1; October 12, 1950, p. 1; November 9, 1950, p. 1; *New York Times,* November 1, 1950, p. 32.

49. Alexander's was a somewhat erratic campaign: he spent much time charging that the military spent more money on travel and "housekeeping" than on weapons. *New York Times,* October 31, 1950, p. 22; *Daily Oklahoman* [Oklahoma City], October 14, 1950, p. 8; October 19, 1950, p. 30; October 20, 1950, p. 21; October 21, 1950, p. 1; October 25, 1950, p. 6; October 27, 1950, p. 8.

50. Duff had entered a demurrer against McCarthy in June. Philadelphia *Inquirer,* September 26, 1950, p. 14; September 29, 1950, p. 28; October 7, 1950, p. 7; October 11, 1950, pp. 22, 23; October 29, 1950, p. 22; November 1, 1950, p. 2; *New York Times,* June 19, 1950, p. 1; October 31, 1950, p. 22; November 4, 1950, p. 7; Robert Bendiner, "Anything Goes in Pennsylvania," *Nation,* Vol. 171 (October 28, 1950), p. 386.

51. Cleveland *Plain Dealer,* September 15, 1950, p. 1; October 5, 1950, p. 27; October 13, 1950, p. 9; October 22, 1950, p. 14; October 30, 1950, p. 6.

52. *Ibid.,* October 19, 1950, p. 4; October 21, 1950, p. 14; *New York Times,* October 29, 1950, IV, p. 2; Lubell, *op. cit.,* pp. 183–189. On the CIO-PAC's difficulties in mobilizing support for Ferguson: Fay Calkins, *The CIO and the Democratic Party* (Chicago, 1952), pp. 34–36.

53. Detroit *Free Press,* September 3, 1950, p. 3; October 17, 1950, p. 3; October 20, 1950, p. 6; October 27, 1950, p. 27; October 31, 1950, p. 15; November 4, 1950, pp. 11, 12; November 6, 1950, p. 35; November 9, 1950, p. 1; November 15, 1950, p. 1.

54. Office memo from "vk," March 10, 1950, File 2, Drawer 5, Tydings MSS., University of Maryland; William Curran to Tydings, May 4, 1950, *ibid.;* questionnaires in File 2, Drawer 4, *ibid.;* Baltimore *Sun,* July 7, 1950, p. 36, July 14, 1950, p. 9; Harry Kirwin, *The Inevitable Success: Herbert R. O'Conor* (Westminster, Md., 1962), pp. 508–509.

55. *New York Times,* October 20, 1950, p. 18; Baltimore *Sun,* September 19, 1950, p. 21. On Maryland politics and the 1950 election, see: Kelley, *op. cit.,* Chapter 4; John H. Fenton, *Politics in the Border States* (New Orleans, 1957), Chapters 8–9; Evelyn L. Wentworth, "County Alignments in Maryland Elections, 1934–1958," unpublished master's essay (University of Maryland, 1961); Wentworth, *Election Statistics in Maryland, 1934–1958* (College Park, Md., 1959); Robert L. Otto, "Maryland Senatorial Election of 1950: Butler vs. Tydings," unpublished master's essay (University of Maryland, 1962); N. Bancroft Williams, "An Exami-

nation of the Factors Leading to the Defeat of Millard E. Tydings in the Maryland Senatorial Election of 1950," unpublished master's essay (Loyola College [Baltimore], 1966).

56. Baltimore *Sun,* September 28, 1950, p. 56; *New York Times,* September 24, 1950, p. 76; Washington *Post,* October 31, 1950, p. 7; U.S. Senate, 82nd Congress, 1st Session, Committee on Rules and Administration, Subcommittee on Privileges and Elections, *Maryland Senatorial Election of 1950. Hearings . . . Pursuant to S. Res. 250* (Washington, 1951), pp. 8–14, 233, 253, 257, 272–280, 327, 365, 370, 386–394, 425–431, 1061–1063; U.S. Senate, 82nd Congress, 1st Session, Committee on Rules and Administration, *Maryland Senatorial Election of 1950* (Washington, 1951), pp. 5, 16, 19–20, 23–25, 27–28, 31–36.

57. *New York Times,* October 15, 1950, p. 32; Washington *Post,* October 11, 1950, p. 18; October 29, 1950, pp. II, 3; Baltimore *Sun,* October 16, 1950, p. 18; November 4, 1950, p. 11.

58. Fenton, *op. cit.,* pp. 172, 178, 182–186, 196, 201; Kelley, *op. cit.,* pp. 140–141; Baltimore *Sun,* July 7, 1950, p. 36; September 11, 1950, p. 25; November 8, 1950, pp. 1, 3; Washington *Post,* November 9, 1950, p. 1; Baltimore *Afro-American,* November 4, 1950, p. 4; November 18, 1950, p. 7.

59. Louis Bean, *Influences in the 1954 Mid-Term Elections* (Washington, 1954), pp. 28–30. However, if the counties are examined *en bloc* rather than in regional groupings, using Spearman's coefficient of rank correlation, rho=0.29, which is not statistically significant.

60. *New York Times,* November 12, 1950, IV, p. 8; January 7, 1951, IV, p. 7; Baltimore *Sun,* November 8, 1950, p. 3.

61. *New York Times,* March 31, 1950, p. 3; May 19, 1950, p. 12; June 11, 1950, p. 42; September 17, 1950, p. 80; Milwaukee *Journal,* October 1, 1950, p. 1.

62. Milwaukee *Journal,* March 19, 1950, p. 12; April 1, 1950, p. 2; April 2, 1950, p. 2; October 1, 1950, p. 1; October 5, 1950, pp. 20, 21; October 9, 1950, p. 18; October 11, 1950, p. 16; October 12, 1950, p. 18; October 13, 1950, p. 5; October 19, 1950, p. 20.

63. *Ibid.,* October 17, 1950, p. 1; October 27, 1950, p. 20; October 29, 1950, p. 1.

64. *Ibid.,* November 8, 1950, pp. 1, 10, 12.

65. GOP gains in two of the cities—Appleton (McCarthy's home) and Sheboygan (Kohler's)—may have resulted from a friends-and-neighbors

effect. *Ibid.,* November 10, 1950, p. 26; cf. Washington *Post,* November 28, 1950, p. 17B; Leon D. Epstein, *Politics in Wisconsin* (Madison, 1958), p. 4.

66. Washington *Post,* November 4, 1950, p. 9; *U.S. News & World Report,* Vol. 29 (November 17, 1950), p. 33; Chicago *Tribune,* October 28, 1950, p. 7; October 30, 1950, p. 10; November 1, 1950, II, p. 1.

67. Milwaukee *Journal,* October 22, 1950, p. 1; Chicago *Tribune,* October 22, 1950, p. 13.

68. *New York Times,* August 18, 1950, p. 12; October 25, 1950, p. 43; October 27, 1950, p. 21; Milwaukee *Journal,* October 18, 1950, p. 33; Chicago *Tribune,* October 21, 1950, p. 10; October 25, 1950, p. 18; October 29, 1950, p. 12; October 31, 1950, p. 14; November 4, 1950, p. 7; November 7, 1950, p. 3.

69. *New York Times,* November 10, 1950, p. 20; December 10, 1950, pp. IV, 9; Washington *Post,* November 3, 1950, p. 23; November 4, 1950, p. 1; Chicago *Tribune,* October 16, 1950, p. 1; October 18, 1950, p. 1; October 26, 1950, II, p. 4; October 30, 1950, pp. 1, 10; October 31, 1950, p. 9; November 8, 1950, p. 1.

70. *New York Times,* October 25, 1950, p. 43; Herman Kogan, "Illinois: A Sorry Choice," *Nation,* Vol. 171 (October 21, 1950), p. 363.

71. Indianapolis *Star,* October 1, 1950, p. 1; October 3, 1950, p. 2; October 4, 1950, p. 21; October 8, 1950, p. 1; October 13, 1950, p. 20; October 18, 1950, p. 1; November 1, 1950, p. 27; November 2, 1950, p. 12; November 3, 1950, pp. 4, 13; Detroit *Free Press,* November 10, 1950, p. 2.

72. Donnell called his opponent "a fine gentleman and the son of a fine gentleman." *New York Times,* October 31, 1950, p. 22; Milwaukee *Journal,* October 24, 1950, p. 14; Donald J. Kemper, S.J., *Decade of Fear: Senator Hennings and Civil Liberties* (Columbia, Mo., 1965), pp. 28–32; Ernest Kirschten, "Donnell Luck and Missouri Scandal," *Nation,* Vol. 171 (October 14, 1950), pp. 332–333.

73. Washington *Post,* October 28, 1950, p. 7; Milwaukee *Journal,* October 31, 1950, p. 6; November 6, 1950, p. 12; Sidney Hyman, *The Lives of William Benton* (Chicago, 1969), pp. 440–441.

74. Bean, *op. cit.,* pp. 23–24. Bean found no Catholic factor in Benton's vote. Bowles was charged with "socialism" and "softness" on Communism, and his rival, John D. Lodge, in a televised speech, alternated a photograph of Bowles with pictures of Marx, Lenin, and Stalin; but McCarthy did not attack the governor personally. *New York Times,*

October 31, 1950, p. 22; Bowles, *Promises to Keep: My Years in Public Life, 1941–1969* (New York, 1971), p. 240.

75. *New Republic,* Vol. 125 (October 1, 1951), p. 6; *New York Times,* January 7, 1951, IV, p. 7; Atlanta *Journal,* July 7, 1950, p. 4; Cf. *Christian Science Monitor,* August 9, 1951, p. 1; *Newsweek,* Vol. 36 (November 13, 1950), p. 27.

76. Memorandum by Kenneth W. Hechler, "The 1950 Elections," November 15, 1950, Box 64, Papers of George Elsey, Harry S. Truman Library; Bruce Felknor, *Dirty Politics* (New York, 1966), p. 10; *New York Times,* October 31, 1950, p. 22; November 9, 1950, p. 28; cf. Epstein and Forster, *op. cit.,* pp. 238–250. I am indebted to Professor Alonzo Hamby, Ohio University, for calling the Hechler memo to my attention.

77. Kelley, *op. cit.* This phenomenon may partly explain why (according to some observers) McCarthyite appeals had their greatest effect in urban areas. Cf. memorandum by Kenneth W. Hechler, November 15, 1950, previously cited.

78. Flynn, *The Road Ahead* (New York, 1949); Karl Schriftgeisser, *The Lobbyists* (Boston, 1951), Chapter 13; Raleigh *News and Observer,* June 12, 1950, p. 4; June 17, 1950, p. 1; Madison *Capital-Times,* March 1, 1951, p. 1; LaPalombara, *op. cit.,* p. 308 and *passim.*

79. Glaser in *Public Opinion and Congressional Elections,* p. 206. Liberals tended to run better than conservatives in 1950. Washington *Post,* December 17, 1950, p. 2B.

80. Hechler memorandum, previously cited; cf. Gus Tyler, "The Mid-Term Paradox," *New Republic,* Vol. 123 (November 27, 1950), pp. 14–15; *Nation,* Vol. 171 (November 18, 1950), p. 451.

81. Memorandum, Violet Gunther to ——, n.d. [1950], Series 5, Box 34, ADA MSS.; Lehman Address over WCBS, October 2, 1950, Campaign Files, Drawer 4, Lehman MSS,; memorandum, J. Carter to T. V. Brunkard, September 25, 1950, Drawer 5, *ibid.; New York Times,* October 22, 1950, pp. 43, 59; October 26, 1950, p. 1; October 30, 1950, p. 13.

82. Nelson W. Polsby, "Towards an Explanation of McCarthyism," *Political Studies,* Vol. 8 (1960), pp. 268–271.

83. Angus Campbell and Homer C. Cooper, *Group Differences in Attitudes and Votes: A Study of the 1954 Congressional Election* (Ann Arbor, 1956), p. 78; Campbell, Philip E. Converse, Warren E. Miller, and Donald L. Stokes, *The American Voter* (New York, 1960), pp. 50–

51; Alfred De Grazia, *The Western Public: 1952 and Beyond* (Stanford, 1954), pp. 43–45; Bean, *op. cit.;* Samuel A. Stouffer, *Communism, Conformity, and Civil Liberties* (Garden City, N.Y., 1955), pp. 59, 68–69, 85.

McCARTHY AND McCARTHYISM:
The Cedric Parker Case, November 1949

1. Jack Anderson and Ronald May, *McCarthy: The Man, the Senator, the "Ism"* (Boston, 1952), pp. 108, 110; Madison *Capital Times,* October 17, and 25, 1946; Les Adler, "McCarthyism: The Advent and the Decline, Part I," *Continuum* (Autumn, 1968), pp. 404–410.

2. Roy Cohn, *McCarthy* (New York: New American Library, 1968). I have written two letters to Cohn, asking him to substantiate his vague claims. I have received no response.

3. *Ibid.,* pp. 8–11.

4. Promoters of the Washington dinner interpretation have exaggerated its significance. They mistakenly assumed that McCarthy first thought of exploiting the issue at the suggestion of Father Walsh, and that he never seriously used or considered it before January 7, 1950. Father Walsh, Drew Pearson insisted, "first planted the idea in Joe's mind" (Madison *Capital Times,* May 6, 1957). A recent McCarthy scholar maintains that he "pounced upon the suggestion" (Robert Griffith, *The Politics of Fear* [Lexington, Ky.: 1970], p. 29. Father Walsh's remark, newspaper editor William T. Evjue assumed, "was the inspiration for the launching of the McCarthy campaign against Communism" (Madison *Capital Times,* August 19, 1954). "The suggestion struck a responsive chord in McCarthy," Fred Cook declared. McCarthy's three friends "had no idea at the time of what they had started" (Fred Cook, *The Nightmare Decade* [New York, 1971], p. 141). McCarthy "seized upon the idea," noted Richard Rovere, and this led him to start his national crusade. He did so with the "simple hope that it would help him hold his job in 1952" (Richard Rovere, *Senator Joe McCarthy* [Cleveland and New York, 1959], pp. 120, 123).

5. For more on McCarthy's decline in Wisconsin from 1947–49 consult Michael O'Brien, "Senator Joseph McCarthy and Wisconsin: 1946–1957" (unpublished Ph.D. dissertation in history, University of Wisconsin, 1971), pp. 57–78.

6. Typed copy of memorandum, Joseph McCarthy to School Clerks of Dane County, November 10, 1949, File 4, Drawer 3 (unprocessed),

Papers of the National Committee for an Effective Congress (NCEC), Washington, D.C.

7. Typed copy of Joseph McCarthy, "Important Questions for the People of Dane County" (no date), File 4, Drawer 3, NCEC.

8. *Ibid.*

9. *The Capital Times,* November 11, 1949; *Wisconsin State Journal,* November 12, 1949; *Milwaukee Journal,* November 12, 1949; *Green Bay Press-Gazette,* November 12, 1949.

10. *Wisconsin State Journal,* November 10, 1949; *The Capital Times,* November 9, 1949.

11. *Wisconsin State Journal,* November 10, 1949; *The Capital Times,* November 9, 1949; *Milwaukee Journal,* November 12, 1949; Claude B. Calkin to Joseph McCarthy, November 10, 1949, President's File, 200, Harry S. Truman Papers, Harry S. Truman Library. A copy of the letter was enclosed with Joseph McCarthy to Harry S. Truman, August 3, 1951, *ibid.* Evjue later explained or rationalized this embarrassing discrepancy. Parker became ineligible for membership in the Newspaper Guild, Evjue insisted, when he became city editor of the *Capital Times.* Therefore, although he signed the affidavit, he did not file it with the National Labor Relations Board; Madison *Capital Times,* August 6, 1951. The Madison newspaper had given much publicity to Parker's signing of the affidavit. After he signed it, Parker proclaimed: "This is my answer to the old 'Red' charge" (Madison *Capital Times,* January 31, 1948).

12. Madison *Capital Times,* November 15, 1949.

13. *Milwaukee Journal,* November 11, 1949.

14. Madison *Capital Times,* March 14, 1941.

15. Later Evjue rationalized that when he wrote the editorial "the word Communist had different connotations than it has today. Today a man can be sued for libel for calling a person a Communist. Ten years ago that label Communist was used broadly in the same sense that the words reactionary, Tory, radical, or Red were used, and the average citizen dismissed these charges as politics" (Madison *Capital Times,* August 6, 1951).

16. Typescript of a tape-recorded interview of Miles McMillin by Robert Griffith, July 25, and August 1, 1967, for the Cornell University Oral History Program, p. 74. A copy of the typescript was lent to the author by McMillin.

NOTES

17. Because McCarthy did not document his seven-point attack on Parker, I had difficulty in tracing his allegations. I could not substantiate his second (Farrell Schnering), third (Kenneth Goff), and fourth (American League for Peace and Democracy) charges. He may have found them in an obscure source. In the order of their appearance, his other points can be found in the *Capital Times*, March 14, 1941; *Committee on Un-American Activities, House of Representatives, Hearings*, 76th Congress, 1st Session, Vol. 9, 1939, pp. 5670–5672; *ibid.*, 77th Congress, Appendix IX, Vol. 54-1, 1944, pp. 1746–1748; *ibid.*, p. 625. Using the Wisconsin State Conference on Social Legislation as an example, it can be seen that McCarthy exaggerated and distorted his evidence. Along with many persons later reputed to be Communists, many outstanding citizens participated in the conference. Among them were Thomas Fairchild, the Democratic candidate against McCarthy in 1952, whose integrity was beyond question, and Perry Hill, who in 1949 was chief of the Madison Bureau of the ultraconservative *Milwaukee Sentinel*. Similarly, McCarthy stated that Eugene Dennis and Parker organized and sponsored the statewide Conference on Farm and Labor Legislation. Actually, Parker and Dennis were among many sponsors and there is no evidence that they organized it. The conference was chaired by Paul Alfonsi who later became a conservative Republican state legislator.

18. *Wisconsin State Journal*, November 10 and 12, 1949; Madison *Capital Times*, November 9, 11, 14, 15, and 23, 1949: *Milwaukee Journal*, November 9, 10, 11, and 12, 1949; and December 5, 1949; *Green Bay Press-Gazette*, November 10, 12, and 14, 1949; *Appleton Post-Crescent*, November 10 and 15, 1949. As examples see the *Waukesha Daily Freeman*, November 10 and 12, 1949; *Oshkosh Daily Northwestern*, November 10, 11, and 12, 1949. "Mud for Muckrakers," *Time*, November 28, 1949, pp. 34–38.

19. *Appleton Post-Crescent*, November 15, 1949: *Milwaukee Sentinel*, November 11 and 12, 1949; the *LaCrosse Tribune*, November 10, 1949; *Milwaukee Journal*, November 11, 1949.

20. *Milwaukee Journal*, November 11 and 12, 1949.

21. "Mud for Muckrakers," *op. cit.*

22. *Racine Labor*, November 25, 1949; *Milwaukee Sentinel*, November 10, 1949; Madison *Capital Times*, November 14, 1949; Reprint of a *Medford-Star News* editorial in the *Capital Times*, November 23, 1949.

23. *Milwaukee Sentinel*, November 11, 1949; *Green Bay Press-Gazette*, November 12, 1949.

Notes

24. During the next five years, McCarthy repeated his allegations against Parker and Evjue at least fifteen times. Everytime he rehashed his "old charges about Parker," Evjue dolefully observed on one occasion, "the Associated Press and the United Press dutifully send it out over the country as news" (Madison *Capital Times,* August 6, 1951). McCarthy's language became more extreme after 1949 as he accused Evjue of running a "disguised poisoned waterhole of dangerous Communist propaganda" (*ibid.,* April 28, 1950).

25. *Kenosha Evening News,* November 16, 1949.

26. The *Evening Bulletin* (Philadelphia), December 4, 1949.

27. The *Eau Claire Leader,* December 8, 1949; *Milwaukee Journal,* December 7, 1949.

28. *Congressional Record,* Vol. 96, Part 1, January 5, 1950, p. 86.

29. *Milwaukee Sentinel,* January 22, 1950.

30. *Congressional Record,* Vol. 96, Part 1, January 25, 1950, p. 895.

31. Only three commentators have discussed the Parker controversy. Whether intentionally or not, the entire story and its full implications were not brought out. Jack Anderson and Ronald May (who had formerly worked for the *Capital Times*) severely distorted the affair in their book: (1) They neglected to give the date of the incident, thus leading the reader to believe it occurred sometime after 1949. (2) They discussed it only as an example of McCarthy's reckless attacks on newspapers that opposed him. (3) They mistakenly assumed that Parker and Evjue effectively rebutted his accusations and that his offensive was a failure (Anderson and May, *McCarthy,* pp. 272–273). In 1954, Miles McMillin associated McCarthy's barrage with his later crusade on Communists-in-government. Although his account displayed some insight, it was superficial and distorted and failed to grasp the full implications of the incident (Madison *Capital Times,* December 13, 1954). The controversy was again reviewed by Morris Rubin in 1967 for the fiftieth anniversary edition of the *Capital Times,* but he merely repeated McMillin's earlier account (Morris Rubin, "The Fight Against McCarthy: Finest Hour of *The Capital Times,*" the *Capital Times: Fiftieth Anniversary Edition,* December 13, 1967.

THE POLITICS OF CULTURE:
Hollywood and the Cold War

1. See, for example, Richard Hofstadter, *The Paranoid Style in American Politics* (New York, 1965), and David Brion Davis, "Some Themes of

Countersubversion: An Analysis of Anti-Masonic, Anti-Catholic, and Anti-Mormon Literature," *The Mississippi Valley Historical Review,* Vol. 47 (September 1960), pp. 205–244, and John Higham, *Strangers in the Land: Patterns of American Nativism 1860–1925* (New York, 1963).

2. Michael Paul Rogin, *The Intellectuals and McCarthy: The Radical Specter* (Cambridge, 1967), p. 222.

3. *Ibid.,* pp. 248–260.

4. For studies of twentieth-century American responses to radicalism, see, for example, William Preston, *Aliens and Dissenters* (New York, 1966), Peter G. Filene, *Americans and the Soviet Experiment, 1917–1933* (Cambridge, 1967), Christopher Lasch, *The American Liberals and the Russian Revolution* (New York, 1962), and Robert K. Murray, *Red Scare* (New York, 1955).

5. *Town Meeting Bulletin,* Vol. 12 (April 3, 1947), pp. 8, 13.

6. Les K. Adler and Thomas G. Paterson, "Red Fascism: The Merger of Nazi Germany and Soviet Russia in the American Image of Totalitarianism, 1930's to 1950's," *American Historical Review,* Vol. 75 (April 1970), pp. 1051–1052.

7. *Ibid.,* pp. 1056–1057.

8. See the *New York Times,* October 1, 1946, p. 3, and October 13, 1946, II, p. 1.

9. *Ibid.,* July 26, 1946, p. 17.

10. *Ibid.,* March 5, 1947, p. 3.

11. Eric Johnston, Testimony before the House Committee on Un-American Activities, March 27, 1947, Chamber of Commerce Commission on Socialism and Communism, Francis P. Matthews Papers, Harry S. Truman Library.

12. *New York Times,* May 9, 1947, p. 15.

13. *Ibid.,* May 16, 1947, p. 1. See also John Cogley, *Report on Blacklisting* (New York, 1956), v. I, p. 11. The Alliance had been formed by a group of actors and writers in order to combat "the growing impression that this industry is made up of, and dominated by, Communists, radicals and crackpots."

14. Cogley, *op. cit.,* pp. 11–12.

15. *New York Times,* October 24, 1947, p. 12.

Notes

16. Edward L. Barrett, Jr., *The Tenney Committee* (Ithaca, 1951), p. 196. See also Cogley, *op. cit.*, pp. 18–19.

17. Barrett, *ibid.*, pp. 200, 208–209.

18. *New York Times*, October 1, 1946, p. 3.

19. Cogley, *op. cit.*, pp. 5, 6.

20. *Ibid.*, pp. 21–23. The Hollywood Ten, producer Adrian Scott, director Edward Dmytryk, writer-director Herbert Biberman, and writers Lester Cole, Ring Lardner, Jr., Dalton Trumbo, John Howard Lawson, Albert Maltz, Alvah Bessie, and Samuel Ornitz were all cited for contempt of Congress and jailed.

21. In striking down Eric Johnston's policy in the case of Lester Cole, United States District Court Judge Leon Yankwich likened Johnston to Cotton Mather during the Salem witch trials, describing him as "dogmatic, doctrinaire, absolutist." *New York Times*, December 21, 1948, p. 32.

22. Murray Kempton, *Part of Our Time* (New York, 1955), pp. 205–206.

23. *New York Times*, October 22, 1947, p. 3.

24. The M-G-M film was being titled *Vespers in Vienna*, but its name was later changed to *The Red Danube*. It was not released until the end of 1949. *New York Times*, November 2, 1947, p. 5, and December 9, 1949, p. 37.

25. *New York Times*, November 2, 1947, p. 5. At the behest of the State Department, *Ninotchka* was sent to Italy where it was credited with having helped swing an election that the Communists seemed to be winning. Dorothy B. Jones, "Communism and the Movies," in Cogley, *op. cit.*, p. 214.

26. Jones, *ibid.*, pp. 219–220. John Cogley in his careful study of the roots of blacklisting attempted to assess both sides of the impact of Communist Party influence in Hollywood. "On the positive side," he wrote, "the Communists can be credited with much of the industry's long-delayed awareness of racial and minority problems. Hollywood traveled a long road from the days of *Birth of a Nation* to the days of *Pinky* . . . . many Hollywood people became aware of social responsibilities that might otherwise have gone unnoticed forever." The price was high, he recognized, but their influence had been beneficial. Cogley, *op. cit.*, p. 44.

27. *Ibid.,* pp. 230, 231.

28. Jones, *ibid.,* p. 217. Some of the more notable of these were, Columbia's *Walk a Crooked Mile* (1948), Republic's *The Red Menace* (1949), Eagle-Lion's *Guilty of Treason* (1949), RKO's *The Woman on Pier 13* (1949), M-G-M's *The Conspirator* (1950), and Warner's *I Was a Communist for the FBI* (1951).

29. Siegfried Kracauer, "National Types as Hollywood Presents Them," in Bernard Rosenberg and David Manning White, *Mass Culture* (Glencoe, N.Y., 1957), p. 273; Pauline Kael, *I Lost It at the Movies* (New York, 1965), p. 291.

30. *New York Times,* January 19, 1948, p. 21, and January 26, 1948, p. 15.

31. *Ibid.,* February 20, 1948, p. 20, and May 13, 1948, p. 21.

32. Bosley Crowther in the *New York Times,* May 13, 1948, p. 31.

33. *Ibid.,* May 16, 1948, II, p. 1.

34. *Commonweal,* Vol. 48 (May 28, 1948), p. 165.

35. Kracauer, *op. cit.,* p. 272.

36. *New York Times,* May 16, 1948, II, p. 1.

37. *Ibid.,* May 30, 1948, II, p. 5.

38. *The New Republic, Vol. 118* (May 24, 1948), pp. 30–31.

39. *Life,* Vol. 24 (May 17, 1948), pp. 30–31.

40. Crowther, *op. cit.,* p. 31.

41. American Communists, interestingly, were portrayed in numerous anti-Communist films of this period as gangsters in the best Hollywood tradition, complete with fast getaway cars and machine guns. Evidently, the shadowy, antisocial underworld with its big city and often alien overtones provided an identification that could be readily understood by American audiences. See also Jones, *op. cit.,* p. 216.

42. The suicide theme prevailed in Republic Films' melodramatic thriller *The Red Menace,* released in 1949, while the murder theme of *My Son John* was representative of a number of other anti-Communist films.

43. Kael, *op. cit.,* p. 290.

44. Kracauer, *op. cit.,* p. 272.

Notes

45. Kael, *op. cit.,* p. 295.

46. Quoted in Athan Theoharis, "The Rhetoric of Politics: Foreign Policy, Internal Security, and Domestic Politics in the Truman Era, 1945–1950," in Barton J. Bernstein, ed., *Politics & Policies of the Truman Administration* (Chicago, 1970), p. 213.

47. Speech by John Foster Dulles, November 27, 1951, John Foster Dulles Papers, Princeton University Library.

48. Speech by John Edgar Hoover, May 2, 1950, Stephen Spingarn Papers, Internal Security File, Harry S. Truman Library.

49. *Congressional Record,* 81st Congress, 2nd Session, p. 1954.

THE POLITICS OF SCHOLARSHIP:
Liberals, Anti-Communism, and McCarthyism

1. *The New American Right,* Daniel Bell, ed. (New York, 1955) was reissued as *The Radical Right* (Garden City, N.Y., 1963). The 1963 edition included two new essays and appended commentary to the earlier published essays written by each of the contributors. The citations in this essay are to *The Radical Right,* see pp. ix, 42, 47, 59, 61, 70, 73, 81–83, 85, 99, 113, 115, 162, 165, 209, 216–218, 222, 228, 308–315, 344, 363, 378. This conception of popular irrationality as the source for McCarthyism attained general acceptance within the American historical profession during the late 1950's and influenced as well interpretations about the earlier Red Scare of 1919–20. See, Stanley Coben, "A Study in Nativism: The American Red Scare of 1919–1920," *Political Science Quarterly,* March 1964, pp. 52–75.

2. *The Radical Right,* pp. 95, 165, 228–229, 326.

3. Michael P. Rogin, *The Intellectuals and McCarthy: The Radical Specter* (Cambridge, Mass., 1967), particularly pp. 1–2, 3, 59–192, 216–282.

4. The works that most significantly influenced the emergence of consensus historiography were Daniel Boorstin, *The Genius of American Politics* (Chicago, 1953); Richard Hofstadter, *The Age of Reform* (New York, 1955); and Louis Hartz, *The Liberal Tradition in America* (New York, 1955).

5. The liberal commentators on the presidency are identified, and these themes more extensively discussed, in an unpublished paper, "The Textbook Presidency and Political Science," delivered by Thomas Cronin of the Brookings Institute at the September 1970 meetings of the American

Political Science Association. The paper was introduced into the *Congressional Record* by Senator Gordon Allott (Republican-Colorado). U.S. *Congressional Record*, 91st Congress, 2nd Session, 1970, Vol. 116, Part 26, pp. 34915–34928.

6. Quoted in Clinton Rossiter, *The American Presidency* (New York, 1956), pp. 10, 163.

7. *Ibid.*, see particularly pp. 25–27, 29, 62–81, 94, 159–160. The themes discussed sketchily in Rossiter's book are extended and developed in greater historical depth by Walter Johnson in *1600 Pennsylvania Avenue: Presidents and the People Since 1929* (Boston, 1963). Johnson as well extolled executive leadership and emphasized the need for a strong, manipulative presidency (given the complexity of issues and the limited understanding of the public). Like Rossiter, Johnson was disturbed by congressional attempts to restrict executive authority; in one section he criticized Senator McCarthy's 1954 request for the records of "privileged conversations in the White House" as a "flagrant encroachment on the executive." See particularly pp. vii–viii, 25, 26, 41, 49–50, 56, 83–84, 107–108, 113, 127, 188, 192, 195, 200, 223–224, 240, 246, 286, 293, 295, 303, 312, 318, 323, 324, 332.

8. Rossiter, *op. cit.,* pp. 121, 122. See also Johnson, *ibid.,* pp. 201–212, 214, 216, 218, 223–224, 230, 240, 246, 308.

9. Arthur Schlesinger, Jr., *The Vital Center: The Politics of Freedom* (Boston, 1949), most succinctly expressed in the introduction, pp. ix–x. See also, Alonzo Hamby, "The Vital Center, the Fair Deal, and the Quest for a Liberal Political Economy," *American Historical Review,* June 1972, pp. 653–678. This attempt to establish a viable and vital center led the new liberals to represent Fascism and Communism as similar movements and ideologies. The transformation of anti-Fascism into anti-Communism during the cold-war years is brilliantly discussed in Leslie K. Adler and Thomas G. Paterson, "Red Fascism: The Merger of Nazi Germany and Soviet Russia in the American Image of Totalitarianism, 1930's–1950's," *American Historical Review,* April 1970, pp. 1046–1064.

10. Hamby, *op. cit.,* pp. 656, 657, 662–665, 676, 678.

11. Clifton Brock, *Americans for Democratic Action: Its Role in National Politics* (Washington, 1962), p. 52.

12. Schlesinger, *op. cit.,* pp. 93–97, 100, 116, 126, 166–167, 204, 208–210, 213, 218, 223, 239–240. In fact, during the 1948 campaign, the ADA sought to identify Wallace's candidacy with the Communists. To do this, it published a list of those individuals who contributed amounts greater than $1,000 to the Wallace campaign together with their dossiers

compiled by the House Committee on Un-American Activities. Karl Schmidt, *Henry A. Wallace: Quixotic Crusade, 1948* (Syracuse, 1960), pp. 159, 192, 252–253, 261–262.

13. Letter, Philip Coombs to James Loeb, Jr., April 23, 1948, ADA Papers, Wallace File, Wisconsin State Historical Society (WSHS), Madison, Wis.

14. Loeb quoted in Robert Griffith, *The Politics of Fear: Joseph R. McCarthy and the Senate* (Lexington, Ky.: 1970), p. 120. Press Release, National Board of ADA, September 19, 1947, ADA Papers, Legislative File, Loyalty; Telegram, Francis Biddle (National Chairman, ADA) to President Truman, August 9, 1950, ADA papers, White House Cor.; Memorandum, For Use of National Board-ADA, November 10, 1950, ADA Papers, Legislative File, Loyalty; and Letter, Francis Biddle (National Chairman, ADA) to President Truman, May 22, 1951, ADA Papers, Legislative File, Internal Security; all in WSHS.

15. *The Radical Right*, pp. 76, 92, 361–362, 363. See also p. 222.

16. *Ibid.*, p. 76. This theme recurs throughout the volume, see also pp. 58, 115, 122, 162, 165, 179, 216–218, 225, 307, 344, 363, 365.

17. The major themes of McCarthy's rhetorical charges are contained in what became his most famous speech delivered in Wheeling, West Virginia, a draft of which he introduced into the U.S. *Congressional Record*, 81st Congress, 2nd Session, 1950, Vol. 46, Part 2, pp. 1952–1981.

18. The author in *The Yalta Myths: An Issue in U.S. Politics, 1945–1955* (Columbia, Mo., 1970) and in *Seeds of Repression: Harry S. Truman and the Origins of McCarthyism* (Chicago, 1971) and Robert Griffith, *op. cit.*, discuss in depth the conservatives' relations with McCarthy and their general position on foreign and internal security policy matters.

19. Letter, President Harry S. Truman to Herbert Hoover, November 25, 1950, Truman Papers, OF2750-A, Truman Library.

20. Letter, Herbert Hoover to President Harry S. Truman, November 26, 1950, Truman Papers, OF2750-A, Truman Library.

21. Quoted in Fred Cook, *The Nightmare Decade: The Life and Times of Senator Joe McCarthy* (New York, 1971), pp. 365–366.

22. *The Radical Right*, p. 70.

23. *Ibid.*, pp. 64, 78, 82, 106, 113, 122, 133, 170, 227, 370, 371.

24. Truman quotes are from *Public Papers of the Presidents of the United States: Harry S. Truman* (Washington: U.S. Government Printing

Office), *1948*, pp. 189–190; *1950*, pp. 376–377. More extensive documentation of Truman's consistent resort to this rhetoric is provided in the author's *Seeds of Repression, op. cit.,* and in "The Rhetoric of Politics: Foreign Policy, Internal Security, and Domestic Politics in the Truman Era, 1945–1950," in *Politics and Policies of the Truman Administration,* Barton Bernstein, ed. (Chicago, 1970). See also, Richard M. Freeland, *The Truman Doctrine and the Origins of McCarthyism: Foreign Policy, Domestic Politics and Internal Security, 1946–1948* (New York, 1972) and Susan M. Hartmann, *Truman and the 80th Congress* (Columbia, Mo., 1971).

25. Truman quote on McCarthy and the Republicans is in *Public Papers . . . Truman, 1950,* pp. 234–235. His private denunciation of Wallace is from William Hillman, *Mr. President* (New York, 1952), p. 128. Clifford quote is from Cabell Phillips, *The Truman Presidency: The History of a Triumphant Succession* (New York, 1966), p. 198. McGrath quote is from Edward L. and Frederick H. Schapsmeier, *Prophet in Politics: Henry A. Wallace and the War Years, 1940–1965* (Ames, Iowa, 1970), p. 186.

26. The McGrath quotes are from speeches he delivered in 1949 and 1950 before conventions of college fraternities, fraternal and religious organizations, and national meetings of the American Bar Association, sheriff, and district attorney organizations. They are contained in the McGrath Papers, Speech Files, Truman Library.

27. For a more detailed discussion of this development, see the author's "The Escalation of the Loyalty Program," in Bernstein, *op. cit.,* and "The Threat to Civil Liberties," in *Cold War Critics: Alternatives to American Foreign Policy in the Truman Years,* Thomas Paterson, ed. (Chicago, 1971). See also, Freeland, *op. cit.;* Eleanor Bontecou, *The Federal Loyalty-Security Program* (Ithaca, N.Y., 1953); and Alan Harper, *The Politics of Loyalty: The White House and the Communist Issue, 1946–1952* (Westport, Conn., 1970).

INDEX

A NOTE ON THE CONTRIBUTORS

Les K. Adler, Assistant Professor of History in the Hutchins School of Liberal Studies at California State College, Sonoma, has contributed articles and reviews to the *American Historical Review* and to *Continuum*. He is currently completing a book on American attitudes toward communism during the Cold War. Mr. Adler earned his Ph.D. at the University of California, Berkeley, in 1970.

Donald F. Crosby, S.J., Assistant Professor of History at Santa Clara University, has contributed scholarly articles to the *New England Quarterly* and *Woodstock Letters*. He received his Ph.D. from Brandeis University in 1973. His dissertation was entitled, "The Angry Catholics: Catholic Opinion of Senator Joseph R. McCarthy, 1950–1957."

Richard M. Fried, Assistant Professor of History at the University of Illinois at Chicago Circle, has contributed to *Continuum* and to the *Tennessee Historical Quarterly*. He is presently at work on a study of the Democratic opposition to Senator Joseph R. McCarthy. He received his Ph.D. from Columbia University in 1972.

Robert Griffith, Associate Professor of History at the University of Massachusetts, Amherst, is the author of *The Politics of Fear: Joseph R. McCarthy and the Senate* (1970), which won the 1970 Frederick Jackson Turner Award of the Organization of American Historians. He has contributed to many scholarly journals as well as to the *Progressive,* the *New Republic,* and *Saturday Review.* He received his Ph.D. from the University of Wisconsin in 1967. He is a Woodrow Wilson Fellow (1962) and has received grants from the American Philosophical Society and, most recently, the National Endowment for the Humanities.

Peter H. Irons is presently teaching at Boston State College. A former member of the legislative staff of the United Auto Workers, he has written on the politics of automation and reapportionment for the *Progressive.* He is also the author of a study of Polish Americans and the Cold War which will appear in *Polish American Studies.* He received his Ph.D. in Political Science from Boston University where he studied under Howard Zinn. His dissertation, completed in 1972, is a study of Cold War politics.

Ronald Lora, Associate Professor of History at the University of Toledo, is the author of *Conservative Minds in America* (1972) and a contributor to Menckeniana Quarterly (1970), Lyle Meyer's *Historical Papers* (1973), and Leach and Billington's *American Democracy on Trial* (1968). He is completing a book on American intellectuals, and is editing and contributing to a forthcoming volume, *Surviving the Sixties: Documentary and Interpretive Selections.* A graduate of Ohio State University (Ph.D., 1967), Mr. Lora has been the recipient of grants from the Ohio State University, the University of Toledo and has been a Fellow of the Henry E. Huntington Library.

Norman D. Markowitz, Assistant Professor of History at Livingston College, Rutgers University, is the author of *The Rise and Fall of the People's Century: Henry A. Wallace and American Liberalism* (1973), from which the essay which appears in this collection is drawn. A graduate of the University of Michigan (Ph.D., 1970), Mr. Markowitz has been the recipient of the E.S. Beck Fellowship in American history and an NDEA fellowship.

Mary S. McAuliffe received her Ph.D. in 1972 from the University of Maryland. Her dissertation, from which the article in this anthology is drawn, is a study of the liberal response to the politics of the Cold War. She presently resides in Ames, Iowa.

Michael O'Brien, Assistant Professor of History at the University of Wisconsin Center, Fox Valley, has written articles for *Journalism Quarterly* and for the *Wisconsin Magazine of History*. He is a graduate of the University of Wisconsin (Ph.D., 1971) where his doctoral dissertation was entitled "Senator Joseph McCarthy and Wisconsin: 1946–1957."

David M. Oshinsky, Assistant Professor of History at Douglas College, Rutgers University, is a graduate of Brandeis University (Ph.D., 1971). He has contributed articles to *Labor History,* the *Wisconsin Magazine of History, Commentary, the New Leader,* and *Change.* At present he is working on a study of the response of the Jewish community to the Rosenberg case, and a political biography of Senator Joseph McCarthy.

William R. Tanner is Assistant Professor and Chairman of the Department of History at California State University, Humboldt. He is a graduate of the University of Kansas (Ph.D., 1971), where his dissertation was a study of the Internal Security Act of 1950.

Athan G. Theoharis, Associate Professor of History, Marquette University, is a graduate of the University of Chicago (Ph.D., 1965). He is the author of *The Yalta Myths* (1970), *Seeds of Repression* (1971) and is co-author of *Anatomy of Anti-Communism* (1969). He has contributed articles and essays to *Politics and Policies of the Truman Administration* (edited by Barton Bernstein), to *Cold War Critics* (edited by Thomas Patterson), and to *Public Opinion and Historians* (edited by Melvin Small), and to numerous scholarly magazines. He has received research grants from the Truman Institute for National and International Affairs, from Wayne State University and from Marquette University. His June, 1971, article in the *Nation* received an award from the American Bar Association.